TRADITION AND ECONOMIC PROGRESS
IN SAMOA

TRADITION AND ECONOMIC PROGRESS IN SAMOA

A CASE STUDY OF THE ROLE OF
TRADITIONAL SOCIAL INSTITUTIONS
IN ECONOMIC DEVELOPMENT

BY

DAVID PITT

CLARENDON PRESS · OXFORD

1970

Oxford University Press, Ely House, London W. 1

GLASGOW NEW YORK TORONTO MELBOURNE WELLINGTON
CAPE TOWN SALISBURY IBADAN NAIROBI DAR ES SALAAM LUSAKA
ADDIS ABABA BOMBAY CALCUTTA MADRAS KARACHI LAHORE
DACCA KUALA LUMPUR SINGAPORE HONG KONG TOKYO

PRINTED IN GREAT BRITAIN BY
THE ABERDEEN UNIVERSITY PRESS

PREFACE

INEVITABLY there is a long list of acknowledgements to people without whom this book could never have been written. I owe most to my family for constant sacrifices and encouragements. I owe a great debt to the chiefs, orators and people of Malie (Tuamasaga), Salani (Falealili) and Apia nu'u, especially to the *pulenu'u* and *'āiga Ni'i Samoa*. I am deeply grateful to the Horniman Trust (Royal Anthropological Institute) and the Government of Western Samoa for material assistance. K. O. L. Burridge generously gave me many hours of advice and assistance.

Amongst those whose help and advice I gratefully acknowledge are, in England, Dr. Burton Benedict (LSE), Professor R. Firth (LSE), A. H. Halsey (Nuffield College, Oxford), Dr. G. Milner (SOAS), the staff of the Institute of Social Anthropology, Oxford and the New Zealand High Commission London, the librarians at Rhodes House, Queen Elizabeth House (Oxford) and the London Missionary Society (London); in New Zealand, L. Davis (Island Territories), Professor M. Groves (Singapore), H. Thompson (Secretary of Labour) and the staff of the Turnbull Library and Dominion Archives; in Samoa, Vaiao Ala'ilima (Public Service Commission), Mrs. B. Dahlborg (United Nations Statistician), Aualua Enari (Land and Titles Court), A. Gerakas (United Nations Economist), R. Girvan (Morris Hedstrom Ltd.), Dr. S. Haraldsen (World Health Organization), Dr. P. Heller (Treasury), Lau Ni'i Samoa (Apia), Leupolu Niko (Agriculture Department), Judges P. Molineux and R. Penlington (Justice Department), J. Mathes (Justice), Tautii Laulu (Nofoalii), B. Turner (Nelson Library), M. Watt (Agriculture), P. Young (Justice), the staff of the New Zealand High Commission, the Land and Titles Court, the Justice Department and Statistics Department. I owe a great debt also to Edward Stehlin (then Secretary to Mataafa and Malietoa) who effectively saw to the arrangements for my stay in Samoa. Finally, I must thank the staff of the Clarendon Press, Oxford for much help and assistance.

ST. LÉGIER VAUD,
December 1968

CONTENTS

List of Tables   viii

Abbreviations   x

Introduction   1

1. The Europeans and Economic Development   15

2. Samoan Economic Values   26

3. Production: Subsistence and Sale   56

4. The Economic Aspect of Status   68

5. Property   90

6. Chiefs and Community   113

7. Village Wage Labour in Town   154

8. Village Capital Formation   190

9. Trading Institutions   230

Conclusion   262

Appendices   268

Bibliography   276

Index   291

LIST OF TABLES

1. Consumption of Necessity Goods in Salani, Malie and Apia—January-December 1964   32

2. Consumption of Luxury Goods and Services in Salani, Malie and Apia 1964   38

3. Consumption of Ceremonial (*Fa'alavelave*) Goods and Services in Salani, Malie and Apia 1964   39

4. Expenditure on Capital Goods and Services in Salani, Malie and Apia 1964   45

5. Work in Malie and Salani 1964   48-51

6. Titleholding in Malie and Salani 1964   69

7. *Fa'alupega* (Ceremonial Order) of the *Matai* of Malie and Salani   79

8. Ceremonial Order of Precedence in Malie and Salani   81-2

9. Land Use and Tenure in Samoa   95

10. House-site Land in Malie 1964   96

11(*a*) Sketch Map of Land Use in Malie 1964   100

11(*b*) Distribution of '*Āiga* Gardenland in Malie 1964   101

12. Diagram of Land Rights in Malie 1964   102

13. Changes in Landholding in Malie 1924–64   107

14. Ceremonial Exchange   128-33

15. Co-operative Societies in Samoa   143

16. Work and Hours in the Apia Street Market   149-50

17. Occupations of Samoans 1961–4   155

18. Population Movement, Salani, Malie, Apia 1964   168-9

19. Employment of Migrants to New Zealand 1962   187

20. Savings and Investment in Malie and Salani 1964   202

21. Sources of Loans (Cash and Credit) in Malie and Salani —1964   208

22. *Fa'asāmoa* Specialists   232-3

23. Sales of Samoan Handicraft and Accessory Vendors
     September-October 1964   241

24. Growth of Village Trading 1885–1964   248

25. History of Independent Samoan Taxi Drivers 1964   252

26. Turnover, Profits and Investment in Samoan Businesses
     —1963   253

27. Samoan Trading in Malie (May-July) and Salani (Sept-
     ember-November) 1964   256

APPENDICES

Appendix 1: Inventory of Household Goods—Salani, Malie
     and Apia   268-72

Appendix 2: Village Income and Its Distribution   273

Appendix 3: Map of Place Names Cited   274-5

ABBREVIATIONS

(Full citations in Bibliography)

G		Germany
	GCA	Colonial Archives
	GC	Samoan Government Gazette (1900–14)
GB		Great Britain
	GBCO	Colonial Office
	GBFO	Foreign Office
	GBMPR	Miscellaneous Published Reports
	GBPP	Parliamentary Papers
	GBPR	Parliamentary Reports
LMS		London Missionary Society
	LMSBFJ	Letters
	LMSJ	Journals
	LMSNP	Papers of the Rev. Newell
	LMSMP	Pamphlets
	LMSSR	*Samoan Reporter*
	LMSAR	*Annual Report*
NZ		New Zealand
	NZAJ	Appendices to Journals of the House of Representatives
	NZBM	British Military Occupation (1914–1920)
	NZIT	Island Territories Department
	NZO	Ordinances 1914–61
PIYB		*Pacific Islands Year Book*
PIM		*Pacific Islands Monthly*
SPC		South Pacific Commission
UN		United Nations
US		United States
WS		Western Samoa
	WSAG	Agriculture Department
	WSDF	Department File
	WSLP	Papers Presented to the Legislative Assembly
	WSLT	Land and Titles Court

WSMP	Memoranda Legislative Assembly
WSO	Ordinances 1962–5
WSST	Statistics Department

Any data not footnoted have been obtained from fieldwork. The spelling of Samoan words is according to Dr. Milner's new dictionary (1966).

INTRODUCTION

TRADITIONAL SOCIETY AND DEVELOPMENT—THE NEGATIVE MODEL

In the recent literature on economic development (or under-development) considerable attention has been given by social scientists to constructing explanatory models which incorporate what are loosely called 'social factors'. In many explanations applied to Afro-Asian situations, traditional indigenous social institutions are viewed as significant, even critical obstacles to *per capita* increases in production or consumption (the usual definition of economic development). In most cases this model is based on the assumption that 'traditional', 'primitive' or 'peasant' economies, and the social correlates of economic activity, are different in kind from the socio-economic institutions known in Europe or North America.

This model of a qualitatively different traditional economy first became prominent in the writing of the nineteenth-century economic historians strongly influenced by the Hegelian dialectic.[1] More recently in the works of many anthropologists[2] there has emerged an often romantic view of isolated, small-scale, face to face economies based on altruism and gift-giving embedded in a kinship and jural nexus, in which individualism, acquisition and accumulation are not, or not *per se*, dominant motives. If maximization is significant in these economies it is the maximization of prestige and power. If

[1] e.g. Bucher 1893.
[2] Malinowski (e.g. 1922: 60) and Thurnwald (1932) argued that in primitive societies man's economic interests were governed by his kinship and status interests or by legal or moral rules. Mauss (1954) attempted to show that exchange of goods and services were part of a much wider system of total exchange and that this exchange was dominated by the disbursement of goods to obtain prestige rather than their acquisition or accumulation. These views were demonstrated in the works of Mead (1949), Dubois (1936), Bascom (1948) and in the many accounts of the Kwakiutl potlach in which destruction was held to be an extreme form of prestige-seeking disbursement. More recently Polanyi (1947, 1957, 1959) and a number of American anthropologists (Dalton 1967 contains a representative collection), the so-called substantivists (Cook 1966), have reiterated that prestige and altruism, operating through kinship mechanisms of reciprocity and pooling, are the base of the primitive economy.

there is contact with the outside world the local small-scale economy is subordinate and inferior.[1]

Many sociologists,[2] too, evaluate the development significance of the social context of Afro-Asian economic activity in negative terms. For example, in studies of entrepreneurship[3] (regarded as a key factor by the economists in the late fifties), Afro-Asian pattern variables are considered to lack growth favouring characteristics in economic activity (achieved status, particularism in the distribution of economically relevant tasks, diffuseness in the performance of these tasks) and all innovation roles are said to be hedged by traditional social sanctions. The social psychologists[4] for their part claim that the critical factor in under-development is the absence of an achievement motive, and that innovation is stunted by unsuitable childhood training.[5]

To many contemporary economists[6] (and administrators) these autarkous, kin-based, prestige economies are considered to be anathema to successful participation or competition in the wider cash economy. For instance, Lewis,[7] whose treatment is the fullest and most systematic, claims from the evidence of European history and the contemporary under-developed world, that a certain attitude to economic activity is necessary for economic development to take place. This attitude (which is rather like Weber's capitalist spirit) he calls the 'will to economize' which he defines as 'the propensity to consistently increase the yield of a given effort or resource or reduce the cost of a given yield'.[8] Lewis argues that for this attitude to be present a high valuation must be placed on the accumulation of goods, on hard work, on capital formation, on innovation. The existence of the 'will to economize' also depends on the suitability

[1] e.g. G. and M. Wilson, 1945, Benedict 1966.

[2] The theoretical foundations of this approach were laid by Linton before the war and Talcott Parsons after it. A leading exponent has been Hoselitz (e.g. 1960).

[3] Much of the work using the Parsonian model has been carried out at the Harvard Research Centre in Enterpreneurial History. A collection of representative views is in Aitken 1965.

[4] McClelland 1961. A specific application to Asia is in the *Journal of Social Issues*, January 1963.   [5] Hagen 1962.

[6] The ideas of the anthropologists filtered back into the economists' writings, for example, Boeke 1942, 1953.

[7] 1955.   [8] 1955: 11.

of the institutions of society. Institutions, Lewis claims, must allow a considerable degree of economic freedom and must secure for the individual the right to the reward for his efforts. Lewis also isolates two other prerequisites for economic development, the accumulation and application of knowledge and capital, and the growth of trade and specialization which have ideal types of institutional concomitants. Lewis argues that these attitudes and social prerequisites are not usually adequately developed in under-developed countries.

These views have been applied specifically to Samoa. The most systematic treatment has been by the FAO economist, Stace.[1] He claims that Samoans place a low valuation on the accumulation of goods, on productive knowledge in particular, on entrepreneurship and capitalistic activity in general. The communal nature of Samoan social institutions is stated or implied to inhibit the development of the capitalist spirit. Stace claims that the individual in the village is involved in a web of reciprocal economic obligations, part of his general social obligations, which tend to prevent him pursuing his own ends and accumulating wealth. Individual freedom is further restricted by the ascription of status. The right to reward for effort, as well as wealth accumulation, is prevented by the constant communal demands on an individual's goods and services.

The models of the Europeans in Samoa are similar if less sophisticated. Samoans are considered to have few wants, though, despite the contradiction, many luxury wants, and to prefer leisure to constructive work.[2] One reason why they are able to do this is because they live in a Garden-of-Eden environment. 'On Fridays', wrote a German administrator,[3] 'their plantations are scantily worked and provisions for a week secured, the other six days are days of rest and play pleasantly relieved by hunting, fishing and practising for Church.' A more important reason for hedonism and laziness is that Samoans are not offered any encouragement within Samoan

[1] 1956.
[2] Examples are: *Missions*: Buzacott, LMS J (1837), Monfat 1890: 98 (RC). *Traders*: GBFO 58/90/379. *Administration*: GCA 2/IV/59, NZIT 69/5. The view that luxury demand comes first in a culture contact situation is propounded in Hoyt 1956.
[3] Wohltman 1904.

society. They are constrained by despotic hereditary chiefs and overbearing communal demands so that there can be no private property or individual incentives. To the French missionaries[1] the chiefs were like the wicked aristocracy of the *ancien regime*, the London Missionary Society[2] compared them to unjust Biblical taskmasters, whilst the New Zealanders called them 'extortionist feudal squires'.[3] Communal demands are equally incompatible with economic progress. The 'communistic system', wrote Dr. Turner of the London Missionary Society, 'is a sad hindrance to the industrious and eats like a canker worm at the roots of individual and national progress. No matter how hard a young man may be disposed to work, he cannot keep his earnings, all soon passes out of his hands into the common circulating currency of the clan.'[4] The South Pacific Commission Economist has said much the same thing: 'Communal systems operate against the spur of personal ambition, (and) adversely affect . . . material progress, the proportionate scale and nature of these communal demands being such that it is difficult for an individual to retain funds or useful property, and the earner or producer after successive distributions is usually discouraged from further effort.'[5]

Native society is similarly held to be an obstacle to the efficient use of labour and capital. Traditional institutions are said to prevent continuous and efficient effort and to dull the incentive to monetary reward. Wage-labour migration adds to the problems of village production, depleting rural manpower and concentrating it in overcrowded urban slums.

Capital is regarded by many Europeans as the heart of the problem in Samoa. The Samoan, either because of some hedonistic trait or fatalistic belief in divine providence, or because of the absence of interest in long-term economic goals, prefers consumption to future production. It is also argued that since generosity is a prime virtue, because of the constant demands of kin and chiefs, there is little chance of capital accumulation in the cash economy. Educational and medical inadequacies are often explained in terms of a defective native mentality. From the first missionaries there has been a tendency

---

[1] Monfat 1890: 154.
[2] LMSMP/3.
[3] NZIT 1/23/2.
[4] Turner 1884: 161.
[5] Stace 1954: 2.

to assume some degree of irrationality in Samoan thought, and some at least consider the Samoan does not think logically but relies on magical explanations rather than logical inference and empirical verification.[1] Even when the Samoan is credited with logical thought it is claimed that this is achieved through rules learned by rote rather than by the use of principles of reason. The Rev. Buzacott[2] writes that the people think the alphabet is 'a series of cabalistic sounds and signs peculiar to Christianity, or a form of prayer to be repeated in times of danger'. Nor is this view confined to the missionaries. Similar conclusions, based largely on the low performance of Samoans in intelligence tests, have been made by psychologists.[3] Intellectual capacity is also considered to be restricted by the weak development of formal educational institutions in traditional Samoa and especially by the absence of literacy. These intellectual inabilities are claimed to inhibit especially the acquisition of modern scientific knowledge.

Finally, trade and specialization are thought to be limited by the nature of traditional society. It is claimed that there is only sexual division of labour in village production and that households are virtually self-sufficient. There is little occupational mobility. Where exchange of goods does occur it is not the product of pressures of supply and demand or interlocking specialized activities, but part of a wider social exchange between households and groups. Because economic exchange is limited there is no monetary or market system. Because economic relations are only an aspect of a continuous and close kinship relationship there cannot be concepts of contract, or conveyance (the transference of proprietary rights) and hence individual incentive is further dulled.

Most significantly, the absence of a tradition of trade and specialization places the Samoan at a disadvantage in participating and competing with Europeans in market institutions. In a society without a tradition of specialization, a society dominated by communal institutions, people cannot acquire skills necessary for producing a high class good or provide adequate skilled labour for a sophisticated market. Samoans who 'never think beyond their village' cannot adequately

[1] e.g. LMSB11F5JA.   [2] LMSJ—Buzacott.
[3] Cook 1942(a), (b).

attend to the needs of marketing cash crops where external organization is at a premium. The villagers are usually held responsible for serious marketing deficiencies (poor produce, late or irregular deliveries). Lack of specialist and marketing skills reduce potential profit, but also Samoans are thought to be in a subordinate and unprofitable position in any market relation with Europeans. The Europeans say that this is largely the result of traditions of liberality and inexperience in trading institutions. Samoans, Europeans say, have no acquisitive traits, no constant desire or ability to higgle-haggle, reduce costs, and participate in profit-making entrepreneurial activities, involving innovation, experiment and risk-taking.

The converse to the argument that there is a negative relationship between native society and local economic development is that there is a positive relationship between European values and institutions, and development. In many historical works, certainly in the models of resident Europeans, externally inspired development was a major theme. There were two views on the effects of European society. First, especially amongst local European residents, there was the belief that Europeans were the benefactors bestowing civilization and its attendant wealth on benighted natives. Secondly, there was the view usually held by non-residents, economists, historians, and particularly Marxists,[1] that Europeans and especially merchants were exploiters taking what they could of colonial resources and labour for their own benefit or introducing capital and enslaving the people in the serfdom of wage labour, ensuring political control even after Independence, through a monopoly of investment. Recent analyses have emphasized that exploitation is not necessarily deliberate or malevolent, but is none the less inevitable because the Europeans who controlled the destinies of the empire and who now control the new nations have deeply ingrained colonial prejudices.

TRADITIONAL SOCIETY AND DEVELOPMENT—THE POSITIVE MODEL

This is an attempt to apply a different explanatory model to a situation of underdevelopment through a case study of the Western Samoan economy and society. The first assumption

[1] A good summary is Worsley 1964.

is that any model involving social factors must as a first priority explore relationships between parts of the total social structure,[1] i.e. including the local society and the outside world, rather than the relationships between social institutions and numerical quantities such as output, productivity and consumption. Consequently underdevelopment becomes a problem of a particular social relationship between two sectors: European and Samoan. The flow of goods and services is seen as part of the total pattern of exchange between the two sectors within this broad social structure.

The second assumption is that this exchange is not necessarily or usually, one-sided. The rigid Hegelian or romantic classifications break down partly because the sectors within the total social structure are interdependent. This interdependence is one of supply and demand. Europeans want (or have wanted) tropical goods, a labour supply, colonial prestige or strategic positions, while the local people desire European goods, expertise or capital. These relationships are created and maintained through the constant movement of the local population within colonial territories, and within the total social framework, especially through intermarriage and occupational involvement in the European world.

This social structure is not monolithic. The two sectors are clearly separated in the conceptual framework of residents. On the one hand there is what the Europeans call Samoan or native society, and what Samoans refer to as—*fa'asāmoa*. Most simply *fa'asāmoa* is the values and institutions of people who call themselves Samoans. In general these are the descendants of the original Polynesian inhabitants, who live in kin groups (*'āiga*), in nucleated villages (*nu'u*), under chiefs (*matai*), according to norms which are assumed to be traditional. European society (*fa'apālagi*) is the way of life of those persons (sometimes descendants of Samoans) who consider themselves to be Europeans and who generally live in the main town of Apia or abroad, according to norms which are assumed to be European, American or Australasian. However, these sectors are parts of a whole, rather than discrete or opposed radicals.

[1] The notion of regarding the colonial situation as a total social structure was first suggested by Balandier 1951 and Gluckman 1947. Later applications can be seen in Wallerstein 1966.

There were few, apart perhaps from the most transient European official, who conform in all respects to the polar ideal. Most aspects of values and behaviour reflect elements of both ideals, and many individuals move from one pattern to the other. One Samoan said: 'The European world and the Samoan world are separated by a sea on which anyone can sail.'

This is not to say that the polar ideals are never important. *Fa'asāmoa* was a significant rallying cry for the anti-European factions during the Mau rebellions or the movement for Independence, though this was largely a politician's device rather than a widespread Samoan sentiment. (And the debate itself was largely over political power rather than the retention of traditional custom.) In the economic sphere even the most ethnocentric chiefs envisaged the *fa'asāmoa* economy as an integral part of the wider economy.

The social structure in contemporary Samoa tends towards centrality rather than duality. As in recent analyses of networks,[1] the important elements within the sectors in the social structure are juxtaposed according to their social distance from a central point of reference. The individual, the *'āiga*, the village (or the European town) are all in different situations the centre of a universe. Key relationships particularly in economic activity are often across the structural boundaries separating *fa'asāmoa* and *fa'apālagi*.

The third and major assumption of our model is that through these relationships local Samoan institutions could obtain desired goods and services from the European world. The significant impetus to any movement of goods or services comes from the Samoan rather than from the European sector. Local economic development has been internally generated rather than externally imposed, partly because the European contribution has been weakly developed but also because the Samoan effort is strong and consistent.

Fa'asāmoa social institutions play an important role in generating this economic development. This role depends on two characteristics of *fa'asāmoa*; firstly, internal flexibility of important elements, and secondly, external compatability and co-existence between inflexible elements in the total social structure.

---

[1] e.g. Barnes 1954, Srinivas and Betaille 1964.

The real dynamic is an intense desire for European goods; this desire is partly explicable in traditional terms, and is achieved through production incentives depending on essentially *fa'asāmoa* patterns of reward in terms of status or goods. The flexibility of *fa'asāmoa* is clearly seen in the adaptation of key traditional institutions to the new socio-economic context. Chiefs (*matai*) become managers, kin groups (*'āiga*) become co-operatives, while kinship or friendship becomes the basis for associations in the towns or abroad. Adaptation is one kind of change, addition is another. If new institutions and values are incompatible persons may vary their economic behaviour according to the situation in which they find themselves (this variation can be correlated, as Sahlins[1] has suggested, with the boundaries of the kinship universe). For example in such activities as wage-labour, capital formation or trading, Samoans may act uncapitalistically within the kinship circle, especially during ceremonial, but still run their businesses efficiently or work regularly. But the uncapitalistic behaviour is situational rather than structural. A man may still act capitalistically with his kinsfolk outside ceremonial activities. Institutional co-existence is also apparent in the internal emergence of what are usually called middlemen or brokers who conduct the socio-economic transactions of the village with the outside world. The village officials, pastors, doctors, traders, teachers, whatever their origin, often become deeply involved in *fa'asāmoa* and promote the cause of village wealth and welfare wherever they can in the outside world.

METHODOLOGY

This study is not intended to be a field-work monograph though a good proportion of the evidence, both qualitative and quantitative, is based on data collected from first-hand observation during an extended stay in Samoan communities.[2]

Fieldwork was conducted in two rural villages, Malie (Tuamasaga) and Salani (Falealili). These villages were chosen

[1] Sahlins 1965. Exchange amongst kinsfolk is either altruistic (the inner group) or involves balanced reciprocity (the larger group but intra-tribal) whilst economizing behaviour (his negative reciprocity) is confined to inter-tribal relations.

[2] Five months in Malie, three months in Salani and Apianu'u, two months in New Zealand, during 1963-4.

because they were examples of variations in economic resources and structure. Malie is a populous mixed cash cropping and wage-labour village. It has the poorer physical environment. The soils are stony clay loams which become thin and rocky about two and a half miles from the coast. There are also trace deficiencies of potassium which makes the cacao trees wither. The rainfall is relatively low, less than 90 inches a year, with a well marked dry season when most plants are short of moisture. Most of the bushland has been cleared away and in parts erosion or thick liana forest inhibits cultivation. Land is short and intensively cultivated since much of the hinterland has been sold, and in some areas the soil is overworked. Because of environmental deficiencies Malie is also more exposed to pests and viruses, notably the Rhinoceros beetle[1] and Bunchy-top virus. Marine resources, at least within the fringing reefs, are also depleted as a result of indiscriminate dynamiting of fish, breaking the coral bed and polluting the water. On the other hand, Malie has a large and active pool of manpower[2] swollen by immigration from other villages.[3] It has easy access to the wage-labour and entrepreneurial opportunities of Apia nine miles away and this contributes significantly to village income.[4] Salani has richer physical resources, a more varied soil pattern, fertile alluvium in the Salani and Fagataloa river beds and a deep clay extending to the mountains. These soils, combined with a heavy, evenly distributed rainfall, (150 inches per annum) suit bananas and coconuts and favour *talo* especially. There is a considerable reservoir (approximately three-quarters of all village land) of unused bushland and grassland. But manpower is short[5] and Salani is almost four hours away by bus from Apia over a twisting mountain road. There are, therefore, few wage-labourers or entrepreneurs in the village[6] and Salani is predominantly a cash cropping village.[7] Migrants were studied particularly in the section of Apia known as Apia village (Apia nu'u) which contains approximately 15 per cent of the Samoan population of Apia.

[1] Estimated to reduce coconut production by one-third.
[2] 1,107 (1964) of whom 40 per cent were between 15 and 45.
[3] See Table 18.   [4] See Appendix 2.
[5] The population is (1964) only 472 and only 10 per cent of this population are males between 15 and 45.   [6] See Table 18.
[7] See Appendix 2.

However, the major problem of the involvement of the local socio-economy in the wider world necessitated the collection of evidence outside the narrow time-space framework of these villages.

Two important methods were used to collect data within this wider framework. The first involved first-hand collection of data often involving only a slight modification of traditional anthropological techniques. Visits were made for short periods to villages other than the fieldwork villages to collect relevant information. These visits were often short, even day trips, since the essential preliminaries, the learning of the language, suitable fieldwork techniques, the establishment of contacts were all done beforehand. Often, too, these short visits were merely to fill in a particular aspect of a problem. For example, only a small number of villages in Samoa possess credit unions, but a study of a credit union in a new village only takes a day since it is usually necessary to interview only the handful who belong to the union. Further information on more general aspects of the village social structure can readily be obtained in the main fieldwork village.

Detailed first-hand observations were also made of the urban institutions with which the villagers were in contact. In Samoa the problem of access and participant involvement in these institutions is not as great as in many countries. Fifty years as an international trust territory has hardened Samoan administrators to external scrutiny. In a land so often visited by experts, all visitors are experts whose incorporation into the department is expected. Besides, secrets are very hard to keep in tropical corridors of power which are constantly open to the glare of any passing person. Finally the key institutions are concentrated in a small number of organizations, such as the cash crop marketing boards, the missions, and the courthouses.

The second important method of data collection involved the extensive use of documentary materials. There are considerable published sources on Samoa, but apart from one or two notable exceptions and the work of professional social scientists most yield only candle ends. Naturally the second generation of anthropologists in Samoa are in the debt of earlier anthropologists, notably Mead[1] and Keesing,[2] especially

[1] 1930.   [2] 1934, 1956.

the latter who was a pioneer in the study of social change. Keesing, however, did not touch what is, in Samoa, as in many parts of Afro-Asia, a vast accessible and largely untapped source of information on social change—the unpublished archives of mission, consular, traders', colonial and administrative papers. Most important are the administrative papers in Apia itself, stored away in the cupboards and attics of departments particularly at Mulinu'u and Central Office. Also important are the colonial administrative archives now to be found mainly in New Zealand at the Dominion Archives. The mission papers (mainly in Europe) and the very rare traders' papers are generally important and occasionally are of very great value.

This documentary material served four important purposes in the present study. Firstly, it permitted problems encountered in the fieldwork in the village to be studied in a much wider spatial perspective, drawing in material from villages other than those visited during the fieldwork. Secondly, it allowed statistics to be extracted which threw the small fieldwork samples into clearer relief. Thirdly, it allowed problems to be studied in a time perspective. For example, there are records of the fieldwork villages in the Lands and Titles courts and districts files dating back to 1900, which provide census information, data on the distribution of land and land use, cash crop production figures, as well as material on the economic problems of the village. The documentary record also provided data on relations which occurred only sporadically in time, and before the present fieldwork. For example, the files of the New Zealand army of occupation give information on the workings of Samoan native companies formed on a nation-wide scale by the chiefs to improve economic conditions. Though this alternative means of improving economic conditions may exist in the minds of contemporary chiefs there were no such schemes in operation during the fieldwork in 1963–4. Fourthly, the documentary record provided a means of securing information which normally people would not divulge and of checking information which the fieldworker suspected to be inaccurate. For example, people usually will not disclose their savings in the banks even to relatives. Many will also only divulge the *gafa*, the genealogies of the village in the Lands and

Titles courts when it is necessary to validate a claim to a piece of land or to a title. The checking of information is important, for in Samoa all information and especially statistical information reflects the relationship between the informant and the questioner. People often scale down the amount of any goods or services they possess because they suspect that Europeans in the villages are either tax inspectors checking on village accounts or possibly United Nations officials anxious to disburse goods to poverty-stricken Samoans. Occasionally people scale up the amounts of the possessions if they feel that the European has visited other villages and that their prestige will thereby suffer. Incomes were checked, particularly at the cash cropping boards in Apia or from the merchants' books, whilst genealogical and land claims were checked in the Lands and Titles Court.

There are admittedly important gaps in the documentary record. In a climate in which paper-eating bugs flourish, in a political atmosphere of changing administrations, local instability and savage internecine quarrels, many files are destroyed or lost accidentally or intentionally. However, especially in recent times there are ways of filling in the documentary record through informants in what is sometimes very great detail. Informant history is admittedly subject to many of the biases which affects the veracity of all oral traditions.[1] But there may be checks in the documentary record which may at least indicate the reliability of the informant. And even if the informant gives inaccurate information this may be very significant especially if the informant was himself involved in the events described.

The concentration on specific problems in the total social structure together with the usefulness of documentary materials in this study had an effect on the fieldwork methods used in the rural villages. This part of the investigation did not need to be as extensive as in the traditional social anthropological monograph in the sense of covering qualitatively all aspects of local society in great detail. On the other hand the narrower definition of problems and the concentration on economic aspects required a more rigorous and precise investigation of factors and quantities in the economic process. For this reason strenuous efforts were made to collect as many, and as

[1] See particularly Vansina 1965.

detailed, economic statistics as possible, to quantify the relationships discussed.

In each fieldwork village a full census of all persons and inventory of all their possessions was collected. Maps were made of land use and distribution from field surveys and air photographs, and resource inventories were made of cash and subsistence crops and livestock. Budgets of all incoming and outgoing goods and services were collected in sample *'āiga* containing at least 25 per cent of the population in each village for approximately a three-month period and from all pastors and traders for the whole year. Detailed work activity data were also collected from these *'āiga* over a similar three-month period, and details were taken on village activity over the year. Detailed census, inventory and budget information was also collected from special groups both inside and outside the village; in rural areas, from traders, co-operative societies, credit unions; in Apia from entrepreneurial groups (taxi-drivers, vegetable and handicraft vendors) and wage-labourers (government servants in the Agricultural Department, sales clerks at Molesi store, domestic servants at the Casino Hotel), which included many people from outside the fieldwork villages.

I

THE EUROPEANS AND ECONOMIC DEVELOPMENT

In this first chapter we analyse the contribution which Europeans have made towards Samoan economic development (i.e. levels of Samoan consumption). The European economic contribution has been generally overrated, but also there has been very little exploitation. The Europeans in Samoa have had only a small direct effect on Samoan standards of living, for Europeans and Samoans have generally gone their own economic ways, communicating with one another only when there is an economic necessity, and then usually in a fair exchange of resources in which there was not usually altriusm or exploitation.

CASTAWAYS, TRADERS AND CONSULS—MISUNDERSTOOD EXPLOITERS

The first Europeans in Samoa were explorers but they usually stayed only a few days and left little impression on the country.[1] The first Europeans to live permanently in Samoa were castaways, men of all nationalities, shipwrecked or more often abandoned by their ships because of disease, even desperate convicts from the New South Wales penal settlement. Most commentators,[2] relying on the missionaries' horrific tales, considered that the castaways were a very evil influence introducing liquor, 'the disease' (syphilis) and other European vices. But although some castaways were rogues, their evil influence should not be overestimated. The castaways, until the arrival of the traders and the commencement of regular shipping services,[3] had no access to liquor, and there is no mention of syphilis in Samoa until 1848,[4] a date suspiciously close to the visit of H.M.S. *Dido*. Many castaways in fact lived

---

[1] The best summary is in Kramer 1902 v. 1.   [2] LMSB10F9JA.
[3] In the early 1840s.   [4] Kramer 1902 v. 2: 198.

useful lives in the villages, settling down quickly with a Samoan wife and entering *fa'asāmoa* society. They often brought useful skills to village economic activity, offering valuable advice when the Samoans became involved in trading relations with shrewd European merchants, or in political bargaining with devious European consuls and missionaries. Some castaways became the representatives of the village in the outside world, whilst others became traders or missionaries in the village. Significantly all villagers were glad to have these men in their midst and they often received titles or were accorded the respect of high chiefs.[1]

The castaways were not the only Europeans to live in the villages. The traders,[2] who arrived in Samoa in the late 1830s, sold village produce to passing ships. Not until 1857 did a large European concern (the Hamburg firm of J. C. Godeffroy) establish a comprehensive trading organization with trading posts[3] throughout Samoa. But many of the firm's agents participated, with or without the firm's approval, in village society. Godeffroys, the largest of the trading firms, encouraged this process, believing that a trader could not succeed in his job unless he had a local wife, could speak the language, and get on with the villagers without quarrelling.[4]

Some economic benefits resulted from the presence of traders. Friendly traders provided a valuable introduction to the workings of the market economy. The traders introduced a number of important technological innovations (particularly the drying of coconuts to make copra[5]), as well as useful goods through their retail sales.

The European planters[6] working on estates or on individual plantations had much less contact with, and much less effect on, village society. Generally the plantations did not adversely affect the village economy. The European planters reduced village profits through their superior competitive position in the cash crop market and lowered local wage levels by importing indentured labour from China and Melanesia, although

---

[1] e.g. Murray 1876: 18, LMSB10F9JA.

[2] Traders memoirs are rare but there is Trood 1812, Churchill 1902, Riedel 1938.

[3] Histories of the Company are Schmack 1938, Spoehr 1963 and in the company archives in Hamburg.   [4] NZAJ 1873.

[5] Riedel 1938: 44—in the 1860s.   [6] Arriving mainly between 1860 and 1910.

few plantations, like other European enterprises in Samoa, made any money. There were, however, some important by-products of plantation agriculture. The roads which the planters built were a considerable asset, especially to the villages of North West Upolu. A very important cash crop, cocoa, was carried into the villages from the plantations. Some Samoans learnt valuable skills whilst working on the plantations.

In Samoa the flag followed the trade, and this only belatedly.[1] The European officials in Samoa as elsewhere do not conform to the Marxist-Leninist model of the capitalist imperialist. Prestige and pugnacity in the Hobsonian formula, not profits, were the motives of the consuls who arrived in Samoa in the mid-nineteenth century. The consuls came basically to establish spheres of colonial influence in the Pacific. Living quite separate from village society in the township of Apia, the consuls had a minute effect on Samoan economic conditions. A number of commercial treaties were concluded with the Samoans which to some extent protected Samoan, as well as European, interests. In a few areas the consuls also regulated the sale of land and occasionally provided a gently restraining hand on Europeans through the consular courts. Some Samoans in Apia benefited from municipal improvements set in train by the consuls, and some chiefs were able to use consular patronage in the form of funds or advice in the *fa'asāmoa* wars of the period.

Most of the European community of traders, castaways and consuls who came and lived in Samoa in the mid-nineteenth century were single men, and many sooner or later took Samoan wives. By the end of the nineteenth century a part-European community emerged. There were two distinct groups within this community; an élite group of part Europeans descended from the German traders or planters, and a part Chinese group descended from indentured plantation workers who established small shops and stores in the back streets of Apia. In general the economic activities of this part-European community did not have adverse effects on Samoan economic

[1] The literature on the consuls is considerable. There is the work of the historians Masterman 1934, Ellison 1938, Ross 1964: Ch. 11, Ryden 1933. But the best sources are the contemporaries: Churchward 1887, Pritchard 1866, Trood 1912, the letters and reports in FO 58, the Powell Papers (at the Royal Commonwealth Society, London), and GB, US, G(Consuls).

development. It is true that some part-European merchants or Chinese traders were responsible through their competitive activities for low cash crop prices to villages, or bad working conditions in urban wage labour. But some people in part-European or Chinese groups formed a closer association with the Samoans. Generally this association did not stem, as in the case of the early traders, from common residence in a village but resulted rather from a common opposition to overseas European political or economic hegemony. In times of nation-alistic feeling (especially during the latter part of the New Zealand administration) the part-Europeans have shown a great interest in, and attachment to, *fa'asāmoa* society. They adopted the Samoan tongue, intermarried with villagers and took village titles. As the ties between the communities strength-ened, considerable economic assistance was forthcoming in the form of capital and advice to relatives, and an equitable reward for Samoan labour and resources. These ties have waned in recent years as the overseas European superiority has declined. In the years immediately before and since Independence (1962) many part-Europeans have reverted to a competitive position in all economic activities. But even here there have been important, if indirect, benefits resulting from the economic activities of part-Europeans. Most significantly a marketing structure has been provided for cash crops and there are jobs in local industries. Even when the part-Europeans left Samoa this left the way open for Samoan entrepreneurs.

THE MISSIONARIES—UNINTENTIONAL BENEFACTORS

The economic contribution of consuls, traders and castaways was small, though sometimes significant, and generally under-rated by commentators. A similar comment could be made about the missionaries, who have generally only found champ-ions in their own ranks.[1] The first missionaries, Wesleyans, arrived from Tonga in 1828, but soon after that the London Missionary Society sent out a group of missionaries, and the Wesleyans agreed to leave Samoa to the LMS in return for a similar concession in Tonga. The Roman Catholic Mission was established in 1845.

[1] The literature left by the missionaries is however immense—See, e.g. LMS. The best individual sources are Turner, Stair, Monfat.

The missionaries were primarily in Samoa to spread the gospel from the pulpit and in the classroom, but they also wanted, indeed considered it their Christian duty as harbingers of a superior civilization, to increase Samoan standards of living. Most missionaries felt Christianity itself would assist economic development, by inculcating the habit of 'productive labour',[1] by emphasizing the sanctity of persons and property, by obtaining just prices for the sale of cash crops. It was also felt that Christianity would lead to a decline in certain 'primitive' *fa'asāmoa* customs (especially ceremonial), which led to 'idleness', 'fornication' and 'low productivity'.[2]

The missionaries did not, however, give unqualified approval to increases in the standard of living. The acquisition of some European goods, for example, clothes, soap and medicines, were considered to be very good. Indeed these goods were thought to be aids to industry. But the missions condemned the acquisition of certain goods and there were many elements in mission teaching and preaching which condemned the pursuit of wealth. The capitalist ethic only finds a place in the most calvinist missionary's sermons.[3] This was partly a theological argument, the association of goodness and poverty, but it was also a result of the great feud between the traders and the missionaries in Samoa.

The critics of the missions have claimed that this insistence on poverty was a result of the missionaries desire to exploit the Samoans. 'The missionaries', said one critic, 'ring a big bell three times a day—the first bell—a summons for the natives to bring to the priest all the taros which they have gathered—the second—all the coconuts and bananas—the third—fresh fish.'[4] It is true that the Samoans were constantly asked to be charitable to the Church. Considerable sums were collected as tithes or contributions, mainly at large meetings like the Wesleyan or London Missionary Society Mē.[5] Considerable amounts of goods and services were also given by villages to the missionaries, village pastors or teachers and for the building

---

[1] e.g. Heath, *Samoan Reporter* 1847/4.
[2] e.g. Turner—LMSMP 4/26, Monfat 1890: 99ff., LMSNP/5, *Samoan Reporter* 1870/3.　　　　　　　　　　　　　　　　　　[3] e.g. LMSNP/12
[4] In many cases in the nineteenth century half of income was given; LMSAR, Monfat 1890: 76; but this decreased greatly during the twentieth century.
[5] See LMSAR, Monfat 1890.

and upkeep of village churches. In some areas the mission used village land and labour to run commercial plantations. But although there were some abuses it was not usual for the missionaries to gain personally. Most money was ploughed back into the missions, which were very expensive to run. Apart from the expense of sending and supporting missionaries, mission ships had to be fitted out, printing presses established, seminaries and schools built. The London Missionary Society was forced to approach the City at one time for a loan. The Samoans, in fact, willingly gave the money to the Church which, as we shall see, was an important arena for the demonstration of wealth and status.

The missionaries, then, were not exploiters, and although the primary object of disseminating Christianity had few direct benefits there were still some important by-products of mission endeavour. Initially the missionaries exchanged steel tools for subsistence foods from the villages or gave them as gifts to converts. New crops, including an important cash crop, bananas,[1] were introduced into the villages from the mission school plantations. On these plantations many villagers gained valuable experience in tropical agriculture and commercial practice. The missions assisted in the development of coconut oil manufacture to swell Church contributions and so helped establish the very important coconut industry. When coconut oil or copra ceased to be a village church contribution[2] and became solely a cash crop the missions often protected the villager against the shrewd merchants. Experience in skilled trades, and in accounting, was acquired in the building of the churches, especially the huge cathedrals in or around Apia. Many villages were introduced to savings habits through accounts that were established for church building funds.

There were also significant mission contributions to Samoan health and education. Most missionaries and some native pastors operated dispensaries even though medicines were given, initially at least, to convert rather than cure. Certainly most missionaries were not trained in medicine, and some 'drew an imaginary line around the peoples' bodies at approximately the navel level—if the trouble was above that line

[1] The so-called *fa'i palagi* (Cavendish) introduced in 1837 by John Williams.
[2] About 1870—LMSAR.

it was eucalyptus, if below—epsom salts'.[1] But the missionaries were all more able than the beachcomber doctors who practised in Apia,[2] and men like the Rev. Dr. Turner and Père Vachon[3] (nicknamed *médecin malgré lui*) did important work. Turner's[4] inoculation of a large number of Samoans against smallpox in 1847 stopped any outbreak of a disease which in other parts of the Pacific decimated the population.

Similarly although the aims of mission teaching were to inculcate the gospel or to train pastors, there were still some important consequences of mission education, notably the high rate of vernacular literacy[5] and the provision of a basic education (the three Rs, elementary general knowledge and scientific knowledge) and some training in practical subjects.

There were limits to the mission contribution. The missions, in the vanguard of the nineteenth-century humanitarian movement, constantly claimed how much they would like to do for their 'sacred trust'.[6] But they were always dependent on private contributions and always short of funds. And these funds were deployed first, and sometimes only, in building large and expensive seminaries around Apia away from the villages. This not only diverted funds from other more beneficial projects but also removed the missionaries and their influence from the village scene and village economic activities.

THE ADMINISTRATIONS—BENEFITS MISPLACED

The administrators were a further group of Europeans, who increasingly in the twentieth century intended to bring economic development to the villages. There have been three distinct periods in the history of the administrative economic effort in Samoa. Firstly, there was the German administration (1900–14). Secondly, there was the New Zealand occupation, when the New Zealanders were an army of occupation (1914–22), a League of Nations mandatory power (1922–45), and finally a United Nations trustee (1945–62). Thirdly, there has been the administration of the United Nations experts (mainly from the Technical Assistance Board) who have

---

[1] Burton 1949: 120. [2] GBFO 58/90/323.
[3] Monfat 1890: 352. [4] 1861: 113ff.
[5] Within twenty years of the mission arrival it was claimed that 25 per cent of the population were literate (*Samoan Reporter*, January 1854). [6] LMSB11F6J8.

taken over important jobs in the Public Service since Independence (1962).

Germany received Western Samoa after international agreements in 1899 which parcelled out spheres of influence in the Pacific.[1] International rivalry, the prestige of having a place in the sun, and the profits of tropical agriculture were the main reasons for German annexation and these interests defined to a large extent the administration's economic role. The prestige of a colony consisted in possession, not necessarily economic development, but the demands of profit meant that the administration (which in German times was closely connected with a semi-official trading company) was forced to utilize Samoan resources or labour. The Germans tried at first to co-operate as little as possible with the Samoans, buying land from them and importing labour to establish plantations. They tried, as the consuls had done, to develop Apia and the surrounding district as an European enclave, interfering only in the *fa'asāmoa* hinterland when a breakdown in law and order seemed imminent. But the increased need for land, the difficulties of importing labour, the transfer of *fa'asāmoa* political rivalries and political instability to Apia itself, made these German isolationist policies impracticable. Consequently the Germans decided to develop the Samoan colony in partnership with the Samoans who would supply land, crops or labour assisted by German capital.[2]

There were also currents of anti-mercantilism and humanitarianism in German policy.[3] The German Governors in Samoa, all-powerful in matters of policy, felt that the Germans had a mission (*bestimmung*) to civilize Samoa by importing the best of European (that is usually German) ideas and institutions as well as European goods and services, and by protecting and preserving the best of *fa'asāmoa* society from European influences. The Germans like to call their colony a Protectorate (*Schutzegebeit*). But over-all the civilizing mission

---

[1] There are no good accounts of the German period. But there are good memoirs by contemporary officials—Solf 1907, 1919, Schultz 1926 (Governors), Schnee 1926 (Chief Justice), Riedel 1938 (Trading company). Also Zieschank 1918, Sudsee Handbuch 1911, Genthe 1908, Deeken 1902. The most important source is GCA—the German Colonial Archives.   [2] e.g. GCA 4a, App. 16.

[3] These are outlined in Schnee 1926. They owed much to Solf (Governor 1900–10) and Dernburg, Colonial Secretary from 1906.

was only a leitmotive. Only small subsidies were forthcoming from Berlin[1] and soon the colony was instructed to support itself from its own taxes.

Humanitarianism became more important and mercantilism less important when the New Zealanders took over Samoa as a League of Nations mandate. The New Zealanders were committed by international agreements to a policy of economic and social development. But for at least the first twenty years of the New Zealand administration problems of law and order were paramount and prevented any effective action. The humanitarian pressures increased after 1935 when a Labour Government came to power and especially after 1945. By 1964, aid in the form of both specialist assistance and funds was proportionately higher than in most underdeveloped countries.[2]

Although by the standards of underdeveloped countries the level of external aid has never been low there were significant deficiencies in the deployment of this capital. A major fault has been the separation of the administration from native society. All the European administrations have been highly centralized. The officers lived and worked in a wholly European area of Apia and only rarely ventured into the countryside, some only to go to and from the airport. For many, knowledge of *fa'asāmoa* consisted only of what their house girls or boys could tell them. Centralization became more significant during the various rebellions when the Apia government or even the home government took over completely. Misconceptions and prejudice also kept the administration apart from native society. Few European officers have bothered to learn the language, and most lived insulated from native society with their wives and families in transplanted European suburban estates or in the local hotels repulsing contact with *fa'asāmoa* society. As with the Protestant missionaries the wives were an important influence in the degree of separation, but single men also presented a problem in their association with Samoan society. There were cases of concubinage with Apia women

[1] e.g. in 1904 there was a 90,000 mark subsidy. There is no trace of subsidies after 1904, see GCA 4.

[2] Up to Independence specialist advice was the main form of aid, but since Independence Samoa has received approximately £250,000 per annum (half from New Zealand) as well.

or homosexuality with local boys all of which intensely annoyed and disgusted the Samoan leaders, and in one notorious case led many villagers to join anti-administration revolts.

Another serious deficiency, especially in the early days of the New Zealand administration, and during the United Nations period since Independence, has been the incompetence and unsuitability of personnel. In the New Zealand case, low wages, and in the United Nations case, the absence of experience in tropical conditions, meant that the best men were not attracted to Samoa and certainly not for long periods. Many officers were psychologically unsuited to the many irritations and frustrations of running a tropical administration in the claustral atmosphere of a small island. Many were trying to escape their own society and nervous diseases were common, whilst only the toughest could withstand the constant threat of sickness. By the end of the Second World War, competent men of long Samoan experience like Turnbull, McKay and Grattan, were running the New Zealand administration, but there were always staff shortages and inadequacies.

The main consequences of the insufficiency and inefficient deployment of capital was that the villages received few economic benefits from the administrative presence. Certainly in the German period[1] the road network was extended in North West Upolu, whilst road building and reef blasting was encouraged in all villages. Villages were protected from the exploitation of traders and planters, and alienation and credit was prohibited. The administration also tried to help village production directly. For example, all the chiefs were ordered in 1900 to each plant fifty new coconut trees on untilled land. Measures were taken to control weeds, marauding pigs and pests, especially the Rhinoceros beetle. But very little was done in the field of health and education. A German philanthropist built a small hospital in Apia and free treatment was given to government officials. A small government school for Samoans was established towards the end of the German administration, and the sons of chiefs were trained in the military *FitaFita* guard.

The New Zealanders admittedly did much more especially in the fields of health and education. But still little was done

[1] GCA O 26/12/1900, 14/9/901, 4a.

to assist cash crop production or wage-labour from which revenue for these social services was eventually derived. Expenditure on vital public works, the provision of communications and water supplies to the villages was an insignificant part of government expenditure and many important public works in Samoa were, in fact, constructed by the United States Marines during the war.[1] At Independence (1962) there were still villages without roads and most roads were of very poor quality. Only one-quarter of the villages had piped water and only villages within a few miles radius of Apia had electricity.[2] Generally little money was spent on agriculture although the administration did arrange for the marketing of bananas, an important new cash crop. Some assistance was also given to marketing by controlling the traders' activities and the prices they charged, though this legislation had only a limited effectiveness.

Similarly, the United Nations schemes since Independence have brought few benefits, mainly because of the experts' incompetence or lack of knowledge of local conditions. For example, one American expert hoped to save the Samoan economy by planting in all villages an unknown Hawaiian nut (*Macadamia*) which possessed remarkable qualities as an ice cream topping but which took ten years to grow and had never been tested in Samoan conditions. Another Scandinavian expert proposed to raise local revenue by taxing village land, which he intended to survey, ignoring the fact that a previous attempt at surveying land by the New Zealand administration had resulted in a rebellion. Again, a Danish furniture expert was introduced to utilize the highland hard woods (brought down, he hoped, by imported elephants), and local coconut fibre to make modern chairs. But the experts had not noticed that the Samoans rarely sit on chairs whilst the pantalooned Europeans could not bear to sit on a rough sennit fibre. Consequently the finished product had to be purchased by the United Nations themselves.

[1] e.g. the western cross island road or the airport.
[2] WSDF Statistics Department.

2

SAMOAN ECONOMIC VALUES

THE role of the Europeans in local economic development, though significant in certain spheres, was not critical. If not externally imposed, how was local economic development internally generated? We begin the examination of this question by considering Samoan economic values.

Economic attitudes vary significantly in relation to three categories of goods and services and according to different social situations. First, there are those goods which are considered to be required for normal (*māsani*) everyday needs of food, shelter and clothing, goods which people say are necessities (*mea tatau*). Secondly there are those goods desired as personal luxuries (*mea sili*) or for ceremonials (*mea fa'alavelave*). And finally there are those goods (or services) which can be transformed into future goods and services, that is, goods such as tools (*mea faigāluega*) and money (*tupe*) which serve capital functions.

NECESSITY GOODS

Fa'asāmoa values emphasize a restrained demand for necessity goods.[1] There is an element of fatalism—*tali i lagi vai o A'opa*[2]— the necessities of life will always be provided. But also a rate of steeply diminishing utility or satisfactions is recognized especially with regard to food. To overeat is physically uncomfortable but also greedy (*matape'ape'a*) and this is a cardinal

[1] We use the term necessity goods in preference to subsistence because this corresponds to Samoan usage, and also because in the writings of economists, subsistence usually refers more generally to an economic situation without significant exchange (the usage in Ch. 3), or to economic activity confined to satisfying some biologically determined need (bread line).

[2] Literally 'A'opa waits for rain'. This refers to the village A'opa (Savai'i) on a lavafield where there is no spring water and the people have to rely on rain water, which, it is said, always falls when needed. The story is told of a visiting chief (To'imoana of Fagaloa) who laughed when the villagers had no water to make '*ava* (kava). But when the people put out the bowls, the rain came.

sin. The greedy man is compared to the legendary figure of Niu who ate so much that he choked to death. Greediness is thought to lead to selfishness, and the most abhored of social situations in Samoa, ostracism. The story is told of Pega who hoarded many pieces of *siapo* (barkcloth) but was so mean that he would wear only one piece. This cloth became so filthy that Pega was not accepted by his neighbours. The barkcloth eventually fell to pieces, so that Pega was sent from the village for exposing his penis. Selfishness is also thought to lead directly to poverty,[1] since prosperity and wealth are thought to depend on the pooling of resources in concerted co-operation. The only variations in necessity requirements reflect variations in status. For example it is thought proper for a *matai* (chief) to eat more, and different kinds of food,[2] have a larger *fale* (house), more *siapo* (barkcloth), etc., though even here there are consumption limits which cannot be exceeded.

These *fa'asāmoa* values generally persist in the cash economy especially with regard to *mea Samoa*, Samoan goods (i.e. goods, usually produced locally,[3] and considered to be traditionally Samoan). The introduction of a new and unrestricted range of goods, *mea pālagi*, European goods, led to a great expansion of necessity wants.

There is much evidence in the literature of a continuous increase in the consumption of European goods. There are many descriptions[4] before 1850 of the use of soap, European household and garden implements and boats. Everyday consumption of European foods[5] came later in the nineteenth century especially when canned foods became available, though flour was widely used before 1870. Housing materials, especially corrugated iron, became popular especially after the

[1] For example in the expression *o le manase oge*—literally 'a hungry stomach', which is said to mean that a person who has nothing must have given nothing.

[2] Certain cuts of meat and fish and certain dishes, e.g. *ta'a folosami* cooked breadfruit and coconut cream.

[3] Local production was the most significant criteria of *mea Samoa* and included mainly traditional food goods. There are a few goods regarded as *mea pālagi* (e.g. bread) manufactured in some villages, whilst some Samoan goods (e.g. Samoan tobacco) are purchased from the traders or street vendors in Apia. These goods are not, however, a significant part of consumption in Salani or Malie, though in Apia many Samoan goods are bought.

[4] LMSMP 5/23, B11F8JA, GBFO 58/63, 252 Wilkes 1847 v. 2: 123, Krämer v. 2:46.

[5] LMSMP 2/7, LMSNP 7/24, NZIT 14/5.

Second World War when the United States marines left a considerable legacy of miscellaneous hardware. By 1964 in the three villages surveyed, European goods predominated in the necessity goods sector.[1] The following table illustrates this predominance.[2]

There are three important reasons for the increased desire for, and consumption of, European necessity goods. First is the European effort to introduce European goods. The altruistic Europeans generally felt that European goods were more suitable for Samoan needs than Samoan goods as well as being more conducive to 'civilization', 'progress', 'economic development', etc. For example, the missions made great efforts to introduce cloth, to replace the 'sinful *siapo*' (which was considered to lead to 'immorality' and 'hedonistic idleness'[3]), soap, and a wide range of household implements to help Samoans lead more Christian and productive lives.[4] The New Zealand administration introduced into the villages what it considered to be nutritious foods (orange juice, powdered milk, eggs, cheese, spinach, etc.) and tried to persuade the villagers to erect toilets, build wells and European-style houses. The traders, in search of profit, attempted to induce, trick or cajole the Samoans into buying any and every European good in stock.[5]

Although the Europeans initiated the demand for European goods and to some extent influenced its expansion they did not, by any means, determine the pattern or growth of Samoan consumption. Consumption was internally generated as much

[1] In comparing consumption of Samoan and European goods, the usual economists' method of reducing all items to cash or potential cash value (e.g. Fairbairn 1963, Catt 1955 (a), was not found to be suitable. Some Samoan goods were never sold, and those that were occasionally sold fetched very different prices in Apia or in the village, or in different social situations. Nor could values be measured by labour, as Salisbury did amongst the Siane (1963: 144) as the production of many goods required very little labour, or capital (see Ch. 8). Instead we have used broad indices of incidence of consumption which give a general picture of preferences, and relative magnitudes. For a full village inventory see Appendix 1.

[2] See Table 1. Page 32.

[3] LMSB11F3JF. Sometimes scantiness was considered to be the connection between siapo and sin though usually the connections were not detailed.

[4] LMSNP/5.

[5] As we shall see later (Ch. 9), coercion by alien traders was not possible, but most of the techniques of modern 'salesmanship' (specials, free samples, loss leaders, credit sales) were used at least as early as the late nineteenth century, e.g. Churchill 1902.

as it was externally imposed. There has been, at least in the twentieth century, a consistent effort by Samoans to raise their own standards of living. Demands for more and cheaper European goods have played an important part in the political movements before and since Independence.[1]

Ultimately European goods are chosen because they give greater satisfaction or utility than any Samoan equivalent. This is partly a matter of what might be called taste; for instance all food is considered tasteless without European salt or sugar.[2] Tinned meat and fish, mutton flaps, rice, and pancakes are considered to be most delicious. But although taste enters into the preference for most European necessity goods it is usually only a partial reason for the preference. A more important reason is the idea that most European necessity goods are more useful (*aogā*) than their Samoan counterparts, that is, as in many economists' concept of efficiency,[3] that greater utility is achieved in relation to inputs of resources, labour or capital in any given situation.

Very often European goods replace those Samoan goods where traditional processes of manufacture are laborious and tedious. For example the use of tinned or prepared foods, matches, charcoal or primus burners, saves the considerable time and effort of preparing food and hot oven stones (*umu*). Many people feel that European tinned food, soft and without bones, or pancakes dripping with grease, or bread dipped in cocoa or tea, is easier to eat than Samoan food. One man claimed that the fact that European food can be swallowed quickly is an asset because it prevented flies polluting the food, or dogs or children filching it.

The relative effectiveness of the goods is also an important part of its usefulness (*aogā*). For example, cloth, metal household implements and roofs are more durable than barkcloth (*siapo*), wooden implements or thatch (*lau*). Soap is accepted as a more effective means of removing heartily detested body

---

[1] The Lauati Mau (1905–11) (GCA XVII/2/17b) during the German Administration, and The Mau (1920–38) during the New Zealand administration (e.g. IT 1/20), and since 1962 the Vaega Malo and Faalapotopotaga Filemu.

[2] Salt (*māsima*) from sea-water and local sugar-cane (*tolo*) were used in foods traditionally, but people consider European salt (*salti*) and sugar (*suta*) to taste quite different and much more pleasant than local equivalents.

[3] e.g. Hall and Winsten 1959.

odours than traditional herbs or perfumes.[1] European lamps or candles give more light than traditional candles.[2] Many people feel especially that meat and fish increases a man's brainpower, shrewdness, and ability to get on in the outside world. Some people explain the achievements of Europeans in terms of the food they eat. Some people also feel that European food has curative powers, that bread stops diarrhoea, that sugary goods confer an immunity to fevers. In some cases the usefulness of European goods is only imagined and produces the opposite effect to that desired. Recent medical research has indicated that the high incidence of disease in Samoa is related to the consumption of European goods.[3]

It is realized that the usefulness (*aogā*) of European goods has a 'cost' (*tau*); that cash has to be paid for European goods which involves a sacrifice of Samoan resources or labour in cash cropping or wage labour. One chief said, '*o le malie ma le tu'u malie*'[4]—'Every shark has its price.' Everything in the world must be paid for. Most people do not make precise calculations of the comparative 'costs' of Samoan and European goods, and indeed many people have only a hazy idea of pricing the factors of production and distribution, or of prices prevailing at any given time. People are aware of any technical superiority of European goods, and, as we shall see shortly, the overall demand for certain European necessity goods, is in a sense elastic, that is varying with changes in price or income.

[1] Despite the missionaries' claim that they gave Samoa cleanliness as well as godliness (LMSNP/5) there was traditionally a strong dislike of body dirt and odours (the greatest insults in Samoa all relate to stinking body odours (*vivi*) compared to pigs excrement, etc.) and there were many means of cleaning the body. When bathing the leaves of the *toi* and *fisoa* trees, or a special mud (*u'u*) was rubbed on the body with coconut fibre and after bathing coconut or candlenut oil scented with various leaves was rubbed into the body.

[2] Traditionally the kernels of the candlenut tree (*lama*) were threaded on a small dry coconut leaf, or coconut oil with a coconut wick was used. Today Coleman lamps are preferred. Where available electricity is often used (around Apia) but the people are mistrustful of it.

[3] For example the poor ventilation in European style housing contributes to the high incidence of respiratory disease. European foods are responsible for dental and deficiency problems and the ubiquity of stomach disease is caused by the unhygienic preparation of breads and pastries—Haraldsen 1964(a), (b).

[4] Literally 'For the shark (*malie*) there is the shark gift (*tu'u malie*).' When a fisherman catches sharks he must present the village with the first (and possibly the only) shark. But the villagers must repay the fisherman with gifts of food. As one chief explained it: 'Everybody obtains something, but everybody must give first.'

In many cases, however, the demand for European necessity goods has little to do with comparative cost in terms of cash. This is partly because demand for certain goods (e.g. cloth) has become an established convention, so that European goods are purchased even when there are price or income changes. The continual use of European goods very often led to an irreversible decline in the use of Samoan resources, as people forgot how to use or conserve local resources, or as capital equipment deteriorated. For example, especially in villages near Apia, many people have only a limited knowledge of edible fishes or traditional fishing methods and often there is little traditional equipment being used.[1] Consequently tinned fish is bought when there is money, and omitted from the diet when there is no money.

More significantly the usefulness of any European necessity good is never measured completely against any cost measured in cash or a sacrifice of labour or resources. An important part of the preference for European necessity goods is that they confer or reflect status, i.e. the consumer's social position, in relation to the European world, or in Samoan society itself. First, European goods represent, for a small minority of Samoans who want to assimilate into European society, a sign of European (*pālagi*) status. In particular, trousers, a diet of European food, a European style house with a toilet, are recognized by both Samoans and Europeans as essential symbols of European status. But most Samoans who have little desire to become Europeans also consume European necessity goods on occasions when there are close contacts with European society. For example, when any European visits the village on 'normal business' (*fe'au māsani*), that is when the occasion does not warrant a feast (*fiafia*), European food would be eaten. Again, people living in the village who have close contacts with the outside European world (Government representatives, pastors, traders, *'āiga* with migrants) often consume relatively more European necessity goods, because this is expected of a person who is a representative of the outside

---

[1] Goo and Banner 1963 claim that 265 varieties were known traditionally. In Malie less than thirty of these were known in 1964. In Malie there are twenty-five canoes but most were very small (*paopao*) and many were in a poor state of repair. See Appendix I for other capital goods.

world, or of a person who has close relatives living in the outside world. This is one reason why the consumption of European necessity goods tends to increase in villages near Apia[1] where contacts with the European world and the number of outside officials are greatest. (In many cases European goods are symbols only and are never used. Many '*āiga*[2]

TABLE I

Consumption of necessity goods in Salani, Malie and Apia January-December 1964

	SALANI		MALIE		APIA	
	Samoan goods	European goods	Samoan goods	European goods	Samoan goods	European goods
GOODS[5]	Locally produced	£ spent per capita	Locally produced	£ spent per capita	Locally produced	£ spent per capita
1. Food[5]	X (11)[1]	6	Ø (9·5)[1]	10·25	O (3·2)[1] 5·0[6]	10·5
2. Clothing[5]	O[2]	1·2	O[2]	2·35	O	2·5
3. Household implements[5]	Ø[3]	0·7	Ø[3]	1·1	O	1·5
4. Houses, outhouses[5]	X[4]	0·1	Ø[4]	0·3	Ø[4]	1·0
Totals		£8·0		£14·0		£15·5

Explanation of symbols (all relative to consumption of European goods)

X—A majority of goods produced locally.
Ø—Some goods produced locally.
O—Few or no goods produced locally.

Based on a sample of 100 adults in each village over a three month period.

1. Potential cash values of consumed goods based on a three-month analysis of approximately 100 persons. Meals with no European foods (apart from salt and sugar) amounted to 65 per cent of all meals in the sample in Salani, 58 per cent in Malie, 30 per cent in Apia. See also Appendix 1.
2. Only locally woven hats (*pūlou*). See also Appendix 1.
3. Mainly *papa* (coarse mats) *fala* (sleeping mats). In Salani all '*āiga* had locally made mats of this kind. The figure for Malie was 90 per cent. See also Appendix 1.
4. There was no house completely without European goods (e.g. nails, hooks, etc.) But 95 per cent of all houses and outhouses in Salani (*fale*-dwelling house, *umu*—cookhouse, *faleo'o*—storehouse) had thatch roofs and a shingle floor. The figure for Malie was 60 per cent and Apia 32 per cent. See also Appendix 1.
5. For full lists of goods see Appendix 1.
6. Spent on Samoan goods bought from street vendors.

[1] See Table 1.   [2] See Appendix I.

have beds and chairs in the *fale* (house), or wooden toilets on the reef, waiting for the arrival of a European to be used.)

On the other hand, certain European goods are symbols of Samoan status, marking a separation from European society. For example, increasingly in recent years, the cloth *lava* (kilt), the small square attaché case, the Hong Kong umbrella, have become the sign of the male Samoan, especially when he comes into town.

These symbols of participation in, or separation from, the European world are also often symbols of prestige (*mamalu*), rank (*matai*) or power (*pule*) in Samoan society itself. Generally speaking European necessity goods rate above their Samoan equivalents. According to the reports of the first missionaries, European goods were first thought to be goods of divine origin fit only for the consumption of the most revered persons.[1] Certainly the aura of divinity surrounding Europeans evaporated soon after the establishment of the grog-shops of Apia in the mid nineteenth century, but most Europeans goods continued to be received by chiefs, with whom the missionaries, administrators and traders negotiated. European goods are still associated with chiefs, or with those who possess wealth without rank. Finally, the prestige of particular European goods reflects the prestige, in Samoan eyes, of the country of origin. In the nineteenth century, it is reported that goods from Great Britain, regarded as the great world power, were highly desired. Today, American goods are in great demand despite their scarcity and high price because Americans are considered to be the most advanced people in the world, and a nation most favoured by God. Necessity goods which are status symbols in Samoan society are usually consumed conspicuously. One *'āiga* in Malie only eats European food when people from other *'āiga* are present.

Despite the usefulness and high status of European necessity

[1] Barff and Williams 1830. The London Missionary Society missionaries Barff and Williams arrived at a critical time in Samoan history in the midst of a vicious civil war over the high titles (*tafa'ifā*), and just after one leader has been assassinated (Tamafaiga). Samoans apparently thought, or were persuaded to think, that the missionaries' arrival was a divine intervention on the side of the Malietoa faction corroborating Tamafaiga's murder. The Malietoa faction aligned themselves with the missions and took over the *tafa'ifā*. The word *pālagi* (*papālagi*) was applied to the first missionaries, and all subsequent Europeans—it means literally descended from the skies.

goods, there are limits to the demand for, and the consumption of, these goods.

Firstly, especially in the case of foods, there are limits to which usefulness or status increment can override taste. Some European foods, for example cheese or spinach are repulsive to the Samoan palate despite the glossy handouts of the Health Department extolling the delicious as well as the nutritious nature of these foods. Many people dislike European beds, toilets, and tin roofs. One man commented that European beds give him insomnia, that European toilets give him constipation, and tin roofs give him a headache. Conversely, many people are very fond of certain Samoan foods, especially *talo* or banana dishes served with coconut cream, or breadfruit. Some of these foods are even imported into New Zealand by migrants.

In a few cases, the relative usefulness (*aogā*) of the Samoan good is important in addition to taste. For instance, many people feel that whilst European food may increase brainpower and shrewdness, Samoan food increases strength and virility. Some chiefs feel that the future of Samoa depends on a large strong population rather than skilled manpower. A few people also feel that European foods with their various additives are poisonous, whilst others consider that European houses, especially if the walls are closed in, cause disease as well as encouraging sly sexual habits, malicious gossip or sinister plots. Electricity is also greatly mistrusted,[1] usually with reason since faulty wiring causes many fires and shocks and the whole system once went off for six weeks. Certainly electricity did not produce the 'consumer revolution' which, Lewis has argued,[2] occurs in underdeveloped countries with the advent of electric power. Finally, some people find that certain Samoan goods, for example baskets and mats, are more durable than European objects.[3]

Status, especially the social position of a Samoan relative to the European world also enters occasionally into preferences for Samoan goods. Just as consumption of European necessity goods increases with social proximity to the European world,

[1] Confined to villages near Apia, though a small number of villages had established or were contemplating establishing their own plants, e.g. Sala'ilua, Samata.

[2] Lewis 1955: 29.

[3] Linoleum tended to become sticky in the heat. Plastic bags ripped easily, whilst anything metal rusted.

so the consumption of Samoan goods increases with social distance. For example, during the Mau rebellion[1] (1925–36) when there were widespread grievances against the European administration, or recently when the Apia merchants were unpopular,[2] there were efforts to boycott the traders and consume only Samoan goods. In general such consumption patterns are only temporary protests, preceding or supplementing political action, and disappear as soon as rapport is established between Apia and the countryside. There are also a small number of Samoan necessity goods which are status symbols within Samoan society. Amongst these are special dishes for chiefs,[3] and certain elaborations in dwelling houses.[4]

The most significant restriction on the consumption and demand for European goods is the restricted availability of cash (or other means of purchasing power) relative to the price of European goods. In particular areas or more generally in times of low incomes or high prices, the consumption of European goods declines, whilst the consumption of Samoan goods rises.[5] For example people in Malie, where there are opportunities for both cash-cropping and wage labour, spend much more per head on European necessity goods than in the isolated village of Salani where there is only a restricted cash crop income, few credit facilities, and where European goods cost more mainly because of transport difficulties.

Demand is similarly, though less sensitively, affected by the price of European goods. Small price variations between competing types of a similar good or between competing traders do not significantly affect consumption patterns, though large-scale price changes (such as those caused in Malie by tariff increases, or scarcity of building materials) do have significant consequences for demand. The pattern is partly explained by the fact that overall demand is concentrated on low-price European goods (salt, sugar, flour, matches, etc.). In general

[1] NZIT 1/20.
[2] In 1964 there were many grievances over cash crops which led eventually to the formation of rural sections of a political party—the Organization of Peace.
[3] For example ta'afolasami—breadfruit (cooked) with coconut cream.
[4] For example, the raising of the floor platform.
[5] The areas of lowest income were generally those with the highest prices, since both incomes and prices were affected by access to the market. Prices varied more exactly with distance. Prices in Malie were approximately 7½ per cent above Apia prices, and in Salani 12 per cent.

high-price goods (for example electrical equipment), whatever usefulness or status value they might have, and even when the purchasing power is available are not preferred. Some people express a nervousness of purchasing a single good over ten pounds, though there is no such feeling about single purchases of cheaper goods, which total more than ten pounds. In some cases unfamiliarity with the good, or its performance, is the reason for this reluctance, but more often it is simply the price which is conventionally regarded as prohibitive.

Demand for European goods is not only restricted by prices and incomes, but also by the comparative 'cheapness' of Samoan goods. For example, in rural villages such as Salani, many Samoan goods are in a sense 'free goods' since the goods and the labour have few alternative uses either locally or in the cash economy. In many cases 'production' involves as little labour as picking fruit off the ground (e.g. the mango). To some extent this is also true of cash crops. For example, although coconuts have a potential cash value in Salani, this potential could only be realized in a restricted number of cases. There are many coconut trees but only a small adult male labour force to make copra, only two small traders and little transport for marketing. On the other hand, production for local con-sumption can utilize a much wider labour force than the adult males, since there is no need to make copra. Hence, coconuts for local consumption are not valued at their potential cash price,[1] though the people do not make comparative calculations for every small consumer decision. Indeed the relevant price facts are often unknown to the consumer, or imperfectly under-stood. It is simply a convention that it is cheaper to eat coconuts than to sell them to buy food.

There are also 'free goods' as defined in Malie, since there are many crops which have no value in the European economy, since many categories of labour (children, old people) have very restricted opportunities in the cash economy, and since village work can usually be adjusted to fit in with the demands of urban labour.[2] But cash crops, used for local consumption,

---

[1] Time is not regarded as a sacrificial input either, mainly because gathering nuts, etc, is not usually regarded as work by the youngsters who participate.

[2] Many wage earners who commute daily to town work in the village before and after their job, in the cooler parts of the day. Weekly commuters work in the week-end. See Ch. 7.

have a much higher potential cash value than in Salani, since there is great population pressure on land, and many more opportunities for the sale of crops and for wage labour in nearby Apia. For example, a coconut consumed is valued in cash at approximately the price for which it could have been sold as a cash crop. Even so, in many *'āiga* coconuts are still considered to be cheaper than any European equivalent. It is considered, for example, that it takes far more coconuts, bartered or sold, to pay for European goods for a meal, than to use coconuts directly, especially since young or old people prepare coconut dishes. Coconuts, and other Samoan goods are considered to be 'cheaper' even when they have to be purchased from street vendors,[1] who do not have the overheads, middlemen, transport and overseas labour costs which put up the price of European goods. In Apia especially, where comparative prices are known, preferences reflect small-scale comparative cost calculations, though the social conventions influence preferences, despite cost.

LUXURY AND CEREMONIAL GOODS

The second category of goods distinguished by Samoans consists of goods not considered to be as essential as necessity goods. First, there are those goods used as personal accessories, or for leisure activities, which we shall call luxury goods.[2] Secondly, there are those goods used in ceremonial activities.[3]

As in the case of necessity goods, there has been a strong and expanding preference for European goods in the luxury and ceremonial sector. This may be seen from the following summary of the consumption of luxury and ceremonial goods in the fieldwork villages in 1964.[4]

External stimulus has been one reason for this expansion. The Europeans, from the first explorers, had an image of

[1] Particularly in Apia village where there was very little garden land.

[2] The list includes tobacco, alcohol, many personal ornaments, bicycles, radios, cinema, dances, ice-cream, soft drinks, perfumes, most activities on a trip to town. For a full list see Appendix 1. The only Samoan goods were some scents, tobacco, coconut body oil, and personal ornaments. See Table 23.

[3] Mainly tinned corned beef (*pisupo*), tinned herrings, tins of biscuits, money amongst European goods. *I'e tōga* (fine mats) and a wide variety of Samoan goods were *mea fa'alavelave*. For fuller details on *fa'alavelave* see Ch. 9. See Tables 2, 14 and Appendix 1.

[4] See Tables 2 and 3 overleaf.

4

TABLE 2

Consumption of luxury goods and services in Salani, Malie and Apia 1964
(All figures *per capita*)

TYPE OF GOODS OR SERVICE[3]	SALANI		MALIE		APIA	
	Samoan[3] goods	European[3] goods	Samoan[3] goods	European[3] goods	Samoan[3] goods	European[3] goods
		shillings		*shillings*		*shillings*
1. Radios[3]	O	2	O	6	O	15
2. Food, drink and tobacco[3]	Ø[1]	4	Ø[1]	15	O	62
3. Clothes and ornaments[3]	Ø[2]	1	Ø[2]	4	O	6
4. Reading material[3]	O	3*d.*	O	6*d.*	O	6
5. Cinema[3]	O	1	O	1	O	54
6. Taxis, bus-rides, bicycles[3]	O	14	O	14	O	38
Totals	£1 2*s.* 3*d.*		£2 0*s.* 6*d.*		£9 1*s.* 0*d.*	

Key to Samoan goods (all indices relative to consumption of European goods).

Ø—Some goods locally produced.
O—Very few or no goods locally produced.

1. Mainly locally grown tobacco—*tapa'a*. See Appendix 1.
2. Mainly Chief's ornaments, such as *fue* (fly-switch). See Appendix 1.
3. For full lists of goods see Appendix 1. Sample as for Table 1.

hedonistic Samoans avidly desiring bright beads, and consequently exchanged luxury items whenever they wanted something from the Samoans. Even the missionaries and administrators, although they condemned the 'trifles and frivolities'[1] of the luxury trade, slipped in the odd bright bead or silver topped walking stick to secure a convert or cement an alliance. As late as the 1950s no New Zealand administrator would leave for the villages without a big bottle of lollies. But the most important influences were the traders and merchants who, in general, were anxious to sell luxury rather than necessity goods, because luxury goods usually involved greater profits. As there were only a few

[1] LMSB11F3JF—The New Zealanders placed a high import duty on 'fancy goods'. See WS Trade, Commerce and Shipping Reports 1923–65.

TABLE 3

Consumption of ceremonial (*fa'alavelave*) goods and services
in Salani, Malie and Apia 1964

(All figures *per capita*)

TYPE OF GOODS OR SERVICE[1]	SALANI Samoan[1] goods	SALANI European[1] goods	MALIE Samoan[1] goods	MALIE European[1] goods	APIA Samoan[1] goods	APIA European[1] goods
		shillings		shillings		shillings
1. Tinned or frozen food[1]	O	63	O	81	O	109
2. Other food and drink[1]	X	3	X	6	Ø 17s.[2]	23
3. Money and fine mats[1]	Ø	29	Ø	36	Ø	64
4. Cloth[1]	Ø	4	Ø	5	Ø	8
5. Ornaments[1]	Ø	1	Ø	1	Ø	4
6. Church contributions[1]	Ø[3]	10[4]	Ø[3]	12[4]	Ø[3]	15[4]
7. Transport[1]	O	14	O	20	O	22
Totals	£6 4s. 0d.		£8 1s. 0d.		£12 5s. 0d.	

Key to symbols

X—A majority of goods locally produced.
Ø—Some goods locally produced.
O—Few or no goods locally produced.

1. For full lists of goods see Appendix 1. Sample as for Table 1.
2. Bought from street vendors in Apia.
3. Contributions to the Church Pastor who is maintained by the villagers.
4. Includes all cash contributions to the local church and to the Central Mission funds, but not food contributions to church ceremonies, etc.

traders in any village and a handful of merchants in Apia who controlled sales and advertising, consumer preferences for luxury goods, as opposed to necessity or capital goods, could be considerably influenced and in some cases predetermined.

For example, in Malie all the films seen are either third-rate Westerns, Second World War blood baths or turgid romances. The trader who runs these shows explained that his programmes are determined by what people want and he points to the capacity houses as evidence of this. Most of the people, however, say their main interest is not so much in the film as in the social gathering. Certainly some young men find the films exciting, but most adults find the films boring, and many sleep through performances. There are equally big crowds when the Health Department shows a film on the life-cycle of the mosquito, etc., and nobody appears to be sleeping. Similarly preferences for reading material (mainly comics) and many other luxury goods are largely determined by what the trader stocks.

The pattern of demand for luxuries is, to some extent, externally imposed. However, even without this there is a strong and expanding desire for European ceremonial and luxury goods in general, particularly to replace *fa'asāmoa* items.[1]

The most significant reason for this demand is that European luxury and ceremonial goods are generally status symbols of a higher order in Samoan society than Samoan goods. Bicycles, radios, fine clothes, trips to town or abroad, confer prestige (*mamalu*) on the consumer, whilst the acquisition of European ceremonial goods (particularly tinned food and money) for disbursement through the kinship network is the most important way of demonstrating, enhancing or even acquiring rank. The symbolic value of these goods is reinforced by their association, real or imagined, with highly regarded Europeans, and with chiefs, especially high chiefs who tend to possess most of these goods.

The replacement of Samoan goods in the luxury sector also, though less significantly, reflects a taste preference and the greater usefulness (*aogā*) of the European good.

For example, ice-cream and soft drinks are considered by many people to be much more delicious than most Samoan luxury dishes or drinks.[2] The cinema, radio, and recently television,[3] are considered to be much more entertaining than traditional Samoan theatre (*tīfaga*). Comparative usefulness is important in the preference for European cigarettes,[4]

---

[1] Although there are no precise historical data on the growth of luxury demand, some indications can be seen from the steady growth of tinned foods, etc., in customs returns (WS Trade and Shipping Returns (Annual)).

[2] For example the coconut sprouted on the ground.

[3] A television service was introduced in American Samoa at the end of 1964 but only a few people in Apia have sets.

[4] Important since the early twentieth century. O. F. Nelson (1922–NZIT 1/22) called the Samoans 'cigarette fiends'.

which are easier to smoke than the unwieldy, Samoan 'cigars' (*tapa'a*) which come to pieces, or for *fa'amafu*[1] 'beer', which is more bemusing than the mildly micturient *'ava* (kava). Many Europeans goods are considered to be more useful on ceremonial occasions than Samoan equivalents. Wheeled transport however decrepit is an improvement on the sedan chair (*fata*) or footslogging during the journeys (*malaga*) which are part of most ceremonials. European tinned food not only saves labour in preparation, but also keeps better[2] than Samoan foods during ceremonies which last up to a fortnight. Tinned food can also be used by recipients when they reach home, or for future ceremonial obligations.[3] Money, easily stored, versatile in use, has also to some extent replaced fine mats (and even food) which are difficult to manufacture and which quickly become tattered.[4]

However there are restrictions on the preference for European luxury goods. For instance, many people feel that the use of certain Samoan goods is more proper on certain occasions. For example during ceremonies it is thought that participants should use traditional ornaments,[5] and many prefer traditional scents and flowers on these occasions. Pigs, fine mats (*i'e tōga*), barkcloth (*siapo*, *tapa*) are all considered to be an essential part of exchanges between *'āiga* who have any pretensions to high status, though in all exchanges European money and food are

---

[1] There seemed to be little inclination towards alcohol in the nineteenth century (GCA 2/XVII/a1/V5/65), and there has been prohibition in Samoa since German times designed to protect the natives from the evils of alcohol. From 1920 some Samoans could obtain alcohol officially only for 'medical or sacramental' purposes (IT 37/3/1). But few Samoans obtained permits on these grounds. In most villages the young men made *fa'amafu* beer, consisting of a methylated spirit or surgical spirit (obtained on a black market through hospital staff), or any liquor obtainable, flavoured with orange or some other cordial or sugar. (See Samoa Act 1921, Pt. 13, Amendment No. 2 1956, NZIT 1/22.) Other similar types of beer can be bought occasionally in the back streets of Apia, or at the liquor clubs. One estimate claimed that 2,500 bottles of homebrew are sold each week in Apia (*Evening Post* (New Zealand), 3 December 1953).

[2] Food which had gone off was not acceptable in ceremonial exchanges. Samoan foods, such as pigs, which are highly valued and can be stored on the hoof, have also an important place in feasts, but once killed a pig has to be constantly recooked to remain edible. One old man commented that he had not had diarrhoea since tinned foods were used in ceremonials.

[3] Sometimes whole cartons of tinned food are taken away unopened.

[4] Although a mat's value was increased rather than decreased by its age and tattered appearance, there was a point when the mat disintegrated. See Ch. 9.

[5] For example, the orator chief's (*tualāfale*) flywhisk (*fue*) and staff (*fa'atuto'oto'o*).

involved. Local foods, especially staples such as *talo*, are also commonly used during ceremonies less because of propriety than because European foods are too scarce to make a full meal.[1]

The relative scarcity of European goods is, in fact, the most important restriction on consumption and demand in the luxury sector. As in the case of necessity goods, this scarcity reflects the relative cheapness of certain Samoan goods and a restricted purchasing power in the cash economy due to levels of income that are low in relation to wants. But it also reflects the priority of demand for necessities on any available cash. In most *'āiga* expenditure on luxury or ceremonial items is relatively small, and only in the wealthiest *'āiga* of Malie and Apia does luxury or ceremonial expenditure exceed expenditure on necessity goods.[2] In most *'āiga*, luxury personal items have the lowest priority. Most people feel that it is wrong to neglect necessities to enable the greater consumption of personal luxury items, and some people feel that all expenditure on such luxuries is wrong, even a sin (*agasala*), likely to lead to the cardinal sin in Samoa—selfishness.[3] There is a saying—*pulapula a lā goto*[4]—pretty things may have bad consequences. On the other hand, all acquisition of ceremonial goods that will be disbursed is a sign of unselfishness and generosity and is widely admired. In some *'āiga* ceremonial goods (especially when required for the church or funerals) are virtually regarded

[1] Though some people believed that European tinned food was excessively rich and that to eat a great quantity made one vomit.

[2] Veblen's (1953) thesis that conspicuous consumption only takes place where there is surplus cash after subsistence (i.e. necessity goods) would seem to apply to Samoa as well as nineteenth century America. For comparative expenditure tables see Table 2. There were, however, occasional very large ceremonial exchanges widely quoted by European officials, for example when a few years ago the village of Sala'ilua (Savai'i) raised £7,000 for a wedding or when Satupaitea raised £2,500 for the privilege of opening the door of a new church in Apia. There were no similar occurrences in the fieldwork villages in 1964. See Ch. 9.

[3] For example in the saying *Se'i motu le pā'a 'ua iloa*, literally 'The fine pearl shell hook should not be hidden'—that is a man who acquires a luxury object will be tempted because of its value to hide it.

[4] Literally 'the brightness of the setting sun'—that is, although the setting sun may appear very bright, it is followed by darkness, where as one chief put it, 'Satan dwells'. A similar saying is '*o le tava'e*'—'the Tava'e bird looks after it's tail feathers'. The *Tava'e* bird has very beautiful long red or white tail feathers. The Samoans say the bird is very proud of these feathers, and that when attacked it will always back away guarding it's feathers so that it is easily caught.

as necessity goods, though seldom necessity goods of the highest priority.

There are other important restrictions on the demand for ceremonial goods. During funerals especially there is only a limited time to assemble goods or cash, and since most debts are incurred on such occasions credit may be difficult to obtain at this time. There are also socially recognized restrictions. For example, in any exchange there are recognized limits to any *'āiga* contribution, based partly on the comparative rank of *'āiga* involved in the exchange, but also on mutually agreed levels of contribution. In any exchange, contributions are not competitive and there are also socially recognized means for any one *'āiga* to contribute, temporarily at least, less than the expected level, without loss of prestige. Most often an excuse of poverty, or pressing necessity needs, is made, whether or not this is the real reason. The receiving *'āiga* are obliged to accept this, for Samoans say, *Ua leo itiiti le Paia*—it is important to keep goods if giving away endangers life or well-being.[1]

Finally, as in the case of necessity goods, the relative abundance and comparative 'cheapness' of Samoan ceremonial goods restricts demand for European goods. Admittedly certain Samoan ceremonial goods (for example *i'e tōga* (fine mats) and *siapo* (barkcloth)) take a long time to make, but their manufacture involves labour (mainly women) which has very few alternative uses in the cash economy.[2] Again, *'āiga* labour can be called on for ceremonial needs, virtually at a moment's notice whatever commitments there are in the cash economy. Finally, as in the case of necessity goods, many Samoan goods used in ceremonials have few alternatives uses in the cash economy.[3]

CAPITAL GOODS

Necessity, luxury or ceremonial goods make up then the pattern of consumption, but there are other goods and services in demand because they lead to future consumption, through production or through the deferment of present consumption. We shall call these goods, according to standard usage, capital

---

[1] Literally 'The voice of Paia is faint'. This refers to a legend of a woman who gave away so much food that she eventually died from starvation.   [2] See Table 5.
[3] Especially the fibre crops from which mats and barkcloth are made.

goods. This category includes tools and machinery (*mea fa'-agaluega*), that is goods which lead directly to future productivity, and other goods, particularly money (*tupe*), which command purchasing power over potential production or consumption goods. Included also are what is often called human capital, that is productive knowledge and health.

The literature suggests that there has always been a keen demand for European capital goods especially[1] and this is true certainly in the contemporary villages. For example, in Salani, Malie, and Apia, approximately one-sixth of cash income is spent on capital items,[2] despite the fact that the minimum capital needs (i.e. the amount of capital required to produce an acceptable product for the market) of most cash economic activities are not great. All Samoans have access to land and all the main cash crops may be self-propagating,[3] harvested manually and traded in without processing, whilst most wage labour is unskilled. The following table outlines the nature of capital demand in the fieldwork villages in 1964.[4]

This demand for capital goods has a solid base in *fa'asamoa* values. Consideration of future needs has always been important in economic activity. There is a saying—*Fa le taeao e le afiafi*—the man who sleeps in the morning will not eat in the evening.[5] There are other values which emphasize the need for thrift in present consumption, for careful planning for future production,[6] for care in the conservation of resources,[7] and for preserving resources after use.[8]

[1] GBFO 58/63/252, Wilkes 1847/123 (nineteenth century), NZIT 11/18/1, NZIT 11/18/1, NZIT 37/3/1 (New Zealand period).
[2] Lewis 1955: 206 has suggested that economic development in areas such as Samoa requires only 10 per cent of income to be invested; cf. O'Loughlin 1956. Economists in Samoa have generally assumed that indigenous capital formation is inadequate (Catt 1955(a), Stace 1962, Fairbairn 1963).
[3] Particularly coconuts, but also cacao and bananas.   [4] See Table 4.
[5] The time of the principal meal.
[6] For example, the saying *Se'i muamua se fa'asaoa manu vao*—'Before catching birds an offering should be made.' Traditionally before bird hunts there were elaborate ceremonies, including offerings to the Gods, to ensure success. A similar proverb is *Se'i muamua ona ala uta*—'Try the fish line on the dry land first.' *Aua letalanoa i masina vale aua e le po lua se lelei*—'Always be ready for the migrating fish.' To catch certain fish which appeared only infrequently, the fishermen had to have lines and nets prepared well in advance. These sayings, like all proverbs, remain although the activities to which they refer (for example, bird hunts) may have disappeared.   [7] There is a long list of conservation *tapu*—see Ch. 8.
[8] Particularly food, for example, the *masi* (fermented breadfruit) pits. See Ch. 8.

TABLE 4

Expenditure on capital goods and services in Salani, Malie and Apia 1964
(All cash figures *per capita*)

TYPE OF GOODS[3]	SALANI		MALIE		APIA	
	Samoan[3] goods	European[3] goods	Samoan[3] goods	European[3] goods	Samoan[3] goods	European[3] goods
		shillings		*shillings*		*shillings*
1. Tools, fishing equipment, etc.[3]	Ø[1]	5	Ø[1]	10	O	3
2. Education[3]	O	1	O	3	O	5
3. Health[3]	O	1	O	1	O	2
4. Savings[3]	O	41	O	70	O	126
5. Transport[3]	O	12	O	20	O	15
6. Machinery and plant[3]	O	1	O	1	O	1
7. Roads, fences water supply, etc.[3]	Ø[2]	1	Ø[2]	1	O	1
Totals	£3 2s. 0d.		£5 6s. 0d.		£7 13s. 0d.	

Key to Samoan goods (all indices relative to consumption of European goods).

Ø—Some (minority) goods locally produced.
O—Very few or none locally produced.

1. Mainly digging sticks (*'oso*), small canoes (*paopao*). See Appendix 1.
2. Mainly pig fences, and compressed sand roads. See Appendix 1.
3. For full lists of goods see Appendix 1. Sample as for Table 1.

European influences had assisted *fa'asāmoa* values. Some missionaries, especially those in the calvinist London Missionary Society, have inculcated capitalist values, there have been isolated administrative attempts to improve village production performances by introducing European capital goods, and the traders have shown by example the advantages of fiscal skills. But the European contribution has been inherently limited, mainly because most Europeans believe that indigenous capital formation is impossible or very unlikely in the Samoan situation.

Far more significant is the Samoan desire for European capital goods, particularly because they are considered to be more useful (*aogā*) for production purposes than Samoan goods. Steel tools are far more effective than stone or hardwood[1]

[1] See Appendix 1.

tools, and save much time in manufacture. Similarly European fishing tackle, if not more effective, saves long hours of net or rope making. Modern fertilizers and pesticides are generally an improvement on traditional methods. Most significantly, money is much more durable, and can be exchanged more comprehensively than any traditional item.

For certain individuals the acquisition of money is, in fact, an end in itself. There are people in every village[1] who hoard money away or accumulate it in a savings bank in Apia. In some cases these 'savings' are provisions for future expenditure, or for hard times, and occasionally a fat bank balance is a status symbol, though usually 'savings' are private and secret affairs. Many also believe that saving is right and proper in itself. One chief said he saved because it is in the Bible, and because by so doing he will be blessed and he quoted Proverbs 20: 22.[2] Another believed that if he saved money he would go to heaven.

There are also a small but significant number of individuals who want to accumulate cash to invest in continuous profit-making activities, in what economists call entrepreneurial activities,[3] that is in activities where there is constant risk-taking, innovation, experiment and utilization of new techniques to increase profits.

More widespread is the feeling that European education and good health are most desirable. Most people believe that it is right that children should go to school and many believe that children should go to secondary school, or have special vocational training in Apia or abroad. Some feel that education is a Christian duty—'We must try to be wise like Christ and then we will be saved'—and others consider that to go to school is a patriotic duty, so that Samoan intellectuals can take their place with the intellectuals of other independent nations. Finally, for most people, a European education is a status symbol of considerable magnitude, and as we shall see, often opens the door to prestigious jobs or titles.

European medical goods and services are as intensely desired as education, as many Samoans are constantly brooding over real or imagined ills. In general, European medicines are

---

[1] See Table 20.   [2] 'The Lord blesses the rich man.'
[3] For definitions see Belshaw 1955(b), Danhof 1959.

preferred because they are considered to be more effective. Certain proprietory medicines (liver pills, aspirins, various 'fever cures') are very popular and are used indiscriminately for any sickness. On the other hand, medically approved drugs, especially if administered by a hypodermic may be suspected and feared. This fear may be justified as dirty hypodermics in hospitals often results in the puncture becoming abscessed. Also certain Samoan herbal remedies are known to be more effective than European equivalents. For example, the Samoan cure for constipation is demonstrably more effective than castor oil or Epsom salts.

There are, however, restrictions on capital demand mainly, as we have suggested, because of the weak development of opportunities or facilities provided by the Europeans. Low incomes are also important. Generally Samoan capital goods (for example hardwood digging sticks (*'oso*) or small locally made canoes (*paopao*)) are most numerous in low income areas (such as Salani), although these are also areas with the poorest access to the capital facilities of Apia.

WORK

An important corollary of the intense desire for goods, or for wealth with which to acquire goods is the high value placed on hard and productive work. The need for this is a traditional and persistent value in a physical environment where contrary to the European view, the utilization of resources may require considerable application. Hard work[1] was, and is, recognized as a characteristic of adulthood, and of active participation in society. There is a proverb—*Feao me ulupo'o*—'(the lazy man) sleeps with skulls', that is, he has no part in living society and is impotent, like a sick man or a cripple.[2] The hard worker, on the other hand, is compared to the hero-chief Taeinu'u who

[1] Work (*gāluega*) comprised generally any activities of men in which *oloa* goods (food, European goods) were produced or acquired. Women's work was specified by certain types of activity, notably domestic chores (*fa'aleaiga*) lagoon fishing by groping (*naonao*) and mat and basket making. Women's work in the lagoon was recognized as work (*gāluega*) but work in the *fale* (house) including mat and basket making as well as chores was relaxation (*pāganoa*), as were most men's activities around the house or making *'afa* (sennit cord) or preparing for ceremonial activities. See Table 5.

[2] Sick persons and cripples are also called skulls.

TABLE 5

Work in Malie and Salani 1964—Division of time between activities in sample 'āiga[1] (adults)

	MALIE		SALANI		MALIE	SALANI
	Dry season[2]	Wet season[2]	Dry season[2]	Wet season[2]	Average per week	Average per week
	proportion of		proportion of			
ACTIVITY	total time		total time		*per capita*	*per capita*
1. WORK	%	%	%	%	Hours	Hours
(a) Subsistence						
Talo-Taamu production	4·0	2·0	7·0	4·0	5·0	7·75
Coconut production	0·5	0·5	1·0	0·0	0·75	0·5
Banana production	0·25	0·25	0·5	3·0	0·5	3·75
Other foods	0·25	0·25	0·5	1·0	0·5	1·25
Village works[3]	3·0	0·5	4·0	0·25	4·25	5·25
Fishing	1·0	0·5	3·0	1·5	1·0	3·25
Weaving[5]	2·0	4·0	4·0	4·0	5·25	7·25
Cooking[4]	7·5	8·0	8·0	6·5	11·0	10·5
Household chores[6]	3·0	3·5	3·0	2·0	6·0	6·75
(b) Cash						
Coconuts[7]	4·5	1·0	6·0	0·0	3·75	5·0
Cacao[7]	2·0	0·0	0·0	0·0	1·75	0·25
Bananas[7]	0·75	0·25	5·0	4·0	1·0	11·5
Other crops[8]	0·25	0·0	3·0	1·0	0·25	4·25
Wage labour[9]	2·0	1·0	0·5	0·5	4·25	0·75
Fono[10]	1·0	1·0	1·0	0·75	3·25	1·5
Handicrafts	2·0	2·0	1·0	1·0	5·0	2·0
2. OTHER ACTIVITIES						
Ceremonial	4·0	10·0	2·0	14·0	11·0	12·75
Eating[11]	7·5	7·0	6·0	6·5	11·0	10·5
Church[12]	6·0	7·0	5·0	6·0	10·0	13·25
Sickness[13]	1·0	4·0	0·75	6·75	4·25	8·25
Leisure activities[14]	2·0	2·0	0·5	0·5	3·0	0·75
House-minding	0·75	1·0	0·25	0·25	2·0	0·25
Relaxation[15]	4·0	2·0	3·0	3·0	5·0	5·0
Daytime sleeping[17]	3·0	1·0	1·75	1·5	3·0	2·5
Night-time sleeping[17]	37·5	37·0	33·0	32·5	65·0	57·0
Miscellaneous[16]	0·25	0·25	0·25	0·25	0·25	0·25
TOTALS						
Subsistence work	21·5	22·5	31·0	22·25	39·5	48·25
Cash work	12·5	6·25	16·5	7·75	14·25	23·25
Other activities	66·0	71·25	52·5	70·0	114·25	96·5

TABLE 5—(contd.)

Work in Malie 1964—Men's share in work activity[20]

ACTIVITY	TAULELE'A[18]		MATAI[18]	
	Proportion of total Taulele'a time	Share of total activity time	Proportion of total Matai time	Share of total activity time
I. WORK	%	%	%	%
(a) Subsistence				
Talo-Taamu production	5·0	38·0	3·0	10·0
Coconut production	2·0	75·0	0·5	15·0
Banana production	1·0	82·0	0·5	16·0
Other foods	0·5	38·0	0·25	10·0
Village works	7·0	59·0	0·5	3·0
Fishing	1·0	40·0	0·5	10·0
Weaving (Sennit, etc.)	0·0	0·0	5·0	100·0
Cooking	10·0	43·0	1·0	6·0
Household chores	2·0	22·0	0·25	0·5
(b) Cash				
Coconuts[19]	2·0	45·0	3·5	45·0
Cacao[19]	4·0	45·0	4·0	46·0
Bananas[19]	1·0	52·0	3·5	46·0
Other crops	0·5	38·0	0·5	10·0
Wage labour	7·0	85·0	0·0	0·0
Fono	0·25	5·0	3·0	85·0
2. OTHER ACTIVITIES				
Ceremonial	4·0	12·0	6·0	46·0
Eating	7·0	29·0	9·0	35·0
Church	5·0	24·0	5·0	23·0
Sickness	0·0	0·0	4·0	56·0
Leisure activities	4·0	52·0	2·0	38·0
House-minding	0·0	0·0	0·0	0·0
Relaxation	4·0	33·0	6·0	35·0
Day sleep	2·0	33·0	3·0	35·0
Night sleep	37·0	22·0	38·0	29·0
Miscellaneous	0·25	28·0	0·25	25·0
TOTALS				
Subsistence work	28·5	23·0	11·0	14·0
Cash work	14·75	41·0	15·5	30·0
Other activities	66·75	15·0	73·5	32·0

TABLE 5 (contd.)

Work in Malie 1964—Women's share in work activity[21]

ACTIVITY	Young Unmarried Women		Wives[22]	
	Proportion of total young women's time	Share of total activity time	Proportion of total wives' time	Share of total activity time
1. WORK	%	%	%	%
(a) Subsistence				
Talo-Taamu production	4·0	32·0	1·5	10·0
Coconut production	0·5	14·0	0·25	6·0
Banana production	0·0	0·0	0·0	0·0
Other foods	0·5	32·0	0·25	10·0
Village works	5·0	34·0	0·5	4·0
Fishing	1·0	40·0	0·5	10·0
Weaving	4·0	25·0	18·0	75·0
Cooking	7·0	23·0	4·0	28·0
Household chores	6·0	42·0	4·0	36·0
(b) Cash				
Coconuts	0·5	14·0	0·25	6·0
Cacao	1·0	14·0	0·5	6·0
Bananas	0·0	0·0	0·0	0·0
Other crops	0·5	32·0	0·25	10·0
Handicrafts	3·0	25·0	2·0	15·0
Wage labour	1·0	15·0	0·0	0·0
Fono	0·0	0·0	1·0	10·0
2. OTHER ACTIVITIES				
Ceremonial	3·0	18·0	5·0	24·0
Eating	5·0	17·0	7·0	19·0
Church	6·0	23·0	6·0	30·0
Sickness	3·0	38·0	0·5	6·0
Leisure activities	2·5	18·0	0·25	2·0
House-minding	8·0	100·0	0·0	0·0
Relaxation	3·0	17·0	3·0	15·0
Day sleep	2·0	17·0	2·0	15·0
Night sleep	35·0	23·0	39·0	26·0
Miscellaneous	0·25	28·0	0·25	19·0
TOTALS				
Subsistence work	31·0	35·0	31·0	28·0
Cash work	3·0	24·0	2·0	5·0
Other activities	66·0	23·0	67·0	30·0

NOTES TO TABLE 5

1. The sample consisted of 10 'āiga in Malie (51 adults) and 7 'āiga in Salani (40 adults). Adults are those persons mainly over 15 who are called tagata (man) or fafine (woman). The survey was conducted over 4 months in all, in Malie (4 May–3 June and 30 October–30 November), in Salani (15 July–15 August and 30 November–29 December), i.e. one month in each village in both the wet season and the dry season.
2. April–November is the dry season, and November–April the wet. Seasonal change is particularly noticeable on the South Coast of Upolu. Divisions in 1 are based on consumption estimates.
3. Including communal clearing of land, building of paths, general cleaning mainly performed by the amauga, the young men's group, and also boat repairs.
4. Including the collection of fuel.
5. Including basket, mat and tapa making by the women, and the production of ornaments and 'afa (sennit cord) by men.
6. All activities connected with the cleaning of the fale, washing clothes, dishes, etc.
7. All stages of production and marketing, except for the time put in by women watching over drying coconut meat or cacao beans.
8. Talo, and any crops of resources grown for the handicraft industry.
9. Only commuters were included in the sample. There were no other employed persons resident in the sample 'āiga.
10. Includes women's committee meetings as well as the council of chiefs and their committees. Included also is the time taken for business other than economic activities (approximately one-third of total time).
11. Eating at fa'alavelave excepted.
12. Including tautua (service) to the pastor, e.g. cleaning his house, etc., but not time spent at Church ceremonials. This time is included under the heading 'ceremonial'.
13. Including time spent in nursing the sick.
14. All informal sports in the village, organized games were usually fa'alavelave. For example, cricket, billiards, the many games of cards drinking sessions and cinema. Also trips to town for pleasure.
15. Paganoa—lounging in the fale but not sleeping.
16. Ablutions, etc.
17. Daytime during daylight about 6 a.m.–6 p.m.
18. Taulele'a—men without titles. Matai hold titles or, as in the case of the Pastor in this sample, are regarded as chiefs.
19. In the Matai's case, mainly time spent in the village or in town marketing arrangements.
20. Sample of adult men in 10 'āiga (24 persons) conducted during 2 months (May, November 1964).
21. Sample of adult women in 10 'āiga (27 persons) conducted during 2 months (May, November 1964).
22. Includes also 2 widows and 1 elderly spinster.

worked hard in his gardens and achieved the highest titles in Samoa.[1] Steady, conscientious and consistent applications of

[1] There are a number of other legends and proverbs telling of the hard work of great chiefs.

labour are thought to be well rewarded.[1] The material from the fieldwork villages indicates the extent of work activity.[2]

There are also exacting standards of craftsmanship in all *fa'asāmoa* economic activities. Good work is a sign of divine influences (*mana*) whilst defects are regarded as symptoms of maleficient forces. In a few cases[3] the desire for good work results in craftsmanship being taken to laborious lengths and a consequently low level of productivity. On the other hand, it is recognized that there is an optimum time limit for all work after which diminishing returns set in. One chief expressed it this way—'*Ua le sau i le afu, le sau i le tutupu, ua sau i le lalau*'—'the yam must be eaten when the leaves appear or it becomes progressively inedible.'[4]

Limits on hard or sustained work are recognized. One significant restriction is the climatic and crop cycle. The heat of the day is spent relaxing as are certain slack times of the year,[5] especially during the wet season (*vaipalolo*—November-February) when there are few root crops to plant and when garden paths are waterlogged and copra hard to dry. At such times it is considered that most labour is unproductive. The European who does not adapt to the climatic exigencies is a figure of fun. Stories were told with helpless mirth of Europeans, who during the heat of the day sweated in offices, or lay burning their skins on the *faga pālagi* (the European beach),[6] or who during the wet season try to drive over flooded country roads.

There is, however, some work activity during the times of relaxation and at most other times except during meals, ablutions or at night. When sitting in the *fale* (house) all people, including the old and the infirm, are usually busying themselves making mats, baskets or sennit cord ('*afa*) and often at the same time discussing and making decisions relating to economic activity.

---

[1] For example in the expression *Ua ita le mona*—literally 'The mona player always loses'. This refers to the *fa'asāmoa* game of *Tagati'a* a competition where darts were thrown. The inconsistent player (*mona*) would get far behind on points and although he might make a brilliant throw he could never beat the player who consistently made good throws.   [2] See Table 5.   [3] For example, canoe manufacture.

[4] Literally 'Not when the yam has dried up, not when it has sprouted, but when the leaves appear'—that is the time when the yam is best to eat.   [5] See Table 5.

[6] A small beach near Apia (Mulinu'u) where mainly overseas Europeans swim and moor their boats. The beach is avoided by Samoans, even by the nearby villagers who have fishing rights off the beach.

It is also thought permissible for people to have certain types of relaxation during work periods. For example, a man working in the gardens can stop to eat something, have a drink, share a joke or even go to sleep, though if he spends over an hour eating or sleeping he will probably be called 'lazy' (*paiē*). During ceremonials all activity ceases.

The periods of relaxation act, in fact, as an important incentive to hard work. The inactivity of ceremonials is preceded by feverish activities. Relaxation in daily economic activity is not only felt to refresh the worker, but is also an important part of the informal atmosphere of work groups, which workers feel make even the most grinding tasks pleasant. Most work groups are made up of kinsmen, often led by participant chiefs, and work is felt by many to be simply an extension of the pleasantries of family life and it is often enlivened by songs. The kinship basis of work activity adds to the production incentives and control. Any hard worker is rewarded not only by a share in any products of his labour, but also by wider recognition in village public opinion, whilst the sluggard is exposed to '*āiga* and village sanctions and scorn.

In the social structure there are other incentives to hard and careful work. Rivalries between persons, '*āiga* and villages, encourage competition in standards and performance. Diligence, obedience and craftsmanship are means of influencing those who select titleholders or of enhancing an existing title.[1] As a consequence of all this the hours worked by Samoans compare very favourably with those in other Afro-Asian countries.[2]

In general, involvement in the European world has bolstered *fa'āsamoa* work values. The missionaries added biblical injunctions to traditional maxims. And today many Samoans believe that 'hard work' will save their souls, as much as church attendance or tithes. There have been, in the twentieth century at least, patriotic motives as well, first to raise the Samoan standard of living *vis-à-vis* the European, and more recently to outdo the neighbouring island and traditional enemy, Tonga. Most significantly of all, the desire for cash and the

[1] See Ch. 4.
[2] A male in Malie works approximately 1,500 hours a year on cash and subsistence food production. Cf. Conklin 1957.

5

competition and standards of quality in the market have placed a premium on hard, productive work.

There are admittedly some restrictions on work incentives in the cash economy. In recent years low cash crop prices, the decimation of crops by hurricanes, pests and diseases, and apparent Government apathy have disillusioned many cash croppers. Many blame the Europeans and suspect deliberate exploitation. As we have said, exploitation was true in the Samoan situation only in a limited sense, and in most instances Samoan and European disillusion was rather the result of misunderstandings which reflected the social separation of Samoan and European society. One good example is the banana industry where Samoan growers have not fulfilled in many years quotas established by the Government-run marketing board. Officials attribute the dearth of bananas to Samoan 'laziness' or inability to organize their labour to enable bananas to reach Apia for the banana boat. The officials do not know that many growers have abandoned banana production in favour of copra or cacao or wage labour, mainly because it is felt that the banana industry cannot survive when the Government does nothing about the Bunchytop virus or low prices. The Samoans do not know, nor does the Government adequately publicize, the measures that are being taken to combat the very resistant Bunchytop virus, or the overseas market origin of low prices.

The decline of work incentives is more apparent in the wage labour sector. In most wage labour jobs work patterns differ from *fa'asāmoa* work patterns. Most urban workers are obliged to work continuously from 8 a.m. to 4 p.m., with an hour off for lunch, a workday directly transplanted from New Zealand. Relaxation and time off for ceremonial activities are only allowed in exceptional circumstances. Work groups in offices, stores, on public works, and in plantations often comprise unrelated Samoans directed by prejudiced and sometimes brutal Europeans or part-Europeans. Work conditions are often poor. People often sweat in ill-lit rooms, without ventilation and sanitation, for wages which, in the absence of trade union activity, are very low.[1] Many urban jobs do not

---

[1] In 1963 81 per cent of all employed Samoans earned less than £200 per annum and 96 per cent earned less than £500 per annum (Source WSDF—Statistics).

recognize or reward traditional skills or differential industry but pay flat wage rates. Workers often have little initiative in their jobs and know little, and care less, about the ends of their activity. There are often strained relations between European employers and native employees and there is very rarely the rapport and intimacy that exists between a leader and his group in the village setting. As a result of all this, workers are constantly moving from one job to another.

In such work groups productivity is probably low, though statistics are unreliable. The European explanation is inherent laziness. But in most jobs which we have described poor work incentives are much more significant restraints on productivity. Certainly wage labourers work hard in the village, before or after wage labour work, in the cool of the day, or during weekends, when *fa'asāmoa* incentives operate. There are also a small number of offices, stores or work gangs where labour relations are good and productivity is high. In one office, for example, a sympathetic European takes into account *fa'asāmoa* attitudes. He allows three hours off during the heat of the day, time off for ceremonial activities and an informal and relaxed atmosphere at work. The work performance of the office is high, the turnover of staff is low, and workers are obviously interested in even the most menial aspects of their work. There is a loyalty to the European boss and directives from him are scrupulously carried out. When vacancies occur kinsmen are brought in, and the bonds of loyalty and harmony are retained. There are also in a number of small Samoan firms duplications of the kinship work context which contribute significantly to these firms' survival and profits in the face of severe competition from European businesses.

In Malie in 1964 the figures were 75 per cent and 96 per cent and the average wage of resident wage labourers (33) was £213. By comparison in 1963 only 35 per cent of Europeans (i.e. mainly part-Europeans) receiving wages from Samoan sources received under £200 and 31 per cent received over £500 per annum. Trade unions were officially permitted, but a Government spokesman claimed that there was 'no inclination' to form trade unions. But both during the New Zealand administration, and since, left-wing visitors have been carefully scrutinized and sometimes refused permission to enter Samoa.

3

PRODUCTION: SUBSISTENCE AND SALE

SEVERAL different ways of securing the desired European goods can be distinguished. Individual Samoans sometimes steal what they want from Europeans, though theft is not nearly as common as many Europeans think, and there are strict *fa'asāmoa* laws against theft and stiff punishments against all thieves.[1] Thefts usually only occur from those whom the Samoans think are exploiters (*tagata matape'ape'a*); treacherous traders, brutal foremen, arrogant administrators, or missionaries.

A more important means of securing desired goods or status was by direct political pressures on the Europeans. From the arrival of the first Europeans the chiefs have attempted to persuade or coerce their visitors to disburse goods or invest the chiefs with political power. In the twentieth century during times of low prices for cash crops the chiefs organized rebellions against the administrations.[2]

In addition to political action the Samoans also attempted to secure desired goods by affiliating themselves to the missions. The conversion of the whole of Samoa was a matter of weeks. Travellers were astounded at the extreme devotion of Samoans. As the missionaries themselves recognized, this conversion had markedly material motives. Many Samoans were prepared 'to *lotu* (convert) for a steel axe'[3] or indeed for any other European goods or for better health and medicines, or better education. Conversion for theological reasons seems to have been very rare.[4] Many Samoans also changed their religion between the three major missions if they did not obtain

---

[1] In Malie in 1964 there were 19 thefts dealt with by the village *fono*. In 8 cases the fine amounted to £1 5s. or goods equivalent (1 small pig, 5 talo, etc.). In the other cases the fine was less than £1.

[2] e.g. the Lauati Mau of 1905–6, and the Mau of the nineteen twenties.

[3] LMSJ Platt (1835).   [4] e.g. Turner 1861: Ch. 14.

satisfaction. For example, one man changed his adherence three times to cure an ulcer.[1] Others changed as the missions themselves appeared more or less likely to provide health, wealth or knowledge. A mission's image and attractiveness for converts was partly related to the mission's actual record in disbursement—the Methodists were said to lose many converts because of one tight-fisted missionary—but more significantly it depended on the mission's association with a European nation whose disbursing power was greatly respected. Great Britain in the nineteenth century was thought to be the greatest power in the world, and God's most powerful instrument for endowing the Samoans with the good things in life, an image that was bolstered by the constant parade of gunboats and the arrival of such extravagant gentlemen as Robert Louis Stevenson[2] whose parties were the talk of Apia. Consequently the 'English mission', that is the London Missionary Society, received most adherents. During the nineteenth century particularly, many Samoans also affiliated themselves to charismatic individuals[3], either Europeans or Samoans, who returned from overseas promising a paradise containing vast quantities of European goods. But the incidence of these cargo cults was limited in space and time.

More influential were the new missions, particularly the Mormons who arrived in force after the Second World War. Many people think that the Mormons will provide the Samoans with modern sophisticated goods. The people point to the sparkling modernistic chapels with their flush toilets and basket ball courts which now appear in many villages, or the model village of Saniatu with its hedgerows, paved streets, sidewalks, and street-lighting, or to the earnest, confident, crew-cut missionaries who are always giving away goods. Many people also believe that this is only the beginning of a much larger disbursement. Mormon ideology with its emphasis on a recent, and possibly recurring millennium amongst the 'lost tribes of Israel' (a frequent Samoan conception of themselves) adds to this belief. Some even believe that the Mormons are the harbingers of an eventual American annexation and even employees of the State Department. This adds great

---

[1] LMSB25F5JA.   [2] Moors n.d.
[3] Freeman 1959, LMSNP/6, Daws 1960, GBFO 58/63, NZIT 45/1.

lustre to the Mormon image and persuades many to climb on the Mormon bandwagon since America is now the symbol of greatest affluence and sophistication.[1]

But at least to the common villager religious affiliation, like political action, was too slow and unrewarding a process. Most Samoans felt that desired goods could be obtained more quickly and more effectively by direct production or, more significantly, through cash exchange.

Direct production or subsistence[2] production (that is production or consumption within the '*āiga*) was an important characteristic of the traditional economy, although as we shall see in a later chapter there are also important exchange institutions outside the '*āiga*.[3] Subsistence production has remained important in the period after the arrival of the Europeans.[4] Subsistence production becomes significant when the external demand for cash crops declines. During the depression, the Samoans could not sell their crops, or only at very low prices, and there were no alternative sources of cash.[5] Many people were forced to rely almost completely on subsistence production and most made makeshift imitations of European goods.

Periodically there was also intense competition in the market from local sellers, or strong economic pressures exerted by local buyers. For example during most of the nineteenth century there was competition from European-run plantations.[6]

---

[1] The Mormons in 1961 comprised 6 per cent of the population of Samoa. The LMS have 53 per cent, the Roman Catholics 21 per cent, the Wesleyans 16 per cent. In the fieldwork villages in 1964 10 per cent of the population were Mormon in Malie, 12 per cent in Apia and 4 per cent in Salani.

[2] There have been two important definitions of subsistence in the economic and sociological literature. First as a low level of wealth, as a minimum standard of living, secondly as self-sufficiency, usually implying an absence of exchange institutions. Our usage is nearer the latter, but we would point out that exchange is always found in the subsistence sector although it is exchange within the kinship circle and, in Samoa, usually the nuclear family, according to the norms of these groups.   [3] See Ch. 9.

[4] For an indication of the extent of subsistence production in the fieldwork villages, see Appendices 1 and 2, and Table 3.

[5] For instance in 1934 copra sales were less than 20 per cent the value of 1928 sales (WSDF Statistics).

[6] At the end of the nineteenth century Europeans owned approximately one-third of cultivated land (Map 1899) mostly in Upolu. In 1964 the figure was less than 5 per cent (WSDF Lands and Survey). In 1914 the New Zealanders appropriated the German plantations, and land was handed back piecemeal to villages, though the majority of the plantations remained as a Government Corporation,

Technological superiority enabled the plantations to grow and process a much more valuable product than village producers.

In addition to competition from plantations, the Samoan producers have also been exposed to unfavourable economic terms from all the marketing agencies who bought their crops. The structure of the market throughout has always been monopsonistic, that is to say, sellers of produce at all levels (village producers to village traders and/or Apia merchants, Apia merchants to a line of overseas buyers) have few alternative buyers which means that buyers can therefore dictate terms that are most favourable to themselves. The overseas and Apia merchants, and to some extent village traders, have all on occasion handed on these unfavourable terms to the Samoan village producer at the end of the line.

Consequently the village producer often receives only a small proportion of the overseas price for his cash crop, though economic pressures and political agitation by Samoans have improved conditions greatly in recent years. Most copra[1] and banana growers now receive (1964) about 25 per cent of the price (CIF) at which overseas merchants buy the copra, though cacao growers receive much less.[2]

A further reason for the importance of direct subsistence production has been dramatic changes in the labour structure. The first critical demographic change was the great influenza epidemic of 1918 which may have wiped out one-third of the population.[3] The survivors were forced to concentrate on subsistence for a number of years. A second and more prolonged change has been the recent population increase. Since 1900 the population has quadrupled.[4] Also the Samoans have

village labour replacing the indentured labour (mainly Chinese) which was repatriated (NZIT 61/62).

[1] This is lower than the official price. Official price controls were difficult to enforce mainly because of the small staff and restricted powers of the Copra Board. One of the most important means of evasion was for traders to buy unprocessed nuts (outside the price control) for which the usual price (Malie) was a third of the official price.

[2] As low as 10 per cent of the CIF price.   [3] NZIT 15/1/6.

[4] According to the census of 1921 the population was not significantly above the 1900 population (32,815) but subsequent censuses showed an escalating increase: 40,231 (1926), 55,496 (1936), 68,197 (1945), 84,909 (1951), 97,327 (1956), 114,427 (1961) (WSDF Statistics). Population in the fieldwork villages reflected these macrocosmic changes, though the population in Salani in recent years (since 1945) has increased only slowly because of wage-labour migration.

abandoned the inland plateaux[1] to settle on the narrow coastal fringe where cash crop resources are concentrated, especially the plain of North West Upolu where there are also the attractions of the main town of Apia.[2] In these villages the subsistence demand for root crops (*talo* and *ta'amū*) restricts the amount of cash crop land available, especially as in most villages shifting methods of cultivation are used for roots,[3] whilst subsistence demands for coconuts and bananas[4] restrict the amount of these crops available for sale. Other subsistence crops (e.g. breadfruit, fibrecrops) have less significant effects since they are grown on agricultural land of marginal productivity, such as house-sites. Subsistence is relatively less important in less populous areas. For example, in Malie in densely populated North West Upolu, 30 per cent of all coconuts, 40 per cent of all saleable bananas are used for subsistence and 20 per cent of all garden land is in root-crops, but in Salani in the thinly populated district of Falealili, less than 10 per cent of garden land is used for root crops and only a small proportion of saleable produce is used for subsistence.

Demand for subsistence resources not only reflects population pressure but also the absence of alternative, particularly marine, resources. In inland villages, or villages without protective fringing reefs,[5] greater reliance is placed on root crops especially where food resources in the forest are also restricted.[6]

A final reason for the importance of direct subsistence production has been the occasional dramatic decline in the

---

[1] Recent archaeological research (e.g. by Professor Green of University of Hawaii, Green 1964) has indicated that there were over fifty inland villages before the nineteenth century. There is some corroboration of this in the literature, e.g. Stair 1897: 57. The present number of inland villages is twelve.

[2] Approximately 60 per cent of the population live in or near Apia.

[3] *Talo* and *ta'amū* were usually planted together in small plots approximately the size of an acre.

[4] This comment applies less to bananas since varieties which could not be marketed were used for subsistence.

[5] Fagaloa and Lefaga Bays, the south Upolu coast from Siumu to Ilii, the lava field and Palauli coast in Savai'i and the north coast from Solomea to Pu'apu'a. In villages in these areas there were less of the small lagoon fish and crustacea which are caught in great numbers elsewhere.

[6] In Upolu especially most of the coastal, and much of the hill forest has been cut away or burnt. Food resources in the forest consist of birds, rats, flying foxes, wild pigs, etc.

supply of cash crops, due to natural forces such as storms, pests and plants diseases.

The most severe storms are called *afā*—hurricanes. Samoans say that *afā* occur every five years and hurricanes have been recorded regularly at intervals of from three to six years.[1] *Afā* are by definition destructive of crops, particularly tree crops and therefore cash crops, although most hurricanes affect only certain districts, and Samoans consider that the devastation of crops by a hurricane will occur to them only once in a lifetime. In Malie there have been four severe hurricanes since 1800.[2] Every year also there are very heavy rains and high winds in the 'wet season' (November-March) which blow over banana trees and encourage fungus in the cacao groves and in copra. The Malie people estimate that the wet season weather will reduce cash crop production by about 10 per cent, though they hope that only old trees, that is trees past their best, will be blown over.[3] Important subsistence crops, particularly root crops, are not so greatly affected by hurricanes, rains or storms and are always extensively used in hard times.

More important than storms or hurricanes have been pests and diseases which have periodically affected cash crops. In some villages it is estimated that approximately 30 per cent of all coconuts are eaten by the introduced black rat (*mus epimys rattus*) which has no natural enemies, and as much as 20 per cent of all trees have been destroyed by the Rhinoceros beetle, introduced in 1902.[4] In Salani, and many other villages on the south coast, the Bunchytop virus is in the process of wiping out the banana gardens, whilst cacao trees are attacked in many villages by rats and various cankers. The destruction by pests and diseases has been accentuated by the ineffectiveness of official pest control. The people try make-shift solutions

[1] For example, LMSB23F5JD, Kramer 1902 v. 2:112, NZIT 87/7.

[2] 1850, reported in LMSB23F5JD; 1890, presumably the famous 1889 hurricane which destroyed six European warships in Apia harbour; 1941 reported in NZAJ A4/1945/16. Another severe hurricane has just occurred (1966).

[3] Severe drought is very rare. The people in Malie cannot remember hearing of a drought in Upolu, though the people of Salani say there was a drought in the nineteenth century when all the rivers dried up. This is reported in Kramer 1902 v. 2:112.

[4] In Malie the figures were less than this—an estimated 20 per cent destruction by rats, 10 per cent Rhinoceros beetle. Cf. WSDF Agriculture.

(destroying Rhinoceros beetle larvae, binding trees with strips of tin or leaves to prevent rats climbing them, etc.), but in general these are only effective on the rare occasions when there is official advice or capital to supplement village attempts. There are few successes because there is too little rapport between the officials and the villagers. For example, it may not be explained to the villagers why an official with a sprayer on his back is wandering amongst the banana plants and he will be stoned.

Although subsistence production has remained important particularly in certain periods of Samoan history or in certain villages, production for cash sale has expanded continuously and now dominates the village economy. The fundamental reason for this expansion has been the intense desire for European goods which we have described. Two important facts made local or village production of the desired European goods difficult if not impossible. First, most European goods and services require, or are thought to require, raw materials or manufacturing skills which Samoans do not possess. More significantly, European goods are, in a definite sense, regarded as goods which have to be aquired from outside the village. *Mea pālagi* (European goods) are, by definition, goods which Europeans in Apia or abroad have manufactured. European manufacture enhances the goods' efficacy as a status symbol and this status varies often with the status of the country of origin. Goods from America, for example, are most highly valued irrespective of any other criterion such as quality. European goods produced locally in the village are always of lesser status and are not consumed locally or else regarded as *mea Samoa*, Samoan goods.[1]

Thirdly, there are external social and economic pressures which have pushed Samoans towards, and in some cases forced Samoans into, the cash economy. There were the demands of the Europeans for cash or cash crops. The missions much preferred to have 'native contributions'[2] or 'tithes' in any European currency rather than in coconut oil which was

---

[1] For example the many introduced fruits and vegetables in the village, most of which are known to be introduced. Locally produced furniture was similarly placed in a *mea Samoa* category. See Appendix 1.

[2] By this is meant the money given to the mission central funds and not funds spent in the village, on the church or the local pastor.

difficult, as well as embarrassing, to market. There is evidence[1] that chiefs were persuaded to use cash in tithes, and to involve themselves in cash earning activities as much for mission convenience as for the christian virtues of commerce extolled in mission sermons.[2] There is evidence, too, of mission encouragement to traders, whatever was said in sermons, at least until the fierce arguments between the missions and the German traders in the late nineteenth century.[3] Throughout the nineteenth and early twentieth century tithes have tended to be a fixed proportion of income. The Roman Catholics and the Mormons expect a literal tithe (i.e. 10 per cent) and although the London Missionary Society and the Methodists place no restriction on their 'contributions', the expected proportion tends to be similar.

Administrative taxes added to the need for cash. A poll tax payable in cash was introduced by the Germans in 1901 on all Samoans 'big enough to cook and make copra'[4] partly to find revenue but also to force the Samoans into the cash economy.[5] Taxes were originally 4 marks[6] for each male, but were progressively increased by both the Germans and the New Zealanders who followed them, and new taxes were added.[7]

During the Mau rebellion (1925–36) when the Apia administration could exercise little authority in the countryside, direct taxation ceased,[8] and the administration collected its revenue from tariffs and duties. Also in recent years, as European missionaries have withdrawn, mission tithes have decreased

---

[1] LMSMP 4/26 is an example.

[2] For example LMSNP.

[3] For example LMSB11F7JA. The first traders were sometimes ex-missionaries (George Pritchard) or missionaries' sons (John Williams, Jr.). The argument with the German traders was due partly to political antagonism (the missionaries were mainly English or French) but mainly to the introduction by the Germans of a debased South American currency, purchased cheaply in Bolivia. The missionaries received this currency in tithes but found that no bank would accept it. They were forced to spend it with the German traders who alone would accept it and then at only 50 per cent of its face value. NZMPPI.   [4] GCA 1/17b.

[5] This was the idea of the Governor Dr. Solf who felt that the Samoans would become civilized by working in the European world (GCA 1/17b).

[6] At the time *circa* 4*s*. sterling.

[7] In 1913 the taxes were 24 Marks per chief. There were also taxes on dogs and all vehicles. The New Zealanders added a medical levy in 1920 for a short period.

[8] Officially in 1936. It was impossible to collect taxes from 1928 to 1936.

in importance. Today contributions to the Church are, in the villagers' conception, status-payments (most funds now stay in the village), part of the general pattern of conspicuous consumption rather than externally imposed obligations. But, since Independence, as Samoa has faced a balance of payments crisis and revenue shortages, new taxes have been imposed[1] or contemplated, and old taxes stiffened.

Samoans, then will not, or cannot manufacture the desired European goods locally and in any case they need cash for taxes and tithes at least. But the degree of involvement in the cash economy also depends on the market demand for Samoan resources, on the opportunities the Samoans have to participate in the cash economy.

The first important overseas demand was for coconut oil, later supplemented and superseded by copra. Copra remained the only important village cash crop in the nineteenth century, and the most important crop in the twentieth century.[2] The demand came most significantly from European soap and candle manufacturers who found wax too dear, and the European middle class consumer too genteel for the unpleasant odours of tallow. Later more industrial and commercial uses were discovered, especially when methods were found of extracting from the dried nut a clear colourless oil without the rancid taste and smell of shipped oil.

Although demand expanded with new discoveries and the expansion of the consumer market, there was also stiff competition from other Pacific suppliers and particularly from South East Asia. While the Hamburg firm of J. C. Godeffroy

[1] e.g. school fees. In 1964 a UN expert recommended a land tax on all village land. Many Samoans were also pulled into the income tax circle whenever they became wage-labourers or traders, etc., instead of, or as well as, cash croppers. Income tax inspection and the collection of cash crop duties has also stiffened in recent years.

[2] Copra-making was introduced by the German merchant Weber about 1865, and copra superseded coconut oil by about 1875. Production figures are unreliable for the nineteenth century though the value of production increased steadily to over £ST100,000 by 1880 though dropping away sharply during the recession at the end of the nineteenth century (GBFO 58). Production climbed again during the German period and remained steady at an average of just over 10,000 tons per annum until after the Second World War, apart from relatively small downturns during the 'flu pandemic (1918), the Depression and the early years of the Second World War (WSDF Statistics). Available figures for the fieldwork villages suggest a reflection of these trends.

and its successor the DH & PG[1] had its base in Samoa, Samoan copra had a place in the European market despite the generally bad reputation of 'South Seas copra'. In the twentieth century war and depression adversely affected the external market, but during and after both World Wars when oil was in short supply there were boom conditions. Some stability was achieved from 1948 to 1957 when contracts at fixed prices were signed with the British Ministry of Food and prices have stayed high since then, mainly because of the difficulties of other producers, and the expansion of new markets notably in Japan.[2]

The export banana (*fa'i pālagi*—musa nana) was first introduced[3] by the missionary John Williams in 1839 but remained a subsistence crop until the New Zealanders opened up the New Zealand market.[4] Because of shipping difficulties and more recently competition from other producers (notably Tonga), returns to growers were uncertain until the Administration arranged guaranteed prices. Cacao introduced from the German plantations in the 1880s was also only grown sporadically by Samoans until the 1920s.[5] Demand was weak before the Second World War because of the bad reputation of Samoan cacoa, and although there were boom conditions immediately after the war, prices have slipped dramatically in the last few years. Many other cash crops[6] have been tried on the export market but none has made any impression. The only other important demand has been recent local demand for food crops mainly in Apia.[7]

[1] The full name was Deutsche Handels und Plantagen Gesellschaft der Südsee Inseln zu Hamburg. The DH & PG remained until 1914.

[2] In 1963 40 per cent of copra went to the United Kingdom, 10 per cent to West Germany, 15 per cent to New Zealand, 15 per cent to Japan (WSDF Copra Board).   [3] Other varieties are indigenous.

[4] NZIT 87/13. A trial shipment was sent in 1923 but the difficulties of transporting the perishable fruit prevented export until a refrigerated ship was bought in 1928. Production climbed steadily even during the Second World War when there was a shortage of shipping, and immediately afterwards when villagers were involved in more lucrative cash crops. The boom years in the late fifties and early sixties (in 1958 there were over 800,000 cases) were the results of improved transport and expanding markets in New Zealand.

[5] Production in the villages was less than 1,000 tons until after the Second World War after which it rose to over 3,000 tons during the 1950s (WSDF Statistics).

[6] See NZIT 87/14–67. Amongst export crops tried in the villages have been pawpaw, rubber, cotton, kapok, cane, tonka beans, bêche-de mer, arrowroot, talo, breadfruit, avocado, macadamia nuts.   [7] See Table 16.

In the economist's[1] view the Samoan position in the world economy is fragile and exposed to the instabilities inherent in 'overspecialized dependence'. But to many Samoans the overseas market is not discouraging. These people are convinced that the world wants their products, which they think are well made and eminently desirable as consumption items. When the market is bad, wicked or incompetent Europeans in Samoa or overseas are thought to have manipulated the economy so as to prevent European consumers obtaining Samoan products. Many Samoans believe that recessions in the market are temporary phenomena which disappear when the wicked or incompetent Europeans are removed by good Europeans or the pressure of consumer demand for Samoan products. Consequently although production slackens when there is a downturn in the market, production is never dramatically curtailed. Even during the great depression most villages went on producing copra and annual production never dropped below 8,900 tons (1934), less than 15 per cent below the average annual copra production in the period 1910–40. During the depression years (1931–6) banana production increased in output and value, and there was a shift into other cash crops, notably cacao, so that time spent in overall cash crop production probably did not decrease significantly.[2] Upturns in the market are greeted without surprise, for the Samoans believe that no price is too high for their products. Cash production increases (though not usually dramatically) in times of rising prices as Samoans believe they are getting a more proper reward for their product and their efforts. For example, in the boom years immediately after the Second World War (1945–51) the average annual production of copra was just over 13,000 tons and only one year (1948–18,181 tons) was outstanding. During this period banana production declined steadily.

Cash production was, then, the most important means by which Samoans could acquire the desired consumption of European goods. Factors of supply and demand singly or collectively allowed or restricted Samoan participation in the

---

[1] The best accounts are those of the FAO economist Stace 1956.

[2] NZIT 87/14–67. Apart from 1935 cacao production increased steadily from 1931. In 1935 there was a swing back to copra production which had a near record tonnage that year (12,501 tons).

cash economy. On balance, to most Samoans the restrictive factors (population explosion, storms, pests, diseases, unfavourable markets) are not critical, but isolated in time or space, or, like the population expansion, offset by cash production increases. As one chief put it: 'It only rains now and then, and only in one village or part of the garden.'[1] Conversely the most important factors which lead to cash production increases, the attraction of the market and particularly the desire for European goods, are constants in Samoan thinking.

[1] A reference to the fact that rain in Samoa characteristically falls as small convective showers sometimes only a few square yards in area.

4

THE ECONOMIC ASPECT OF STATUS

DIRECT production is, then, of lesser importance in Samoan economic activities than cash production. In this and following chapters we will examine the social context of cash production. We shall attempt to show that *fa'asāmoa* social institutions are often a favourable milieu for the expansion of cash cropping. The individual in the context of *fa'asāmoa* social institutions has very significant production incentives, resulting, as in the ideal capitalist system, from guaranteed rights of access to the factors of production (land, labour, capital) and rights to the rewards for productive effort.

These rewards, or returns to the producer, can be regarded in all societies including Samoa, as constituting, analytically at least, two distinct types. First there are the rewards of high status,[1] and secondly there are rewards in goods or cash profits. The functioning of status rewards as production incentives require that high status reflects high achievement in economic activity and not ascribed factors such as birth.

MATAI TITLES

The most important *fa'asāmoa* status results from the acquisition of a *matai* (chief) title, the most important rank in Samoan society. A *matai* title connotes mature manhood, and allows behaviour symbolizing manhood, superiority, and prestige (*mamalu*). A title allows precedence in distributions of food and drink, a seaward position in seating arrangements, etc.[2] The *matai* title can be seen, in many respects, as an extension of the *rites-de-passage* begun at puberty. For all men are expected to

---

[1] By status we mean simply any social position, 'the rights and obligations of any individual relative both to others and the scale of worthwhileness in the group. (Nadel 1951: 71).

[2] On the order of precedence see Table 8.

become *matai*,[1] and most men become *matai* of some rank before they die. The number of *matai* titles has expanded as the population has expanded and in 1964 there was a similar proportion of titles (about 6 per cent) to Samoan population as in 1904.[2] Old titles have been split as many as twenty times and new titles have been created to meet the increasing demand. The most split titles are in Savai'i (Papali'i in Sapapali'i (20) Asiata in Satupaitea (19)) but Salani has a title that has been split twelve times (Fuimaono) and Malie a title split nine

TABLE 6

Titleholding in Malie and Salani 1964

TYPE OF TITLEHOLDING	MALIE		SALANI	
	Number	Percentage of total titles	Number	Percentage of total titles
Matai holding single old[1] titles	9	15	4	12
Matai holding split old[4] titles	25	46	18	55
Matai holding newly[2] created titles	13	23	7	22
Matai holding titles from outside the village	6	10	3	9
Matai holding more than one title	4	7	3	9
Matai absent[3] from the village	13	23	11	33
Total number of titles	55		32	

1. That is titles held in the village before *circa* 1900. The *matai* lists are in GCA XVII/BI/VI, GCA III/2.
2. That is since *circa* 1900. This category includes in Malie two titles which are split amongst four holders.
3. That is not resident in the village during the week.
4. Seven old titles were split in Malie, four in Salani. One title (Fuimaono) has twelve holders.

[1] The ceremonies of the installation of a chief (*saofa'i*) resembled in many respects ceremonies at other *rites-de-passage*, particularly in the pattern of exchange. See Ch. 9.

[2] The total number of matai and the proportion of matai to untitled people were 1904, 2,544 (7 per cent); 1921, 2,654 (9 per cent); 1926, 2,985 (9 per cent); 1936, 3,100 (6 per cent); 1945, 3,497 (6 per cent); 1961, 6,043 (6 per cent) (Source: GCA 2/IV/5a/24, NZIT 38/1).

6

times (Fa'amausili). Table 6 indicates the nature of titleholding in Malie and Salani.[1]

In general the pressures influencing the expansion of titles has been internal, titles usually splitting when more than one son resides patrilocally,[2] and new titles usually being created when residence is uxorilocal or neolocal. But European approval has contributed to the expansion. When the population began to increase significantly at the beginning of the twentieth century, the missionaries and the New Zealand administration, reputedly to increase their influence, encouraged the multiplication of titles amongst adherents and supporters,[3] and the principle became firmly established in the European law applying to Samoa. The main result of the establishment of this principle has been that *matai* status has become available to any person who wants to acquire a title.

The acquisition of a title is not, however, automatic. Most titleholders[4] in Malie are selected initially by a council (*filifiliga*) of the *'āiga potopoto* (that is all those persons claiming a relationship to the title, though not necessarily to the titleholder, through descent, marriage, adoption or voluntary affiliation).[5] The *'āiga potopoto* council usually consists of the senior members of the *'āiga* resident in the village (*'āiga atoa*) to which the title is said to attach. The initial selection has then to be approved by the *taulupega* (the *'āiga potopoto* not resident in the village), the council of village chiefs (*fononu'u*), and in some cases by specific *'āiga* outside the village, especially the *'āiga* known as *tamafafine*.[6] The only exceptions to this rule are a small number

---

[1] See Table 6.

[2] In Malie 62 per cent of married males resided patrilocally. In Salani the figure was 72 per cent.

[3] Influence in Samoa, in mission and administrative reports, was always measured in chiefs rather than population. The key European figure was the LMS missionary H. Griffin who, under the New Zealanders, became the Secretary for Native Affairs. See GCA 2/XVII/B/121, Gurr 16/9.

[4] Sometimes called the *matai 'āiga* titles. These titles number (1964) approximately 98 per cent of 7,000 titles.

[5] Selections were always represented as unanimous choices. The choice was made in informal discussions by eliminating contenders until only one name remained.

[6] That is an *'āiga potopoto* which was considered to be related to the appointing *'āiga* usually through a woman. In general the relationship was considered to be established when the title of the appointing *'āiga* was first held. Usually the *tamafafine* was a particular sister or daughter of the first titleholder. *Tamafafine* is also applied to any kin related to the *'āiga* through a woman, In the *'āiga*, into which these women have married, the women's natal *'āiga* had certain latent rights,

of high titleholders who are selected by traditional groups of chiefs. When there is a dispute, as there often is, the argument can be taken to the Lands and Titles Court in Mulinu'u, Apia,[1] which has the final right of arbitration.

At all levels of selection or approval, economic ability especially in cash cropping is the most significant qualification for a *matai* title.

There are certainly other considerations. According to some observers,[2] notably Mead, the eldest son, or surviving brother's or sister's son, usually, though not automatically, has the prior right to succeed to a title. Whilst this may have been true at Manu'a, where Mead and her followers worked, or of nineteenth-century Samoa generally, it is not true of contemporary villages in Western Samoa. Certainly all Samoan *gafa* (genealogies) have a high incidence of senior successions.[3] In most cases, however, seniority is a social rather than a biological fact. There is a definite tendency for those who succeed to a title to become senior in the genealogical record and in village estimation whatever their biological position. The incidence of seniority increases as the genealogies go back in time.[4] The same process affects contemporary titleholders. One recently installed chief in Malie who I knew to be a very distant relative of the previous titleholder, was reported to me by the *tulāfale* who kept the *'āiga gafa*, to be the second son of the previous titleholder. Six months later the newly installed chief was the eldest son in the genealogy.[5] Approximately

---

particularly in land (see Ch. 5). Most anthropologists writing about Samoa have either been mystified by *tamafafine* (Mead's dispersed descendants in the female line, 1930) or have confused the semi-permanent traditional relationships between *'āiga*, in which rights to approve a titleholder were involved, with the temporary relationships established between *'āiga* and affinal relatives (cf. Gilsen 1963).

[1] The Court was established in 1903. Every title in Samoa has been brought to court sometime in the last fifty years and especially in recent years. In 1963 nearly 600 disputes over titles (total approximately 7000) were brought to the Court's notice. The Court is staffed (1964) by Samoan judges with a European judge presiding. His effectiveness is reduced because proceedings are in Samoan which he does not understand.

[2] e.g. Mead 1930: 144, Holmes 1957: 120. See Williamson 1924: III for a summary of the early literature.

[3] e.g. Kramer 1902 v. 1: 166 ff.   [4] Kramer 1902 v. 1: 166 ff.

[5] There were other cases where affinal relatives became brothers, and younger brothers, elder brothers in the *gafa*. The movement always seemed to be within the same generation.

one half of the fifty successors to titles in Malie and Salani were either very distant consanguineous kin, or affines, or adopted sons. For example, there was a quarrel in the Mauala family in Malie when a section of the '*āiga* appointed an adopted son to one of the vacant split titles. The village *fono* and later the Lands and Titles Court upheld the original choice on the grounds that the candidate was the most able man available. In this case the adopted son had full *fa'asāmoa* rights since the '*āiga* had presented his genitor with food and a fine mat.

Cases are recorded of people without any relationship, and even Europeans succeeding to an '*āiga* title.[1] In the Leupolu family in Malie a man was appointed by the *filifiliga* of the '*āiga potopoto* to one of the Leupolu titles. The man, though born in the village, had never resided there nor formally affiliated to an '*āiga*. A disgruntled competitor complained to the Lands and Titles Court. His complaint was dismissed because the great majority of the '*āiga* and the village were very impressed by the new titleholder's ability as a cash-cropper. The new titleholder, however, gave several fine mats to his '*āiga* to signify his adoption. In Alamagoto village near Malie a man of part-Samoan descent who had been registered on the electoral roll as a European was elected to a title. The opposing members of the '*āiga* were able to cite administration ordinances prohibiting Europeans from holding titles. The Lands and Titles Court, however, in an informal session decided that the able young man should hold the title because of his recognized ability.

Age also counts to some extent in determining when a man should acquire a title. Youth is thought to be an unsuitable time to have a title, because youthful power is considered to be either ineffective or unduly harsh. The actions of youths are compared to the threat of a *gata* (a snake), whose bite, though not poisonous,[2] still hurts. Conversely age is thought to be a

---

[1] Cases of Europeans holding titles are also reported in Trood 1912: 53, Dana 1935: 28. GCA 2/XVII/6a. From 1930 Europeans, i.e. citizens of any nation other than Samoa, or persons born in Samoa and registered as Europeans have not been permitted to hold titles. But the law does not seem to have had a great effect.

[2] No snake in Samoa is poisonous. *Ua fa'afo a gata* is the proverb, literally 'The threat of the snake'. It is also said that a man with all his teeth will govern harshly.

fit time for honour and the exercise of authority, though it is recognized that the disease of *mūmū*[1] (filaria) can quickly deprive a man of his mental and physical faculties whatever his age, and make him unsuitable for a title. Such a man is *ua pulapula a lo goto, o le 'upega le talifau*, like the setting sun or the tattered fishing net, honourable but ineffective.

The wish of the dying or retiring encumbent also carries some weight with those who make the appointment.[2] Wishes are politely accepted, especially if the *matai* is sick or dying, and are respected if the *matai* himself is regarded as an astute man. But the wish of the *matai* cannot be imposed on the *'āiga* or village. *Matai* often resort to devices to secure the succession of a favourite, who will be allowed to stand in whilst the title-holder claims or feigns temporary illness or incapacity. But this can only be a temporary expedient, the *'āiga* soon want a real titleholder not a surrogate, whilst the village chiefs resent the influence in village affairs of an untitled man.

There are several significant reasons why economic ability is highly valued. First, production skills are the mark of the mature man. To become an adult man, Samoans say, one merely has to be able to clear bush (*mamā o le vao*), to plant *talo* and support a family.[3] Cutting away the thick green jungle of lianas and trees is heavy work but it does not require any particular skill. On the other hand, the attainment of maturity is thought to depend less on crude labour power than on the possession of special labour and managerial skills which will increase cash crop production.

Secondly, production skills result ultimately in an increase

---

[1] Elephantiasis (Filaria Bancrofti) is characterized by progressive apathy and swelling of the limbs and scrotum. 95 per cent of Samoans are said to have the disease which usually begins to affect people in their thirties. NZIT 89/1/12, 8/12.

[2] Traditionally it was customary for a *matai* to make a will (*mavaega*), a solemn pronouncement in public on his inheritance. The Germans encouraged the use of written wills especially to pass on titles, as they thought (erroneously) that this would lead to fewer quarrels. GCA 1/176/v2/100. The New Zealanders discouraged the use of wills, because it was felt that titles were not the personal possession of the *matai*.

[3] Age or sexual development had very little significance in the *rite-de-passage* to manhood. Males who could not clear bush (e.g. cripples or sick persons) were never called men (*tagata*). The *rite-de-passage* (marked traditionally by circumcision) usually took place four or five years after puberty. Today this is usually when a boy is 15 years old.

or maintenance of *mamalu*[1] (prestige, honour) for the whole *'āiga* or village.

Traditionally an important means of increasing or maintaining *mamalu* was by diplomacy or warfare.[2] *Fa'asāmoa* diplomacy or warfare involved most significantly food production. The greater the food production of any *'āiga* or village the more troops could be victualled, the more allies could be bribed into loyalty, for victory depended on the allegiance of manpower rather than its actual deployment. Battles were seldom fought; once one side obtained a recognizable majority, the other side usually conceded. If the armies met at all in battle, it was in brief skirmishes and lightning raids from fortified positions. More usually one side would quickly acknowledge the other side's superiority by flight,[3] whereupon the victorious side (*mālō*) would destroy a number of *fale*[4] (houses) or gardens, or simply slash a banana tree or eat a dead foe, both supreme symbols of victory. Battles were in a definite sense only a symbolic expression of existing economic facts.

Since the end of the nineteenth century the Europeans have stopped *fa'asāmoa* warfare. In contemporary Samoa *mamalu* is now achieved or maintained by competitive ceremonial disbursements. Untitled men demonstrate their economic abilities by contributing (*tautua 'āiga*)[5] to these ceremonial distributions.

In ceremonial distributions local cash croppers have the greatest opportunity to make an impression and secure *mamalu*. Most ceremonial distributions take place during *rites-de-passage* especially death (*lagi*). On such occasions only a man who is a resident can assemble ceremonial goods quickly enough— for burials have to be within twenty-four hours[6] and other

[1] *Mamalu* in Samoan has a meaning similar to mana in other Pacific societies, cf. Firth 1941. In contemporary Samoa, however, it has no supernatural connotations, and has come to mean 'impressiveness', or prestige, though this prestige depends as Firth has noted (1941) on effectiveness in economic activity and on political power (*mālō, pule*).

[2] For accounts of Samoan wars see Pritchard 1866: 56, Stair 1897: 246, Turner 1884: 194, LMSB11JAF4. On the wars with Tonga see Ella 1899.

[3] Even fleeing before battle, e.g. a battle in Aana in 1848 GBFO 58/63/233.

[4] Sometimes whole villages would be razed, e.g. GBFO 58/63/233. Destruction of property was a common feature of intervillage feuds and fights as well.

[5] The contribution itself was called *monotaga*. Samoans say *o le ala; le pule o le tautua*—'*Tautua* is the road to the title'.

[6] This is both a *fa'asāmoa* rule and a European law.

ceremonials are often at short notice—and only a cash cropper can purchase the European goods (particularly tinned foods) which are the *sine qua non* of feasts.[1] Consistently good performances in these contributions impress those who select titleholders, the local *'āiga*, and also the *taulupega* and *tamafafine* (the relatives from outside the village) who are likely to receive presentations on such occasions.

A hardworking young man can also impress the other *matai* of the village. Contributions for large ceremonials are prepared under the direction of the village council (*fono*). In ceremonials involving inter-village competition (e.g. Church openings, cricket matches) where village prestige (*mamalu*) is at stake, the *matai* are glad to have a young man who can increase the size of the village presentation. Finally the village council (*fono*) is the group dealing with the outide *pālagi* world. Cash cropping skills are considered an important part of the qualification for joining a group continually concerned with bargaining and skirmishing with traders and merchants over prices and terms.

The wage labourer does not have such a good chance as the cash cropper of obtaining a title. Unless he sends back money regularly, and returns occasionally, an absentee is likely to be considered a *tagata'ese*, a stranger, or even a *pālagi* or *afakasi*—a half caste. The exile might still be welcome in his own parent's *fale*, but other members of the *'āiga* are likely to be uncertain of his virtues as a titleholder. There is a saying in Malie '*Ua fa'atamala o le tautua, faatasi taule 'alea, atu lua matai*'—'The man who neglects his *'āiga* when he is untitled, will neglect them more when he is their *matai*.' Encumbent chiefs are particularly opposed to the returning migrant. They fear he will shirk his *fa'asāmoa* duties in the village, and might try to introduce *pālagi* customs. There were great objections to one returning migrant in Malie because he arrived back in the village wearing trousers, the furthest symbol of social distance from *fa'asamoa*.

Consequently although returning migrants often have more money than local cash croppers, this cash is regarded differently from the cash or the cash potential of the local man. For example, in Malie a wage labour migrant came back to the

[1] See Tables 3, 14.

village from PagoPago (American Samoa) with nearly $600 but he was defeated for a vacant title by a resident cash cropper who was lucky if he could raise £30 a year for ceremonial contribution. The cash cropper was known and trusted, he had the backing of gardens and children whose potential was fully realized and thought to be the more fitting background for a new chief. But enough cash can still secure the title. 'For £500', said a high chief in Malie, 'no *'āiga* would ignore a relative no matter how *vavale* (slimy) he is.'

Mamalu and productive capacity do not, however, depend entirely on production skills for ceremonial disbursement. Both also depend significantly on a man's ability to have children. Fertility is characteristic both of traditional gods, still applauded in myth and legend, and of Old Testament patriarchs[1] whose constant begetting is the most popular biblical text in the village. Impregnation is the most important means of transmitting or increasing *mamalu* and the male genitals are considered to be the source of it.[2] More significantly fertility is the ultimate source of production increases, since the size of agricultural production, subsistence and cash crop, is largely a function of manpower. Even the very young can contribute significantly to agricultural production, for example, by gathering nuts. Children also help swell the *'āiga* income more indirectly, not only by wage labour, but also through adoption, when economic rights in other *'āiga* can be established or maintained.

Again the man in the village can use this source of *mamalu* to greater advantage than the wage labourer in the town. There are relatively more women available for marriage in the village as there are relatively few wage labour opportunities for women in the towns. Moreover, most women who migrated to the town are either not anxious to enter into a permanent liason which will stop them working or are more anxious to move further into the *pālagi* world by migrating abroad, or

---

[1] The popularity of the Old Testament is not only a result of the influence of calvinist missionaries; many Samoans also believe that they are a lost tribe of Israel.

[2] As in the Maori, *mana tagata* (Gudgeon 1905). According to one informant the old Samoan warriors would expose the genitals of their leader to give their army greater effectiveness (*mālō*). *Mālō*, meaning great effectiveness and political power is said to be derived from the word meaning the girdle which covers the penis.

marrying a *pālagi*. And even if they do marry a Samoan, they are not anxious to have large families, for the additional manpower which increases wealth in the village, decreases the individual's wealth in the town where jobs are short and where most families are dependent on a single small pay-packet.

Finally, in an important way the Land and Titles Court bolsters the rights of local residents to local *'āiga* titles. The Court recognizes *tautua* (contribution to *'āiga* activities) as the most important qualification for a *matai* title, mainly because it is considered that the *'āiga* owns (*pule*) the title. The priority of *tautua* is upheld even when the *'āiga* itself wants to appoint a candidate on other grounds. Judge Marsack, who together with high-titled Samoan judges, has been responsible for this precedent, has laid down that the Court should regard 'blood relationship' as conferring 'no . . . obligation' whilst '*tautua* . . . is of the utmost importance'.[1] The Court has also laid down that *tautua 'āiga* (service to the *'āiga*) 'necessarily involves' continual residence in the village.[2]

MOVEMENT OF TITLES

Economic ability then, especially in cash cropping, is a most significant qualification for a title and consequently a very significant production incentive. But the acquisition of a title is not normally the end of a man's ambitions or activities. Amongst most *matai* there is also a great desire to move to more highly regarded status positions.

The most frequent method of achieving a higher status for a particular title is to increase the *mamalu* (prestige) attaching to the *'āiga* and its title. This is done, as in the case of acquiring a title, by excelling in ceremonial distribution. Any increase in *mamalu* leads not only to an increase in the reputation of the *matai* and *'āiga* in the village but also to a rise in the title's position in the formal orders of precedence in the village.

Traditionally, the most important order of precedence was the *fa'alupega* (the announcement of titles at the beginning of ceremonies) and the *gafa* (genealogies). The manipulation of *fa'alupega* and *gafa* to reflect increased *mamalu* was performed by the *tulāfale* (orator chiefs), whose verbal authority could

[1] Marsack was Chief Judge of the Court from 1947 to 1961. Marsack 1961(a): 10.   [2] Ibid.

not be challenged. In the last fifty years the *fa'alupega* and *gafa* have become less important means of validating the *mamalu* of a title. In the early years of the twentieth century, the London Missionary Society gathered together the *fa'alupega* of all villages and published them, and more recently the Mormon mission and Land and Titles court have collected many *gafa*.[1]

In some villages, the London Missionary Society *fa'alupega* particularly, froze the existing rank structure, and prevented the correlation between *mamalu* (prestige) and precedence. But in many villages means have been found of circumventing the *fa'alupega* or *gafa*, or developing new means of demonstrating rank. For instance, in many Catholic villages the authority of the London Missionary Society *fa'alupega* is openly defied. Even in staunch London Missionary Society villages, such as Malie, ways have been found of using the *fa'alupega* (one *matai* described it as 'the bible') and still allowing *mamalu* (prestige) to determine precedence. The *fa'alupega* in Malie has in the highest position, not a single title but a group of titles, *Falefitu*, supposedly consisting of seven *tulāfale* (orator) titles. But there is documentary evidence to show that the *Falefitu* has contained at one time or another most of the titles of the village, as many as ten at a time. In 1964 the *Falefitu* contained the six most important chiefs of the village. The following table outlines the changes which have taken place in *fa'alupega* in Malie and Salani.[2]

The *gafa* which the Europeans have collected are generally ignored as they do not have an association with the established Church, and as it is well known that neither the Mormons nor the Land and Titles court usually permit access to their records.

More significantly increasing *mamalu* (prestige) has been symbolized by proximity to certain superior symbolic positions in the temporal or spatial distribution of things or persons in the village. For example, increasing amounts of *mamalu*

---

[1] The first *fa'alupega* were published in Germany by Kramer in 1902 (Kramer 1902 v. 1), but Kramer's work was not read extensively in Samoa. The LMS *fa'alupega* first appeared in Pratt's dictionary in 1909 (Pratt 1911: 92), but the complete *fa'alupega* was published separately about 1920 (*Fa'alupega* 1958). The Mormons who arrived about 1890 collected *gafa* to enable converts to be able to bring their ancestors into the church.   [2] See Table 7.

TABLE 7

Fa'alupega' (ceremonial order) of the Matai of Malie and Salani

Position number	1964[1] *Fa'alupega*	Position number	1897[2] *Fa'alupega*
1. MALIE (*Matai* names in capitals)			
1	Tulouna[3] oe 'AUIMATAGI	1	Same order, but note the changing members of this
2	Tulouna lo outou FALEFITU	2	group[3]
3	Afio[4] mai SA MAULA IVAO	3	No. 4—1964
4	Afio mai le matua o FAAMAUSILI	4	No. 3—1964
5	Afio mai lou Tapaau FA'ASISINA	5	Newly created
6	Susu mai MALIETOA na faalogo i ai Samoa	6	No. 5—1964
7	Afio mai Taito o le FUAIALII	7	Newly created
8	FALEUPOLU	8	Newly created
9	LAFITUANA'I	9	Newly created
2. SALANI (*Matai* names in capitals)			
1	Tulouna[5] a oe le Gafatasi Afio mai FUIMAONA ma ou alo tutusa	1	No. 7—1964
2	Susu mai LEASIOLAGI o le Sa'oao	2	No. 1—1964
3	Afio mai SIFUIVA o le Matuaalii	3	No. 2—1964
4	Afio mai TUPUA ma le aumaga a Atua ma Aana	4	No. 3—1964
5	Tulouna a le sa TANEAVAE o le alii mau o Faleupolu	5	No. 4—1964
6	Tulouna lo outou aiga SA TAELE'AVA ma lau tofa le matua o TOFUA'IOFO'IA	6	No. 5—1964

1. The same as *Fa'alupega* 1958.
2. As reported in Kramer 1902 v.1: 224, 287.
3. The translation is (1) 'Most respectful greetings to Auimatagi'; (2) 'Most respectful greetings to Falefitu, the House of Seven Orators.' This refers to the group of orator chiefs who traditionally elect the highest titles in Malie, and control most of village affairs. Though the *matai* say this group has always existed as it is today there is documentary evidence to show that the group has changed significantly during the last sixty years. Kramer in 1897 recorded the seven chiefs as Toelupe, Leupolu, Leapai, Tuloa, Laulua, Maligi and Saunia'au (Kramer 1902 v.1: 225). But in 1903 five different chiefs (Taito, Lalolaugi, Tauanu'u, Si'a and Tuiatafu) signed a letter (GCA xvii/BI/VI), and in 1941 (WSDF District Affairs, Malie File) ten chiefs including chiefs from both the 1897 and 1903 lists and new chiefs signed a petition (Seaga, Toelupe, Si'a, Leupolu, Le'afa, Leapai (2), Lupetuloa, Auimatagi (2)). In 1964 the Falefitu contained six chiefs—from the *'āiga* of Lalolagi, Faamausili,

[*continued overleaf*

Le'afa, Leapai, Auimatagi, Toelupe—generally considered to be the most able chiefs in the village. Auimatagi was also the name in 1964 of an '*āiga*. It was also applied to Malietoa, though his *matai* title was in position six. This was in recognition of his succession to the abolished *Tafa'ifā* (kingly titles).

4. The translation continues (3) 'Most reverent welcome to the family Maualaivao'; (4) 'Most reverent welcome to the elder Fa'amausili'; (5) 'Most reverent welcome to the High Chief Fa'asisina'; (6) 'Most reverent of all welcomes to Malietoa whom all Samoa obeys' (*Susu* is an indication of Malietoa's high *Papa* (*Ao*) title); (7) 'Most reverent welcome to Taito, the seed of high chiefs'. (8) and (9) are titles *igoa-ipu* not called in the *fa'alupega* but used in the *'ava* ceremony and during distributions of food.

5. The translation is (1) 'Most respected noble ancestor, most reverent welcome to Fuimaona, descendent of the most noble' (this is a reference to Salamasina, a woman who was the first to hold the *Tafa'ifā* and from whom Fuimaona is said to be descended); (2) 'Most reverent of all welcomes to Leasiolagi, the leading title'; (3) 'Most reverent welcome to Sifuiva, the senior chief'; (4) 'Most reverent welcome to Tupua, the leader of the young persons of Atua and Aana who chew kava' (this was an honorific position accompanying the high title Tupua); (5) 'Greetings to the family Taneavae who live with the people' (Taneavae is a *tulāfale* title, originally said to be a jester to Tupua for the entertainment of the people); (6) 'Greetings to the family of Taele'ava and to the Eldest Ofo'ia'.

are reflected in a man being *mua*, that is high (in some cases low) in the ceremonial order of distribution of food and drink, or high in the scale of cuts of meat and fish, nearest the front (usually the seaward side) in any seating arrangements, nearest the *lagi* (sky, home of the ancestors) in his dwelling house,[1] having the greatest number of personal *tapu* surrounding the person. Conversely the lower the *mamalu* the greater the proximity to inferior symbols, a lowly position in food distributions, proximity in spatial arrangements to the landward positions, or the ground, where women or untitled men sit or sleep. For example, the following is the ceremonial order for portions of food in Malie.[2] Increasing *mamalu* is also reflected in increasing power and authority (*pule*) in village or '*āiga* affairs.

A second method of acquiring rank is to move to a higher title. Most ethnographic descriptions of Samoan society have stated or implied that there are two grades of title, a superior grade (*ali'i*) and an inferior grade (*tulāfale*). The missionaries talk of the *ali'i* lords and *tulāfale* servants,[3]

---

[1] That is the highest house foundation.   [2] See Table 8.

[3] cf. Kramer 1902 v. 1: C2, Gurr 16a/18.

TABLE 8

Ceremonial order of precedence in Malie and Salani

	CHIEFS[1]					
FOOD	Highest ranking chiefs			Lowest ranking chiefs		
Pig	Ribs (*Tualā*)	Neck (*Ivi muti ulu*)	Shoulder (*alagā-ima*)	Back (*o'o*)	Topside - - - (*itūmeatele*)	Legs (*alagāvae*)
Turtle	Head - - - - - - - - - - - - - - - (*Ulu*)			Forequarters - - - - - - - - - - - - - - - (*Sagamua*)		
Bonito	Head (*Ulu*)	Sides - (*Io alo*)			Back - - - - - - (*Io tua*)	
Shark	Tail (*I'u*)	Dorsal Fin Side - - - - - - - - - - - - - - - (*Nono*)			Belly - - - - - - (*Lau Alofa*)	
Poultry and Fowl	Legs - (*Saga*)			Wings - - - - - - - - - - - (*Apa'au*)		
All other food and drink	First (*Mua*) -- *Pālagi* Food[2] Special Dishes[3]					

See notes overleaf.

bearers, barbers and buffoons. Mead and Keesing[1] repeat that the *ali'i* was 'highest ranking' 'supernaturally tinged' 'ultimately powerful', whilst Davidson has claimed that the *ali'i* have today a monopoly of political power.[2]

Apart from a small number of titles,[3] and certain ceremonial activities,[4] these distinctions of grade have very little significance in Samoan life today. Indeed many chiefs in Malie and Salani do not know whether they hold *tulāfale* or *ali'i* titles and some hold titles which are known to be neither, or both, or a combination of both. Again *tulāfale* and *ali'i* titles are distributed more or less equally throughout the rank structure. For example, an examination[5] of the titleholders who were called to the Constitutional Convention of 1960 and the Legislative Assembly of 1963 shows that *ali'i* and *tulāfale* titles are represented by approximately equal numbers.

[1] Mead 1930: 11, Keesing 1956: 40.   [2] Davidson n. d: 81.
[3] e.g. the titles of Malietoa, Mataafa, Tamasese.
[4] For example, *tulāfale* had the rights of custodianship of the *gafa*.
[5] WSDF—Mulinu'u.

TABLE 8 (contd.)

UNTITLED PERSONS

FOOD	Men	Women	Children	Other
Pig	Bottomside (itū-pale-asu) Head (Cooks) (Ulu)	Back Topside (muli)	Remainder	Abdominal Wall— Tāupou (alo)
Turtle	Back - Hindquarters (Tua)			Tāupou (Sagamuli)
Bonito	Belly - (Ma'alo)			
Shark	Belly - - - - - - - - Body - - - - - - - - - - - - - - - - - - Head—Tāupou (Io)			(Ulu)
Poultry and fowl	Breasts -- (Fatafata)			
All other food and drink	Last (Tua) - Cooks may be first			Tāupou may be first

Key - - - - - - - - - - - Indicates a temporal order of precedence only.

1. The horizontal position of the portion of food indicates approximately the grade of chief who will receive it. For example the back of a pig (o'o) will go to a chief who occupies approximately the middle position of those present.
2. That is when only a limited amount of pālagi food is available.
3. For example: tipi tipi—baked talo in coconut cream, ta'a falosami—baked breadfruit in coconut cream.

The rank structure, at least for titles attached to 'āiga can be said to constitute a continuum of rank rather than distinct grades. An ambitious matai can then move up the rank structure by taking on any vacant title above his own. But although the dominating influence of created prestige makes the rank structure fluid, titles moving up or down as mamalu waxes or wanes, there is a time lag between the demonstration of prestige (or absence of it) and its acknowledgement in rank. This applies particularly when, usually through death or sickness, a title becomes vacant. The Samoans say 'the heat remains in the stone when the fire has gone out', that is the rank of a title will remain for a short time when the force generating *mamalu* (prestige) has ceased to operate. Consequently a *matai* who succeeds to a title above his own has initially the prestige and rank created by the previous holder,[1] although this position can only be maintained if prestige bearing disbursement is resumed on an adequate scale.

Two methods of moving to a higher title can be distinguished. First the old title can be relinquished. This is not the preferred course either for the *matai* titleholder or the *'āiga* in which he holds the lower title. The *'āiga* does not want to lose a competent leader, and although it has no powers to prevent a resignation, it can damage the reputation of the *matai* by circulating rumours of his overpowering greed, ambition (if he is leaving the village), or his treachery (*fa'alata*). Nor does the *matai* necessarily increase his personal *mamalu* in relinquishing the lower title. The previous prestige record of the higher title is no guarantee of manpower, and *'āiga*, especially when there is a changeover of titleholders, tend to be levelled off by fission[2] or migration. A *matai* might well succeed to an *'āiga* title with only a similar production and prestige capacity to his previous *'āiga*, and without the ties of loyalty he has created previously. Only occasionally do capital resources (for example fertile lands, or a hot air copra drier) make the new *'āiga* a better proposition.

An alternative is to acquire additional titles. It is estimated[3] that 5 per cent of all chiefs hold multiple titles, usually double titles, sometimes triple titles and occasionally quadruple titles.[4] The great attraction of multiple titles is that the extra

[1] Generally speaking the higher the title the longer a position could be maintained. Some Samoans say that in the highest titles, pre-eminence in rank remains for several generations.

[2] When a title becomes vacant many claimants usually appear and are often successful in carrying off part of the *'āiga* under a new title, split from the old title, or newly created. Disappointed claimants often migrate to the towns, to live down their failure or more usually to add cash to their claim for a title. See Table 18.

[3] WSDF The Justice Department hold a register of *matai*, although only an estimated 75 per cent of *matai* have registered. A *matai* has to register in order to be able to vote.

[4] Of multiple titleholders (estimated 275) nearly 90 per cent hold double titles and 9 per cent triple titles, there are three known quadruple titleholders (0.9 per cent). As proportions of all titleholders the percentages are approximately 4.5 per cent (double titleholders), 0.45 per cent (triple titleholders), 0.045 per cent (quadruple titleholders) (WSDF Justice Department). In Malie there were four (total 55 matai) and in Salani three (total 32 matai) double titleholders.

manpower can increase productive capacity and hence *mamalu*. But there are difficulties in multiple title-holding. If the villages in which the titles are held are far apart a *matai* cannot adequately supervise production or attend to the duties,[1] economic and social, which are expected of him. Persistent neglect of these duties can result in the *matai* losing his title. Consequently multiple titles are usually held in the same, or neighbouring villages. For example, of the thirty-one multiple titleholders in the districts[2] around Malie and Salani, twenty-four (77 per cent) hold their titles in the same village or in the villages within a ten mile radius, and none hold a title outside the island of Upolu.

A further difficulty is the reluctance of most '*āiga* to share its *matai* and his *mamalu*. Sometimes an '*āiga* makes the acceptance of its title conditional on the *matai* relinquishing his other title, a view that is supported by the Lands and Titles Court who insist on residence and *tautua* (service to the '*āiga*) as a qualification for a title. In other cases the '*āiga* compromises, dividing the title between a prestigious but generally absentee *matai* and a local resident. But usually if the prospective candidate has an impressive reputation as a cash cropper he will be chosen, even if he wants to keep his original title. In the appointment to all titles economic achievement counts for most.

Most *matai* obtain additional '*āiga* titles, that is titles awarded by an '*āiga*, and involving rights and obligations in that '*āiga*. There are also a small number of greatly desired titles, often called *Ao*.[3] These titles are appointed by traditionally recognized groups of chiefs representing villages or districts,[4] and are

---

[1] The duties of the *matai* are outlined in Ch. 6.

[2] That is the constituencies of Falealili and Sagaga-le-usoga.

[3] I recorded ninety nine in Western Samoa, that is approximately 1.5 per cent of all titles.

[4] These chiefs were often *tulāfale*. They were known generally as *Tama-a-'āiga*, '*āiga tetele*, *tumua* or *pule*, or by the individual name of the group. For example, with Afega, a neighbouring village, Malie had the right to appoint the *Ao* title *Gatoatitele*. In Malie the orator chiefs known as *Falefitu* or *Auimatagi* co-operated with the Afega chiefs known as *Tuisamau* to make this appointment. The group was known collectively as *Laumua*. There is no adequate treatment of *Ao* titles in the literature. Mead confuses the *Ao* titles with *ali'i* titles which could be '*āiga* titles (Mead 1930: 11) whilst Keesing (1956: 23 ff.), though recognizing that the *Ao* titles were distinct (his 'royal' titles), assumes that these titles were always held by the same '*āiga* or *sa* (Samalietoa etc.)

purely honorific, though they are recognized as bestowing the greatest honour of all Samoan titles.

The Europeans who came to Samoa called the four greatest *Ao* titles[1] 'kings', and assumed that these titles were similar to medieval European monarchies. The assumption was also made by twentieth-century anthropologists,[2] as well as by missionaries and administrators, that these titles belonged in perpetuity to the *'āiga* whose titleholders held them when the Europeans arrived. The Germans, when they abolished the kingship and prohibited the awarding of the four great *Ao* titles, made the encumbent holders hereditary high chiefs, (*ali'i sili* or *fautua*),[3] and the New Zealanders continued this policy. Some Samoans accept the European transformation of the *Ao* titles, but there was much opposition both during the Mau rebellion (1925–36) and the Constitutional Convention of 1955 and 1960. During these Conventions[4] an attempt was made by high ranking *tulāfale* to resurrect the traditional powers of villages and districts to appoint *Ao* titleholders to the most important positions in the new state. The New Zealand administration, largely unaware of the nature of *Ao* titles and feeling that opposition was simply a renaissance of the Mau rebellion, prohibited this procedure. But the *tulāfale* chiefs managed to make the most important positions in the new state elective by all *matai* or the members of the Legislative Assembly.[5] When Independence came (1962) the highest positions in the new state, the executive Heads of State,[6] the Prime Minister,[7] the Council of State, were all men who had succeeded to the highest *Ao* titles.

[1] Known individually as *Pāpā* and collectively as *o le Tafa'ifā*.
[2] For example, Keesing 1956: 23—also GCA XVII A, NZIT 67/2.
[3] The German aim (1900) was to make the chiefs subject to the Kaiser's authority by depriving them of their monarchial status and making them employees of the Kaiser. *Ali'i sili* or *fautua* (introduced in 1912) came to be translated as High Adviser. GCA XVII/A 143.   [4] Western Samoa, Constitutional Convention 1955, 1960.
[5] The Heads of State (*fautua*) were Tamasese and Malietoa, each to remain Head of State during his life. After the death of both, a single Head of State would be elected for a five-year term. Thus far (1966) Tamasese has died (1963) and Malietoa is the Head of State. Since Independence Mataafa has been Prime Minister and Tuimalaeifono the member of the Council of State. But the *'āiga* of these persons (Samalietoa etc.) though they may appoint new holders of their own title (Malietoa etc.) cannot appoint the Head of State or Prime Minister, etc. As one matai said *Ao fautua*—'the Head of State is the new *Ao*'.
[6] Malietoa and Tamasese.   [7] Mataafa.

In all *Ao* titles the most important criteria for selection has been, to an even greater extent than ordinary *matai* titles, economic achievement.

Traditionally *Ao* titles were acquired by *fa'asāmoa* war and diplomacy, that is by achieving superiority over other contenders and their supporters, largely through the weight of an alliance. In the nineteenth century wars became more important as the European consuls and missionaries supplied guns and tactical advice to rival chiefs to further European political or evangelical ends. But arms were prohibited from the end of the nineteenth century, and international rivalries ceased when Samoa was allocated to Germany. As in the case of *'āiga* titles, rivalries took the form of competition in the distribution of property.

There are admittedly a handful of *Ao* titles which are confined to relatives,[1] but even in these cases it is very unusual for a man to be unable to find at least one long-lost relative, real or putative, in the village or district. The most important consideration in the selection of *Ao* titleholders is, as in the case of *'āiga* titles, the potential *mamalu* which the titleholder will bring to the district, and also more immediate benefits, especially the provision of regular large feasts. Both these desiderata require cash-earning ability. It is generally reckoned that an installation feast (*saofa'i*) for an *Ao* title costs £200 and smaller feasts (about £100) are expected at least every two years. In addition the *Ao* titleholder is expected to assist, in an advisory capacity or financially, village or district projects including ceremonials.

The *Ao* titleholders, however are not involved, like the *'āiga matai*, in the day to day obligations of running the *'āiga*. Consequently *Ao* titleholders very often live away from the district in which they hold their title. Many *Ao* titles are awarded, in fact, to people who live in Apia and who have attained eminence in the *pālagi* world of merchants and politics. Successful participation in this world is in itself a qualification for an *Ao* title, and many *Ao* titleholders are local part-Europeans[2] or

---

[1] There are six all controlled by traditionalist villages in Savai'i.

[2] Though this (by the Samoa Status Act of 1963) was a punishable offence unless the European had adopted Samoan status, a course very few Europeans or part-Europeans took.

occasionally overseas Europeans. A more significant qualification is the relatively high salaries which these positions of
eminence usually entail and which provide enough money to
pay for the privilege[1] of the title.

There are, however, a number of cash cropping *matai*,
resident in the villages, who hold *Ao*[2] titles. These *matai* all
have either multiple titles, or very considerable garden resources in one *'āiga*, so that they can meet the demands of holding an *Ao* title. Most *matai* prefer to raise the level of their
ordinary titles which connote daily *mamalu* (prestige) and power,
in contrast to the more sporadic honours of the *Ao*.[3]

UNTITLED PEOPLE

Titles also act as a production incentive for those who are
not generally eligible for titles, that is women and children.[4]
Women and children bask in the reflected *mamalu* of the titleholder and it is in their interests to increase the productivity
of the *'āiga*. There are also in the village social groups[5] of
women and young untitled men in which the members of the

---

[1] One senior United Nations official was awarded an *Ao* title in Manono,
but not understanding *fa'asamoa* customs he imagined this was an honorary
title. He was very surprised to have to pay the bills which went with his title.
He eventually pleaded that United Nations officials were not allowed to give
presents, an attitude which significantly lowered the *mamalu* of that body in
Manono.

[2] One estimate (by a Malie chief) was that 25 per cent of *Ao* titleholders were
locally resident cash croppers.

[3] For example two of the wealthiest cash croppers in Samoa, Va'ai Kolone
(Vaisala) and Luamanuvae Eti (Salelologa), have not *Ao* titles but have simply
the highest ordinary titles in their villages.

[4] In Samoan symbolism women have always an inferior (back-*tua*, last-*toe*) position. Their interference in matters concerning titles was felt to bring bad luck
(*aituemea*). The Samoans say in this connection—*Tapai tagata le pilia*—'There
must be no lizards about when the *afato* grub is being taken.' The lizards (women
or children) will eat the edible grub. That is women and children will spoil the
success of such delicate matters as those concerning titles.

[5] These were *Faletua ma Tausi* (wives of *matai*), *āvā taulele'a* (wives of untitled
men), *aualuma* (unmarried girls past puberty), *'aumāga* (untitled men). These
women's groups today have few functions, and generally all women belong to
Tomiti Tama'ita'i, the Ladies committee (or subcommittees of it) which is very
active in organizing health, welfare and ceremonials in the village. The young
untitled men's group (*'aumāga*) still works together on communal projects, and
acts together on formal occasions, though the young men often form part of the
subcommittees of the village *fono* (council of chiefs). The main ranking symbols in
these groups are distributions of food and seating arrangements.

'*āiga* are ranked for any occasion according to the rank of their *matai*.

Occasionally women also take a *matai* title,[1] though the Samoans think this usually inappropriate, and should only be done if the woman is 'keeping the seat warm' for a relative who is too young or immature to take up the title, or if she wants to act and be virtually regarded as a man in village activities. Again, especially in '*āiga* where migration or an untimely death leaves no experienced men, a woman often has the *mamalu* associated with the title, and exercises the greater power but allows a young man[2] to hold the title and represent the '*āiga* in the village *fono*. Finally, there are in every village special titles for a small number of unmarried girls (*tāupou*) and untitled men[3] (*mānaia*). These titles are regarded as village possessions,[4] though the rights of appointment usually belong to the *matai* with the highest rank and the greatest *mamalu*. The titles are in a definite sense an additional and greatly desired symbol of the *mamalu* of the '*āiga*,[5] and young men and women may work very hard to secure this honour. A *mānaia* title can also be achieved without belonging to the most prestigious '*āiga*. There were examples where the *mānaia* was simply the most expert gardener amongst the untitled men.

ECONOMIC DISABILITIES

If economic ability is the most important qualification for a title, the loss of these abilities is an important reason for a *matai* to lose his title.

There are certainly other reasons for the removal of a title, notably as we shall see,[6] when a *matai* abuses his powers. A more frequent reason for loss of title is when a *matai*, through senility or *mūmū* (filaria), begins to lose his physical and mental powers, and becomes unable to run the affairs of the '*āiga*.

---

[1] There are a number of reports of women holding titles. Before the Europeans came a woman Salamasina held the *Tafa'ifā*, the greatest *Ao* titles. Kramer 1902 v. 1 : 170, Gurr 16/9. There were in 1964 four titleholders in Samoa.

[2] The custom is called *tuaigoa*.   [3] *Sa'otama'ita'i*, cf. Keesing 1938.

[4] e.g. *Tāupou* title Tamasa'ilou, Salani.

[5] The *tāupou* or *mānaia* had very few functions in the village beyond preparing food and '*ava* on ceremonial occasions, though the *tāupou* 'the village virgin' of the ethnography traditionally played an important part in attracting and creating dynastic connections which could increase *mamalu*.   [6] See Ch. 6.

The critical time in the Samoan conception is when the *matai* cannot walk up to the gardens to give advice on planting. Generally *matai* will recognize their inability to continue and convene the *'āiga filifiliga* (*'āiga* council) to appoint a successor in the normal way. Most *matai* do not hesitate to resign. Though they relinquish their *matai* title, they are awarded a new title *igoa fa'asausaunoa* (the pilot of the canoe) to which are accorded the dignities of the highest *matai* title. *Matai fa'asausaunoa* often serve as important advisers to the new *matai* and the village *fono*. However, if a *matai* refuses to retire when the general opinion in the *'āiga* is that he is too old or sick to continue, then the *'āiga* can, through the village *fono*, remove the title from him.

The other reasons for removing a title from a *matai* also involve a default of economic duties in the *'āiga*. *Matai* who have migrated to New Zealand or the United States, and who are not returning in the forseeable future, are sent brief notes telling them they have been deprived of their title, though a wad of banknotes may allow the *matai* to hold on to his title temporarily. Economic irresponsibility may also be a reason for the removal of a title. For instance, a *matai* in a village near Apia was dismissed for placing the *'āiga* into great debt, another because through neglect he allowed a valuable consignment of cacao beans to go rotten. On the other hand, if an able *matai* commits a serious offence, for which, in theory, he should lose his title, the *'āiga* will often make strenuous attempts to secure his acquittal. For example, in Salani recently a very able *matai* committed the very great *fa'asāmoa* crime of sleeping with the wife of a high ranking *matai*. He was tried by his peers in the *fono* and sentenced to banishment from the village. He retired to a village of refuge a few miles from Salani, but his *'āiga* in Salani agitated for his return. After a year the Salani *fono* allowed him to be reinstated on the condition that an adequate feast was provided. Since the offending *matai* was an able cash cropper he was able to provide the feast.

5

PROPERTY

In the last chapter we attempted to show how status, especially the *matai* title, is an important production incentive. But all Samoans, whether titled or not, also want to acquire goods, especially European goods, for everyday consumption or for personal luxuries. The achievement of this want depends most significantly for the individual on his rights of access to the factors of production (land, labour, capital) and especially on his rights to the cash or other rewards for productive activity, which enable him to fulfil his consumption objectives.

The individual has in *fa'asamoa* society significant rights in production factors and in the rewards for productive activity. There are in contemporary Samoa concepts of private property, and individual rights in goods and services adequate enough to act as significant production incentives.

PRIVATE PROPERTY

First, there are many goods and services which traditionally were classified as private property as usually understood in English law, that is goods or services over which 'one man claims and exercises sole and despotic dominion',[1] over which he has rights of use, consumption and disposal.

Ultimately, Samoans consider that the individual person and his services are his own private property. Forcing a man to use his person against his will is compared to taking away a limb, that is, depriving a man of something which is naturally and properly his own. There are also a large number of goods, which were conceptualized as part of, even attached to, the person. Traditionally, these goods consisted of frequently used material objects such as clothes, sleeping mats, ornaments and tools.

The expansion of the cash economy has enlarged this

[1] Blackstone 1773 v. 2: 2.

category of goods as more items have appeared on the traders' shelves and particularly as cash itself has become readily available in the villages. The Europeans also, believing fervently in private property as the keystone of prosperity and happiness have added to Samoan values. Many Samoans now believe that all European goods should be privately owned and most Samoans now possess a wide range of purchased private property and usually considerable hoardings of cash.[1]

An important characteristic of this private property is its proximity to the person. Traditionally, most private property was worn or, like sleeping mats, was in frequent contact with the body. People say that this demonstrated the absolute quality of ownership. 'Your *lāva* (kilt) is like your skin,' said a man in Malie, 'it cannot be taken away from you.' This kind of demonstration of ownership continued after the introduction of European goods. But as the volume of private property increased and unwearable objects came to be owned, new means of demonstration of ownership appeared, though according to Captain Wilkes and others,[2] some people continued to try and wear all the goods they possessed with often embarrassing results. Since the late nineteenth century most people have acquired suitcases or trunks with locks in which personal property is stored.[3] People say that in these trunks goods are as safe as if one were wearing them. Cash, the most important personal possession, is occasionally kept in these trunks, but more often it is kept on the person, in a shirt pocket or a purse, or secreted under a pile of sleeping mats or in a hidden tin or jar.

Secondly, there is a wide range of goods in which a person has, if not absolute ownership at least significant rights, particularly rights to make decisions regarding use in production or consumption.

These goods comprise mainly the goods of the individual's immediate household,[4] in or around the house (*fale*) in which

[1] See Appendix 1.

[2] Wilkes 1847 vol. ii: 78 describes a woman who went to church swaddled in yards of calico cf. LMSB15JAFC.

[3] This can be seen from the photographs of Scheurmann 1927 taken in 1900. For contemporary ownership see Appendix 1.

[4] This group (*'āiga* or *tagata fale*) sometimes corresponds with the larger *'āiga atoa* which generally consisted of a number of *fale*. In approximately 80 per cent of *fale* in Salani (70 per cent in Malie) the group consisted of an elementary nuclear family often (41 per cent—Salani, 39 per cent—Malie) with grandchildren.

he lives. There are few restrictions on the use or consumption of such goods. Adults can use household chattels or food on the house-site (*laota*) as they wish, provided they do not misuse permanent property. Only children are expected to ask permission before using the household chattels and have few rights to refuse the demands of an adult for labour.

These rights of private property or use were reinforced traditionally by supernatural and secular sanctions. Most private property was surrounded by *tapu*. Breaking a *tapu* meant that a spirit (*aitu*) would bring sickness, misfortune or even death to the offender. These property *tapu* were quite distinct from *tapu* which were the correlate of *mamalu* (prestige) and rank,[1] and applied to the person and personal property of all individuals irrespective of rank. These property *tapu* were in many respects an extension of *tapu* surrounding the person. One man in Malie said 'My watch is like my faeces. Nobody will touch it.'

Tapu apply automatically to private property but they are also specifically applied to an object especially when the general effectiveness of the *tapu* is in doubt. For example, in Malie the breadfruit from a tree on a man's household land was constantly being pilfered. He uttered dark threats about what would happen to the thief. This worked for a time but then the thefts resumed. The man then put a plaited coconut leaf on the tree, which he said meant that the thief would get an ulcer on his penis. There was no more theft.

European institutions have generally made the traditional *tapu* more effective. The Christian god replaced the *fa'asamoa* high gods (*atua*), as the provider of the world and its wealth, and not the amorphous evil spirits (*aitu*), which brought disease and misfortune. The Christian condemnation of theft, in fact, adds force to the threat of *aitu* borne sickness. 'If I disobey the seventh commandment', said a young man in Malie, 'I shall get T.B. from the *aitu* and when I die Jesus will not want me.'

There are also secular sanctions against all kinds of theft. For example, any theft, even of a worthless item, involving two people within a single '*āiga* is settled by the council of the '*āiga*. The usual settlement is the return of the stolen article and an apology. Between persons of different '*āiga* the matter

[1] cf. Steiner 1956: 106 ff.

is settled by the village *fono* at one of its regular meetings. Usually food fines[1] are imposed for first offences according to village regulations, though persistent theft warrants more drastic punishments including ultimately banishment. Thefts involving persons of different villages are settled by special inter-village councils and usually involve great exchanges of food. Inter-village thefts often lead to serious political trouble, even warfare, and a quick settlement is thought to be very necessary.

The introduction of a European judicial system has generally bolstered *fa'asamoa* secular sanctions. The courts provide a new arena for argument and independent arbitration. European conceptions of theft make no distinction between persons of different relationship or residence, so that any person can prosecute any other. But there are a number of restrictions on the use of European courts. The courts themselves are in Apia, physically distant from most villages. Again European judges are considered to be sceptical of all Samoan evidence and only willing to impose inconsequential punishments. Finally, it is felt that European justice co-related the serious-ness of the theft with the cash value of the stolen article. Most articles stolen in the village are only of small cash value, though some can be very valuable in the *fa'asamoa* scale of values. As a result of all this, some Samoans feel that European punishments seldom fit the crime.

Most court cases are from villages near Apia, or cases in which an amicable solution could not be reached in the village. Very often these are cases between members of the same *'āiga* and usually occur because the offended relative feels that an apology is not enough compensation for the injury which he has suffered.

COMMUNAL PROPERTY

There are, then, distinct concepts of private property in contemporary Samoa, backed by effective sanctions. There

---

[1] The *fono* usually fined double the value (in the *fa'asamoa* scale) of the goods stolen. Fines were usually pigs and *talo* and in more serious cases fine mats and cash as well. The rate of exchange for fines was equivalent to exchange rates in other sectors of the economy. There were nineteen cases of theft in 1964 brought before the Malie *fono* involving a total £25 in fines, of which £15 were in cash and the remainder mainly in pigs and *talo*. The exchange rate was pig — £2 to £5 depending on size. *Talo* — 5s. to £2 depending on size. See Ch. 9.

is also a wide range of goods and services in which Samoans have if not rights or ownership, then at least significant rights of use, similar in many respects to the Roman law concept of usufruct.

Most of this usufruct property is, because of price or labour time involved, too scarce to be individually owned, or has technological requirements involving a large labour force. In traditional Samoa the important scarce goods were canoes. Since the arrival of the European there has been a great increase in the price of goods, and consequently of scarce or potentially scarce goods—though actual scarcity has depended on the level of wealth. During the depression, it is said whole villages shared such goods as *lava lava* (kilts), but as economic conditions have improved only a small number of very expensive items, for example, buses, trucks, copra driers, have remained scarce enough to be communally owned. Communal goods, requiring a large labour force, consisted in traditional Samoa mainly of a wide range of fishing equipment. Today only the large fishing net (*tolomatu*) is used frequently.

This usufruct property is considered to be owned by the *'āiga* or village, usually the former. All members of these groups have right of use, subject to the approval of the chiefs who manage these assets. In most cases this permission is dependent simply on the demonstration of an individual's ability to use the goods properly. For instance, a man will not be allowed to drive a truck, or sail a canoe, unless the chief feels that he can do so without endangering such a valuable and expensive piece of equipment.

The most important *'āiga* or village property, is the land which produces both cash crops and subsistence food. The following table indicates the pattern of land use and tenure in Western Samoa.[1]

Fa'asāmoa rights in land vary with the type of land used. In some cases rights amount to an equivalent of the Common Law fee simple or beneficial ownership and provide in all cases access to the land and its products, adequate enough to encourage sustained economic activity.

The first kind of *fa'asāmoa* right recognized by the villagers is over house site land (*laota*). As can be seen from the accompanying map of Malie,[2] this land is mainly in the village itself,

[1] See Table 9.　　　　　　　　　　[2] See Table 10.

Table 9

Land use[1] and tenure in Samoa

Land ownership	Cropland	Pasture	House-site land[2]	Cultivated forest	Bushland	Scrub	Swamp	Lava-field	Total	Proportion[3] of total area
	sq. miles	sq. miles	sq. miles	sq. miles	sq. miles	sq. miles	sq. miles	sq. miles	sq. miles	%
Fa'asāmoa[4] land	159.3	17.0	6.5	22.1[5]	606.1	23.9	2.3	44.2	881.4	81
Proportion[3] of total *Fa'asāmoa* land	18%	2%	1%	2%	69%	3%	—	5%	—	
European freehold land	14.8	1.7	1.0[2]	3.7	17.6	1.1	0.3	—	40.2	3
Government land	22.7	7.0	0.6[2]	2.6	137.8	2.3	0.2	0.1	173.5	16
Proportion[3] of total government land	13%	4%	—	2%ᶜ	80%	1%	0.05	—	6.42	
Malie	3.0	—	0.12	0.5	2.8	0.15	0.05	—	6.42	
Proportion[3] of total land	47%	—	2%	7%ᶜ	44%	—	—	—	—	
Salani	2.1	0.5	0.12	0.4	4.7	0.07	0.08	—	7.67	
Proportion[3] of total land	27%	7%	—	5%ᶜ	52%	—	—	—	—	
Total Western Samoa	197.0	25.7	8.1	28.4	761.5	27.3	2.8	44.3	1095.1	

1. *Source*—Lands and Survey Department based on a 1956 survey except for Malie and Salani which were surveyed as part of the fieldwork.
2. Residential land.
3. To the nearest per cent.
4. Officially termed 'Customary Land'.
5. Shifting cultivation, mainly *talo*.

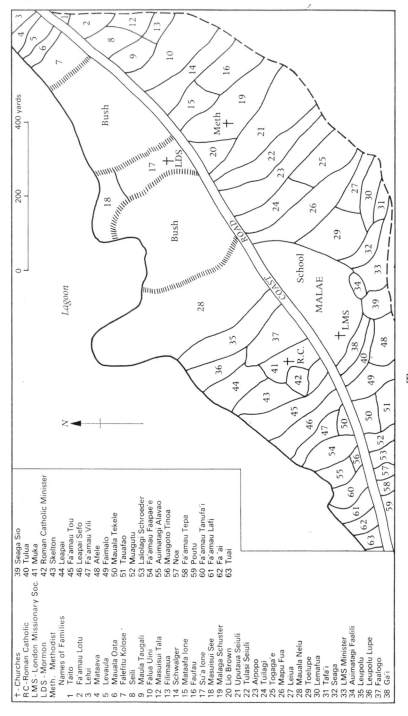

+ - Churches
R C - Roman Catholic
L M S - London Missionary Soc.
L D S - Mormon
Meth. Methodist

Names of Families
1 Taito
2 Fa'amau Lotu
3 Lelui
4 Mataava
5 Levaula
6 Mauala Oata
7 Falefitu Kolose
8 Seili
9 Maula Taugali
10 Faiua Uini
11 Masuisui Tala
12 Filimaua
13 Schwalger
14 Mataafa Ione
15 Faufau
16 Su'a Ione
17 Masuisui See
18 Malaga Schuster
19 Lio Brown
20 Uputaua Seiuli
21 Tulasi Seiuli
22 Aipopo
23 Tuilagi
24 Togaga'e
25 Mapu Fua
26 Leiua
27 Mauala Nelu
28 Toelupe
29 Lematua
30 Tafa'i
31 Seaga
32 LMS Minister
33 Auimatagi Faalili
34 Leupolu
35 Leupolu Lupe
36 Faalogo
37 Ga'i

39 Seaga Sio
40 Tulua
41 Muka
42 Roman Catholic Minister
43 Skelton
44 Leapai
45 Fa'amau Tou
46 Leapai Sefo
47 Fa'amau Vili
48 Afele
49 Faimalo
50 Mauala Tekele
51 Tauafao
52 Muagutu
53 Laloiagi Schroeder
54 Fa'amau Faapae'e
55 Auimatagi Alavao
56 Muagoto Tinoa
57 Noa
58 Fa'amau Tepa
59 Poutu
60 Fa'amau Tanufa'i
61 Fa'amau Lafi
62 Fa'ai
63 Tuai

TABLE 10

House-site land in Malie 1964

stretching about half a mile back from the coast. House site land is cut up into small sections with clearly marked boundaries. On house site land, sleeping, cooking and storage houses are built and some food trees, notably bread fruit, are planted. Every young man when he marries is entitled to a house site. Usually he obtains it from his natal '*āiga*, or if he marries uxorilocally from his wife's '*āiga*. But he can obtain house site land from any '*āiga*, from the village itself, on former bush land, unused parts of the *malae* (village green), or on the beach. In addition to the right of occupation a man also has a recognized right to hand on the house site land to his wife, or his direct descendants.

Generally, no specific rent is expected for this land if certain conditions are fulfilled. The occupant has first to obtain permission to reside on the land and to build a house. People think that the chief, who is considered to manage the land, should automatically give permission for residence on house site land. A second condition is that house site land should only be used as a dwelling site and to provide subsistence food or cash crops. Houses built on the site should be of an approved style and the foundations should be of a regulated height. House site occupants are also expected to abide by the general rules of the village and specifically to keep the house and land tidy, and the household quiet after the curfew. The occupant is expected to respect the authorities who grant him the right to occupy the house site and to participate, when asked, in the affairs of the '*āiga* or village.

If the house site occupant does not abide by any of these conditions he can, theoretically, be removed from the land. But apart from cases where serious crimes entail banishment, or where permission from a *fa'asāmoa* authority has not first been obtained, removal is, in fact, rare. If a man has blood relations or affines in the village, if he has lived in the village for more than five years, he is considered to have the right to remain permanently, to provide a home for his wife and children, whether or not he acknowledges the village authority. In one case in Malie ('*Āiga* Auimatagi) the village fono refused the right of a senior titleholder to remove a young family from land which they did not own but on which they had planted coconuts. To remove a man for not respecting the village chiefs, or for not participating in ceremonial is considered to be cruel (*leaga*) and even sinful (*agasala*).

There are, however, some pressures which can be brought to bear on the non-conformist house site occupant. Occasionally the threat of eviction may be used, for the threat itself is something of an insult. For example in Apia nu'u a man ('*Āiga* Tuiletufuga) erected a cookhouse on a piece of land without the senior titleholder's permission. When told that the house would be dismantled he complied with the chief's wishes. There are other more important sanctions. In the hot and humid Samoan climate wooden and thatched houses fall into disrepair within two or three years. Some housing materials usually have to be obtained from other '*āiga* and village labour is needed for rebuilding. These village resources for labour can be used as a lever to ensure compliance. European courts can also be used. An awkward house site occupant might find himself reported for having Rhinoceroses beetles on his land, and he will probably be prosecuted since most lands are infested with beetles. In most cases where a house site occupant tries to lease land to a trader the matter will be taken to the Lands and Titles Court. The Court usually confirms the occupants tenure, although the house site land is regarded as being under the jurisdiction of the chief. The court usually directs that the man leasing the land or trading on it, should give a proportion of his rent or profit to his chief, or to the village.

The introduction of European institutions bolsters individual access to house site land in ways other than reinforcing *fa'asāmoa* rights through the courts. During the middle and the end of the nineteenth century,[1] the Europeans, especially the Germans, bought a considerable amount of land in or near villages, particularly to establish trading stores, build churches, or to facilitate the transport of goods grown on inland plantations. In the twentieth century the New Zealand administration appropriated much land in the villages as part of the captured German estates and also took over land to build schools and for public works. Since the Second World War as Europeans have withdrawn from the countryside, some of these freehold or government lands have come on to the market

---

[1] Judge Gurr (File 10A) says that over 2,000 acres of village land was bought, most of which was confirmed by the 1893 International Land Commission.

and have been purchased by, or leased to, local Samoans. Rights over these lands are similar for all practical purposes to the European conception of ownership in fee simple, and have been held in the European courts to be outside the jurisdiction of *fa'asāmoa* authorities. In another case in Apia nu'u, where the problem is most frequent, a chief (*'Āiga* Folau) bought back a piece of land which his *'āiga* had previously sold to Europeans and which had been registered as freehold. When the chief died intestate (in European law) the *'āiga* claimed it back as part of their *fa'asāmoa* patrimony, but the Land and Titles Court awarded it to his descendants (in European law).

The second and most significant kind of Samoan land right was over garden land (*fa'ato'aga*), that is the land lying behind the village on which cash crops and subsistence crops are cultivated. As can be seen from the accompanying map of Malie,[1] the great majority of garden land is considered to belong to the various *'āiga* of the village. In Malie the *'āiga* owns various parcels of land, each containing coconuts, cocoa or bananas and several *talo* plots towards the bush line. This can be seen in Malie if the maps of land use are compared with the map of the distribution of *'āiga* garden land.[2] Those *'āiga* not having a portion of banana land, usually have some arrangement by which they can obtain bananas. The LMS pastor (9) receives bananas as part of his parishioners' contribution, the Fa'amau fala (25) *'āiga* receive them from related Fa'amau *'āiga* as part of reciprocal *'āiga* exchanges, and the *'āiga* Schroeder who are involved in wage labour, buy bananas.

The people say that this distribution ensures that all the villagers share in good and bad land, though the pattern is also the result of population expansion, and the development of new land by branches of the *'āiga*.

In theory, a man inherits land rights from his *'āiga*, but in practice there is very little restriction on access to land. Descent[3] rules are very flexible. Generally, a man has the right to affiliate to any *'āiga* in which he has a relation. Samoan

[1] See Table 11. [2] See Table 11.

[3] The descent rules described by anthropologists in American Samoa would appear to be different to Western Samoa. Mead 1930: 24, Holmes 1957, Davenport 1959, Ember 1962.

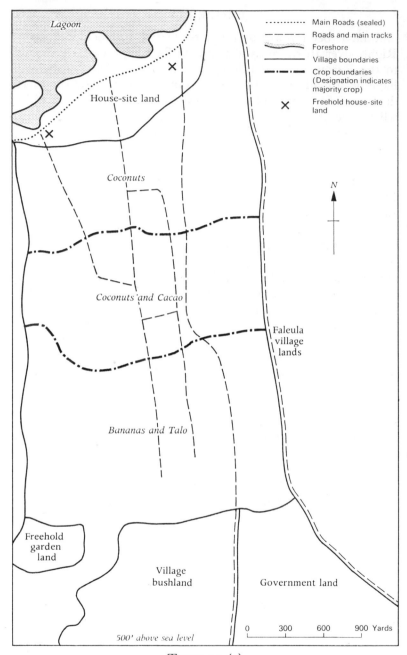

Lagoon

House-site land

Coconuts

Coconuts and Cacao

Faleula
village
lands

Bananas and Talo

Freehold
garden
land

Village
bushland

Government land

500' above sea level

Main Roads (sealed)
Roads and main tracks
Foreshore
Village boundaries
Crop boundaries
(Designation indicates
majority crop)
Freehold house-site
land

N

0   300   600   900 Yards

TABLE 11 (a)

Sketch map of land use in Malie 1964

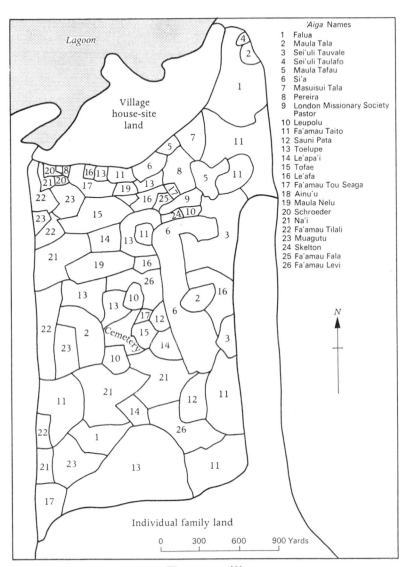

'Aiga Names
1 Falua
2 Maula Tala
3 Sei'uli Tauvale
4 Sei'uli Taulafo
5 Maula Tafau
6 Si'a
7 Masuisui Tala
8 Pereira
9 London Missionary Society
   Pastor
10 Leupolu
11 Fa'amau Taito
12 Sauni Pata
13 Toelupe
14 Le'apa'i
15 Tofae
16 Le'afa
17 Fa'amau Tou Seaga
18 Ainu'u
19 Maula Nelu
20 Schroeder
21 Na'i
22 Fa'amau Tilali
23 Muagutu
24 Skelton
25 Fa'amau Fala
26 Fa'amau Levi

Lagoon

Village
house-site
land

N

Individual family land

0   300   600   900 Yards

TABLE 11 (b)

Distribution of 'Āiga *gardenland, Malie 1964*

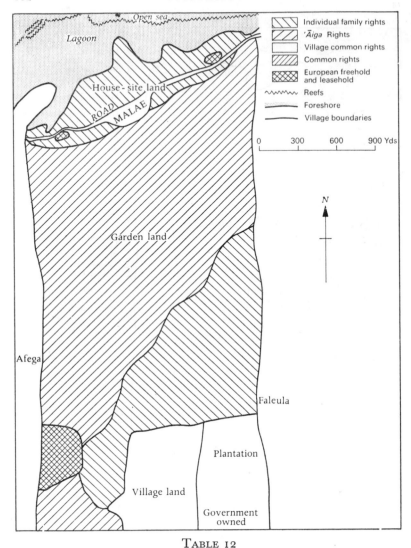

Individual family rights
'Āiga Rights
Village common rights
Common rights
European freehold and leasehold
Reefs
Foreshore
Village boundaries

TABLE 12

Diagram of land rights in Malie 1964

fecundity has meant that a man has a wide range of choices for affiliation. Most Samoans in most villages can find some long lost cousin thrice removed on whose land he can make a garden. Secondly, a man can marry into an *'āiga*. Occasionally garden land is formally transferred to a man as part of the wife's dowry, but more usually he simply participates in the affairs of his wife's *'āiga*.

Even if a man does not have a relation in the village or, as is happening frequently in the crowded villages of North-West Upolu, near Apia, this relation has very little land to spare to make a garden, it is possible to affiliate to an *'āiga* without there being any known relationship, provided the person is resident in the village. There were two cases in Malie (*'Āiga*, Maula, Fa'amausili) where land was given to village residents without requiring *'āiga* affiliation, *tautua* or rent. This practice, however, was stopped when one of the men (a European) claimed the land was a gift, and therefore his freehold, and when the claim was upheld in the European courts. Sometimes there will be an exchange of goods between the two *'āiga* concerned[1] similar to the exchanges in cases of adoption. In some cases where a man claims *'āiga* garden land the situation is expressed, sooner or later, in a descent idiom. People say after a short time that non-relatives are relatives, and that relatives are more closely related than they are in fact.

There are few restrictions on the rights of cultivation of *'āiga* garden land. On plots near the house sites, individual families use the resources much as they would on the house site. The chief has more control over the distant garden plots. It is the chief's decision initially as to what areas of land should be cultivated and usually he gives advice also on planting methods and arbitrates whenever there are disputes. But it is up to the individual cultivator to interpret these directions and to make any operational (i.e. small scale) decisions. For usually the *'āiga* labour force splits up into individual families for all kinds of cultivation. Most chiefs prefer to let the young men in the *'āiga*, certainly those with families, go their own way in the gardens. For the chief's great pleasure is not gardening, but sitting in the village and arguing and debating in the *fono* about local and national politics and government.

In every village there are young families[2] who farm by themselves on *'āiga* land and only return to the village for

[1] That is usually his natal *'āiga* and the *'āiga* to which he wishes to affiliate.
[2] See Table 12.

important ceremonial occasions. Often these young families cultivate the banana and *talo* plots which are further from the village than the more ancient coconut groves. In many villages, too, young single men live for long periods on the bush line, cultivating *talo* for the village or the Apia market. In some villages the whole of the village lands[1] have been cut up by the chiefs into individual farms.

Rights of tenure and cultivation on *'āiga* land are dependent in theory on the cultivator fulfilling certain duties. He is expected to obey general village rules and to participate to some extent, in *'āiga* activities. In particular, a cultivator is expected, when requested, to render service (*tautua*) to the chief and to set aside trees or crops (*sā*) for *'āiga* ceremonials. There are definite restrictions on the duties involved in *sā* and *tautua 'āiga*, and these duties seldom affect in practice, the rights of tenure and cultivation. It is very difficult for a chief to remove a man from his garden land. Most people feel that removal from garden land is a very harsh act indeed, especially if a cultivator is removed from cocoa or coconut land, where trees take years to mature. It is thought to be a fundamental right of every man, especially men with families, to work the land to provide for their families. The chief himself is usually reluctant about removal because it involves a loss of *'āiga* man-power and prestige. Inevitably, also rumours circulate of the chief's harshness, greed or favouritism. The village *fono* is also usually very cautious about expelling a man from his land for an expelled man will either seek alternative lands in the village, causing a rift in the village, or seek lands outside the village, blackening the reputation of the village in the outside world.

Finally, in addition to rights of cultivation, a man also has the rights to bequeath *'āiga* garden land. In the event of the death of the head of a family, the traditional custom was that the widow could return to her own village though her children remained on the land under the new *'āiga* chief. In contemporary Samoa, the widow and children usually stay on the land even if the widow remarries, provided they fulfil the normal conditions regarding the use of garden land.

Introduced European institutions generally bolster *fa'asāmoa*

---

[1] For example, Vaisala, Saleleloga.

mechanisms ensuring security of tenure. First, the Lands and Titles Court provides a court of appeal for villagers threatened with removal.[1] Most cases which come to the Land and Titles Court have been approved by the village *fono* and there are usually good *fa'asāmoa* grounds for removal, usually because the man has not only refused *tautua 'āiga* (service to the '*āiga*) but has also committed an offence which warrants banishment. The Lands and Titles Court generally refuses to sanction banishment, as this has been specifically prohibited by administration ordinances since German times. The village chiefs are either instructed to punish the crimes by *fa'asāmoa* means informally recognized by the Europeans (e.g. food fines), or submit the case to the regular European courts. The only time when banishment is approved is when a young man sets himself up as a rival chief in the '*āiga*. Generally, the village chiefs abide by these Lands and Titles Court directives, partly at least because they want other chiefs to know that they are generous and ready to accept advice. Occasionally, however, chiefs will resort to subterfuges to punish the offending cultivator, such as banishing him for a short time or uprooting temporary crops, such as *talo*. There are limits to such punishment since the offending cultivator may go back to the Lands and Titles Court. The chief is then exposed to the ridicule showered on the deceitful and might even lose his title.

Individual rights in garden land have also been strengthened by European efforts to introduce individual tenure. The Europeans believe fervently that the greatest obstacle to economic development in Samoa is the communal nature of land holding. Secure individual tenure was thought to be a 'proper' and 'civilized' institution[2] necessary for economic development, and also perhaps it simplified alienation. Since the beginning of the New Zealand administration there have been concerted attempts either to introduce individual tenure[3] based on fee simple or leases, or to see that individuals are properly protected in the *fa'asāmoa* system. These administration schemes of individual tenure have only had a limited direct

[1] The court handled 75 land cases in 1961, 103 in 1962, 118 in 1963. More significantly, in 1963 the court dealt with over 400 cases informally, and settlements were, in fact, made out of court.

[2] NZIT 69/199.

[3] Notably General Richardson's scheme on the Tongan model (NZIT 1/23/8).

success. The chiefs are always suspicious of a foreign administration and generally refuse to co-operate with it. But administration pressure undoubtedly did make the chiefs introduce, or maintain in the *fa'asāmoa* system, individual rights, partly at least in order to retain chiefly influence in the village *vis-à-vis* the administration.

Individual rights, then, in garden land, are extensive and secure. It has even become possible in the villages to acquire land without affiliating to an *'āiga*. The accompanying map indicates the kinds of land acquisition that have taken place in Malie in recent years.[1] First, land can be acquired by a limited amount of *tautua* (service) to an *'āiga* or village. Generally this involves duties such as helping tidy the *'āiga* land once every month. A more significant means of acquiring land is by direct payment of a rent to the *'āiga* concerned. Although there are records of renting in traditional Samoa[2] its regular occurrence would appear to be a modern innovation. Renting generally involves lands bearing temporary crops such as bananas or *talo*. The reason for this is that most people think that in renting land permanently they will alienate it. It is firmly believed in the modern village, that the Lands and Titles Court regards land use, especially land use over a number of years, as the most important criteria for securing permanent tenure, especially if permanent tree crops are involved. It is also widely recognized in the village *fono* that the longer a tenant stays on the land, the more likely people are to forget who are the real owners of the land, or at least which are the correct boundaries. Sometimes land is rented for specific periods such as ten years, but generally the letting is for the period for which the land is needed by the lessee and not needed by the lessor. It is recognized by the village *fono* that notice of three or four months is required on either side before quitting the land.

The rents are generally paid in kind, usually from the rented land itself. Rents are often used for ceremonial purposes, and rents are usually demanded and paid when the *'āiga*

---

[1] See Table 13.

[2] LMSB20JAFC. The rate for housesite land in Malie is 4 to 5s. per month, 10s. per month for a *fale*. For garden land the rate varies according to the production potential of the land. In the four cases of renting I saw the rent was approximately 10 per cent of the cash value of the goods produced.

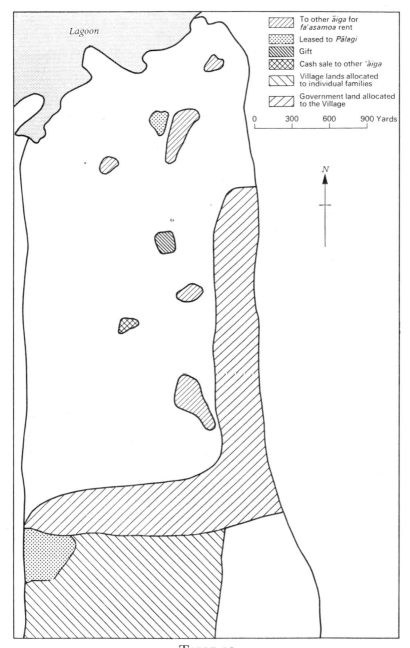

Lagoon

To other *āiga* for *fa'asamoa* rent

Leased to *Pālagi*

Gift

Cash sale to other *'āiga*

Village lands allocated to individual families

Government land allocated to the Village

0   300   600   900 Yards

N

TABLE 13

Changes in landholding (1924–64) in Malie

letting the land has ceremonial needs. There is no specific recognized rent, but the tenant is expected to contribute to ceremonial much less than the ordinary '*āiga* member. In the '*āiga* who rented land in Malie and Salani, the rent worked out to approximately 10 per cent of the total production (or cash equivalent)[1] of the rented land. In cases where the land is being rented by a person who does not reside in the village, or participate in village activities, a specific annual rent is charged, usually a little lower than current Apia market rates for leasehold land in the vicinity. Usually, special permission has to be obtained from the administration authorities for the letting of land to strangers, especially non-Samoans.

Thirdly, land can be acquired outright by gift. Traditionally, land was given to outstanding warriors or as personal tributes to high chiefs. In contemporary Samoa, a young man may sometimes still acquire land in this way, particularly through some conspicuous act of bravery or service. More usually, land is given to persons who have succeeded in the outside world, and whom the village wants to have resident.

Fourthly, land can be acquired by a specific grant from the village *fono*. Such grants are usually made from land which has been handed back to the villages by Europeans. The process of returning land to the village began in the late nineteenth century when an International Commission disqualified many European claims to land.[2] The Germans, in the period 1907–14, also sold land back to many villages when the future of the Samoan colony was in doubt.[3] Most prodigal, however, was the New Zealand administration.[4] The New Zealanders were constantly embarrassed by the large amount of fertile German plantation land inherited as war reparations[5] and the accusation that they were as rapacious as the Germans had supposedly been. Land was first given back as a reward for the good behaviour of chiefs, especially their abstinence from participation in the Mau rebellion (1925–36). Just before the Second World War large chunks of land were given back as gifts. After it land has been given on the stipulation that the

[1] Where goods were not to be sold the proportion was roughly calculated by weight or size.   [2] From 1893—the records are in Samoan Government.
[3] GCA 2/XVII/B/V2.   [4] NZIT 21/8/42, 1/32.
[5] That is after the First World War. In fact the New Zealanders captured the German estates in 1914.

chiefs should grant the land for the use of individual families
in the village.

Fifthly, a small amount of land can be bought on the open
market or in the villages. Some of this land is European freehold land approved by the 1893 Commission in or around
Apia. Freehold land is purchased through advertisements in
the local newspaper or through one of the town's two lawyers.
But the majority of land available for sale is *fa'asāmoa* village land[1] which is sold when some local *'āiga* desperately
wants to raise cash. In such cases the village *fono* recognizes
rights in this land to be similar to rights in house site land.
In the few cases which have come before the Land and Titles
Court the village *fono* decision has been confirmed despite the
legal anomalies of *fa'asāmoa* freehold.

Sixthly, it is possible to cultivate bush land remote from the
village by squatting, that is without any reference to a village
authority.

In these garden lands held without affiliation to an *'āiga*,
individuals can with few exceptions, do what they wish with
the land. Efforts are sometimes made to expel squatters or
incorporate them in an *'āiga* but these efforts are generally
unsuccessful as few people care about plots of land which are
usually separated from the village by an hour's sweaty tramp
through the mosquito-ridden rain forest.

A more significant restriction is on the exchange of land
with outsiders. This is partly a *fa'asāmoa* convention. There is a
reluctance to allow persons from outside the village to use
village lands. The main fear is that land use, especially near the
village boundaries, will lead to a decrease in village land and
certainly quarrels between villages. Sometimes, it will be claimed
that village lands could not be alienated because of ancestral
associations, though most people think this is a rhetorical
device.

European influences contribute also to the restriction on
exchange. Many Europeans, missionaries and administrators,
have believed that Samoans should be protected from rapacious Europeans. In 1893, under the direction of an International
Commission set up after the Berlin Conference in 1889,
Europeans were prohibited from purchasing Samoan land

[1] See Table 13.

outright. Under the German and New Zealand[1] administrations the rights of Europeans to acquire leasehold land were
progressively whittled away. Europeans always assumed that
the Samoans were glad to have this protection, but, in fact,
many Samoans have had mixed feeling on the subject. Before
1893 Samoans made considerable sums of money on the land
market and financed successful wars from land sales. For all the
examples of acres of Samoan land sold for a worthless blue
bead, there are many more examples of Europeans who bought
the same piece of land from several Samoans or bought worthless swampy mud flats or bought land without adequate proof of
ownership. The 1893 International Commission accepted less
than 10 per cent[2] (by area) of European claims to land, usually
on the grounds that the sale was not made by the rightful
owner. Moreover, Europeans who lost their cases had no
claim on the Samoans from whom they bought their land.

More or less clandestine land sales, or at least leases,[3] went
on during the German and early New Zealand administration,
as most administration ordinances were difficult, if not impossible, to enforce. Profits to Samoans were very large as
prices were inflated by the artificial restriction on supply.[4]
But European demand petered out during the depression.
The simple fact was that the Europeans were very much less
anxious to purchase Samoan land than in the late nineteenth
century when colonial fervour necessitated the founding of
tropical plantations. The desire for Samoan land decreased
even more after the Second World War, as the Europeans
began to retreat from rural Samoa, at least as far as the bars
and civilized conveniences of the port town of Apia. But although the need for restriction on exchange had vanished,
if indeed it had ever existed, *fa'asāmoa* land in 1964 could not
officially be exchanged, even amongst Samoans.

The third kind of land right recognized in the village is in
land which any person in the village has the right to use without
restriction. This common land generally includes the u_nculti-
vated bush land (*vao*) beyond the gardens up to the mountain

---

[1] Notably the Samoa Act (NZIT 1/65).
[2] Gurr Papers n.d. 10a.   [3] NZIT 69/199.
[4] Prices rose steeply from £3 (sterling) an acre for good garden land near Apia
in 1885 to as high as £500 per acre in the early twentieth century, NZMPP 3A/23.

ridges, land used for obtaining house building materials, or for hunting birds and small mammals. Common land also includes the main bush tracks (*ala*) crossing the island ridges or along the coast, the village green (*malae*), the foreshore (*matāfaga*), the lagoons and reefs (*a'au*) from where many subsistence marine products are obtained. All village residents have the right to use these lands, provided they do not break any village rules or the special rules which attach to each kind of common land. Persons who commit certain kinds of crimes[1] are not allowed to approach the village green until they have expiated the crime. Traditionally this rule appears to have had religious significance since the village green was a sacred enclosure, into which *tapu* persons, menstruating women, sick persons and criminals were not allowed. The special rules for admission to common land are now designed simply to ensure the conservation of resources. Fouling of footpaths, throwing broken bottles into the lagoon, lighting fires in the forest are the most important prohibitions in contemporary Samoa. Breaking these rules can entail a temporary restriction on use.

Bushland owned by Europeans and Government roads and properties are treated similarly to *fa'asāmoa* common land. There is usually no means of stopping villagers entering European-owned land at will, especially government land which is seldom fenced. Nor, generally, could plantation owners stop poaching on their bush lands. Apart from a small number of private roads all roads are public ways, though the Samoans do not recognize, understand or abide by the government's traffic regulations. There are, every year, hundreds of traffic accidents in every village.

The fourth kind of land right is in the open sea ('*au peau*) or along the mountain ridges (*mauga*). The open sea, that is the sea outside the reef or lagoon, is understood by all to be free for the use of all men. Mountain ridges are considered to be village property and village boundaries are said to run along the ridge tops. From the villages these ridge tops appear as sharp lines in the sky, though in fact the ridge tops often contain plateaux and valleys. In practice, on the rare occasions when such deep bush is used, all the villages treat the ridge

---

[1] For example, murder or adultery with the wife of a chief.

tops as common land. But since the Europeans have driven
roads along and through the ridge tops, and there have been
chances of compensation or cash cropping, there have been
many arguments about precise boundaries, and attempts to
include mountain crest land within village lands.

Rights of access to land are, then, clearly recognized and
obtainable in the village. Land rights also entail rights to the
rewards of productive effort on the land. *Fa'asāmoa* usage of
land does not distinguish between the land and its products.
The product of land use becomes, after production, private
property, belonging to the person who uses and has the rights
of use in the land. The benefits of labour on all land farmed by
individual families is due to these families.

6

CHIEFS AND COMMUNITY

IN the last chapter we considered property institutions in Samoa, that is the structure of rights *in rem*, in the objects themselves. But these rights also involve significantly rights, either jural rules or rights in practice, in relation to other persons. We now examine the question of how these social relations, particularly the demands of chiefs and kinsmen, affect production incentives and production increases.

First, although the chiefs have great prestige and economic ability, they do not have significant powers over, or rights in, the goods and services of untitled people who have the ultimate authority or sovereignty in the Austinian sense. However, the chiefs are often in fact a significant influence in production increases.

RESTRICTIONS ON MATAI POWER

In the nineteenth century there are certainly reports of extensive chiefly powers, of divine chiefs apparently as absolute as the divine kings of Egypt and Mesopotamia.[1] The divine power (*mana*) carried with it absolute judicial prerogatives and unfettered rights over the gods' gift of land and resources. Goods produced were for the propitiation of the gods, and labour to honour their representatives, the chiefs. But this evidence is unreliable as it is usually based on myths and legends which the Samoans themselves recognize to be fanciful stories rather than an accurate chronicle of events, and on the talk amongst Europeans 'on the beach' in Apia, always a highly magnified and sensational, as well as a hearsay, evidence on *fa'asāmoa*. By the time the anthropologists Mead and Keesing[2]

---

[1] See Williamson 1924 v. 3: 61 ff; also Stair 1897: 76, Kramer 1902 v. 1: 40 ff., Steubel 1896: 122 ff.

[2] Mead did her fieldwork in 1924–5, Keesing the major part of his work in 1929 (Mead 1930: 12 ff., Keesing 1934).

did their fieldwork in the 1920s the chief's authority had apparently greatly diminished, though he had still a 'God-like
arrogance'.[1] To Keesing[2] and other Europeans in Samoa the
explanation for this decline was the influence of the Europeans
and particularly the imposition of European law and order and
administration.

It can be argued, however, that the European influence
did not significantly reduce the power of the chiefs. It is
true that from the middle of the nineteenth century Great
Britain, Germany or the United States, purportedly to protect
their nationals, paraded gunboats or sent soldiers at the slightest
rumble of war, though most 'incidents'[3] were the exaggerations
of edgy missionaries, or misconceptions of the mock warfare
of ceremonial competition. It is also true that the Europeans
made many attempts to reduce the power of the chiefs. The
missions, suspicious of the chiefs' supernatural connections,
did their best to cut away the religious supports of *fa'asāmoa*
authority, by prohibiting[4] all *fa'asāmoa* religious ceremonies,
and by placing in each village a mission trained pastor. From
1900, successive administrations,[5] concerned initially with the
chiefs as a threat to law and order and then as an obstacle
to 'progress', 'economic and social development', etc., removed
as many judicial and executive prerogatives as possible, in-
corporating the chief in the Administration or subjecting
him to its laws.

But apart from a few villages near Apia the Europeans did
not 'tame the chiefs'. There was a far greater danger to European gunboats in tricky island waters and on the sharp coral
reefs[6] than to Samoan thatch houses hidden in the undergrowth,
whilst soldiers soon floundered in the damp jungle and filar-
ious swamps. Nor did the involvement of the chiefs in the
administrative bureaucracy[7] affect the chief's powers significantly. European administrators lived and worked in Apia,

[1] Keesing 1956: 101.   [2] Keesing 1934: 248, 1956: 88.
[3] For example, Gurr No. 13, LMSB11F4JB, F8JA.   [4] e.g. LMSB16F2JE.
[5] e.g. GCA 2/XVII/2/2, NZIT 16/1.
[6] For example, sudden winds which sprang up in 1889 wrecked six warships off
Apia.
[7] From the beginning of the German administration, there were a number of
Government representatives in each village—the *pulenu'u* (village mayor), assisted
in some villages by a clerk or constable (*leoleo*). Until recently there have also been
Judges (*fa'amasino*) with attendants in some villages, while plantation inspectors

remote from village society and could therefore exercise little control over the village representatives. In fact, all administrations have allowed most of their representatives to be appointed in the village, where they remained subject to local authority. As we shall see more fully later,[1] some chiefs even used the administration to increase their own power. There were few sanctions available to the administration. Tiny revenues allowed the representatives only small wages, whilst dismissal was out of the question as the administration wanted to maintain good relations with the villagers. The missions appointed their local pastors, but always in consultation with the local council of church deacons comprising the highest ranking chiefs in the village. In most cases the village pastor, like the Government representative, was subject to, and sometimes the puppet of, the village council.

Restrictions on chiefly power and authority owe more, both in the nineteenth century and in contemporary Samoa, to *fa'asāmoa* conventions and sanctions, than to European controls.

First, even the highest ranking chiefs, whatever traditions surrounded their title, however many powers they were supposed to have in theory, have few means of coercion, to establish or maintain authority. There are not usually police or armies at their call, whilst the steepness of the terrain makes communications and suzerainty difficult even if the means of coercion can be found.

There are distinct limits on the chief's personal rights (*pulematai*—that is rights for personal consumption) over the goods and services of his '*āiga* or over lesser chiefs.[2]

The most important prerogatives of rank are, in fact, only courtesies, the use of the chief's language[3] and respectful

---

(*pulefa'atoaga*) and Samoan medical practitioners still live in some villages. Periodically complex sets of instructions were issued to these officials who, between them, were supposedly responsible for the running of all the villages' affairs (NZAJ 1928/ A/46: 468 ff., Tulafono 1926, Western Samoa, District and Village Affairs 1950). The situation has remained the same since Independence (1962).

[1] Usually the chiefs' power only increases in the colonial situation when it is felt that the chief ought to be an autocrat as the British felt, for example, in Fiji and Highland Burma (Leach 1954: 183).

[2] Most observers have not made the important distinction between these personal rights (*pulematai*) and rights delegated to the chief by the '*āiga* or village (*pule 'āiga* etc.). This is discussed later in this chapter.   [3] See Milner 1961.

behaviour. Whenever an untitled person meets a chief such deference is not usually resented by untitled people. Other obligations of untitled people are hardly more than the filial duties of most societies; the preparation and serving of meals to the head of the house, cleaning the house, nursing the sick and old. Even here it is felt that the chief should not be waited on hand and foot. The sultan of the legends is in real village life a figure of fun, a lazy man with all its implications, a *fafine* (a woman), a *muli mafulu* (fat buttocks).

Traditionally the *'āiga* or lesser chiefs also presented a number of gifts in kind (*mea fa'apolopolo*—tribute) to high chiefs, particularly after harvests, after fishing, or before planting *talo*,[1] building canoes or houses, or making a journey. But this tribute is today only a token gift,[2] voluntarily given, and never a significant demand on any reward for productive effort. The chief who complains of the size of the tribute (*mea fa'apolopolo*) or tries to force a man to give it, is called a greedy man and sneered at by villagers. Traditionally, because he was the gods' representative, tribute was given to the chief to ensure the success of an undertaking (gifts at the beginning of an undertaking), or of future undertakings (gifts at the end of an undertaking). In Malie and Salani today tribute is still designed to ensure the success of an undertaking,[3] not usually through the goodwill of a god, though the pastor (the Christian God's representative) often receives the first gift, but because it is considered that these gifts bring good luck.

Pulematai, personal privileges and rights, certainly increase with rank. The highest ranking chiefs receive the most tribute. But again these personal rights are not so much a prerogative of rank, as a privilege associated with the *mamalu*, the prestige and charisma of a titleholder. The man with the greatest *mamalu* receives the greatest number of personal tributes and the greatest respect. Conversely a man who has little or no *mamalu*

---

[1] Some of these gifts, sometimes called first fruits are mentioned in Williamson 1924 v. 3.: 118, Turner 1884–319.

[2] Possibly only a single small *talo*.

[3] There are many proverbs relating to this subject—*Se'i muamua se fa'asao a manu vao*—'Before catching birds an offering must be made' and *Se'i muamua atu mea i Matautu*—'Something must first be given at Matautu'. This refers to the demon at Matuatu village who ate people who passed him without making an offering. Both expressions mean that success depends on the proper *mea fa'apolopolo* being made.

might miss out completely on his tribute, and be snubbed in the village. In Malie, a chief who had a high rank in the village, was so lethargic and irritable that even his children objected to preparing his meals and washing his clothes, and he seldom received gifts. The personal rights of the chief, like prestige itself, is dependent, in the last resort, on the willingness of *'āiga* members to give goods or service.

There is very little a chief can do to force an untitled person to give goods or services. Certainly there are situations (insulting language for example) where a chief is entitled to beat the person or inflict a food fine. But there are limits to these punishments. A chief who beats a member of his *'āiga* unnecessarily or excessively is condemned in public opinion. In the Samoan conception, the cruel man (*tagata agaleaga*) has no *mamalu* (prestige), for cruelty is a demonstration that the chief has failed to attract gifts through his own reputation.

Again, the chief has no rights over the residence of *'āiga* members or their *'āiga* allegiance. A man who does not like his chief's demands can, without any formality, go to another *'āiga* in the same village or in another village. Often he will go to his mother's *'āiga*, or to an *'āiga* where one of his sisters has married, but he could go to an *'aiga* where he has no relatives. The *'āiga* will usually welcome additional manpower, and are glad to be known as an *'āiga* to which people want to affiliate. Even children (that is boys and girls under the age of 13) can leave the *'āiga* of their own accord because of some grievance, real or imagined. There is always an especially warm welcome for them in the mother's *'āiga*.[1] Alternatively, young men can go to the town or abroad to seek work. A *matai* does not want to lose an *'āiga* member whose manpower contributes to his own *mamalu* and usually he will modify his behaviour accordingly.

In addition to his own personal rights the chief also has rights, delegated to him by the *'āiga* (*pule 'āiga*) or village (*pule nu'u*), to appropriate *'āiga* or village goods usually for ceremonial purposes. We shall discuss the distribution of rights

---

[1] In Malie 53 per cent of adult males affiliated to their father's *'āiga*, 11 per cent to the mother's natal *'āiga*, 23 per cent to the wife's *'āiga* and 13 per cent to *'āiga* in which they had no close relatives. Approximately 5 per cent of all departures from Malie were because of quarrels with *matai*. See Table 18.

9

in the *'āiga* more fully shortly, but we would like to make the point here that the chief cannot commute his delegated rights into personal rights.

Generally speaking the delegated rights are conditional on the *matai* redistributing any goods appropriated and deploying any services to *'āiga* or communal ends. Traditionally the chief was forced to redistribute because the appropriated goods consisted mainly of food which perished quickly in the hot climate. Bad food in ceremonial distribution is an insult and cannot bring *mamalu* (prestige). Also the *matai*, as the gods' representative, was considered to be responsible for transforming the gods' gift of land into consumer goods. Finally, like Polanyi's[1] redistributing chief, the *matai* linked consumers to producers in the absence of marketing relationships.

Since at least the end of the nineteenth century there has been no necessity for the *matai* to redistribute. The product of *'āiga* effort is basically cash which can be accumulated or transferred into durable consumer goods. There are now also adequate market relationships where production goods can be exchanged for consumer goods.

However, it is not to the chief's advantage to accumulate goods or cash derived from the *'āiga*. The *mamalu* (prestige) of a title results from the uninterrupted flow of goods from one *'āiga* to another in ceremonial disbursement. For prestige originates in, and depends on, opinion outside the *'āiga* in which the title is held. A *matai* who accumulates goods which can potentially be used in ceremonial distribution is compared to the person who feasts by himself, a selfish and wretched figure, a man who would *ua ina ona miaga* 'drink his own urine'. By deflecting *'āiga* goods or services to his own uses, the *matai* also jeopardizes future *mamalu* (prestige). If the *'āiga* considers its *matai* is abusing his position, it can immediately stop providing prestige-bearing goods, or divert them elsewhere.

In fact the existence of cash or durable consumer goods increases the personal demands on the *matai*. No longer is the amount of redistribution goods limited by perishability or available labour. Also the expected level of disbursement necessary to secure prestige has risen as more goods have become available in the village. That is to say, the cost of

---

[1] Polanyi 1957; cf. Sahlins 1956.

prestige has become inflated in the usual economist's sense of the word. One *matai* complained bitterly that even the smallest feasts today would have been regarded as a 'royal feast' (*tupu*) fifty years ago. Although this inflation affects the whole *'āiga*, it affects the *matai* particularly, since he has most to lose or gain in the acquisition of prestige. Consequently many chiefs add to the prestige goods, which they can obtain in the *'āiga*, their own personal accumulations of cash or goods.

Again the *matai* has obligations to the *'āiga* or village who are said to 'own' (*ona*) the title. These obligations are primarily a responsibility for production and prestige. But also the *matai*, as the representative of the all-providing gods, is expected to see that the *'āiga* are properly fed, housed and clothed, to protect them from force or injustice, to care for them when they are sick or needy.

All these responsibilities have become more onerous in the cash economy. We have mentioned the inflation in the cost of prestige. Also as the number of *pālagi* goods and services has increased in the village, a higher standard of living has been expected in the *'āiga*. Introduced diseases and *pālagi* education which removes children for a long period from productive effort has increased the burden of dependents, whilst the proliferation of debt and litigation has further widened the circle of the needy. All these demands, which cannot easily be refused, eat into a chief's time and resources. Samoans say *o le matai i le foaga*—the *matai* is the grindstone (of the *'āiga*). I knew several men in New Zealand who had fled from Samoa, not because of oppression from a *matai*, but because they, as *matai*, were overpowered by their obligations in the *'āiga*.

Most significantly of all, because the *matai* title is considered to be an *'āiga* or village possession, the chief's actions are in a definite sense controlled by the *'āiga* or village. If the *fa'asāmoa* polity is not exactly Rousseau's 'campfire democracy', a chief's behaviour, and the decisions which he makes, reflect a majority opinion in the *'āiga* or village. Decisions in the various *fono*[1] are never the unanimous 'diktat' which the Europeans

---

[1] The *'āiga* assembly (*filifiliga*) containing local members of the *'āiga* met whenever there was anything to discuss. The most important assembly, however, was the village *fono*, or subcommittees of it, containing all the titleholders of the village, and (especially in the subcommittees) prominent women and untitled

in Samoa claim they are. There is much argument and opposition on the many informal occasions during which the '*āiga*
and *matai* meet before the formal assemblies. Decisions are,
in fact, made beforehand by eliminating competing courses of
action, until one course is acceptable to all or the great majority.
The formal assembly becomes then the symbolic acknowledgement of an existing state of affairs.

The '*āiga* can, during these informal discussions, decisively
influence a chief's decision, or censure his actions. The Samoans
say the '*āiga* is *fa'amatagi*, the source of the wind, that is the
'*āiga* holds the ultimate authority or sovereignty.[1] As we have
indicated, this is mainly because the '*āiga* controls the *mamalu*
of a title, particularly the production of prestige-bearing
goods. But the members of the '*āiga* can also report the *matai*
to the village *fono*, who can, in turn, use recognized sanctions
against those chiefs who have not fulfilled the obligations to,
or abided by, the decisions of their '*āiga*.

Generally the *fono* will simply implore the offending *matai*
to try and re-establish harmony. Usually the *matai* will take
notice of what the *fono* says, for the *fono* contains representatives
of all the '*āiga* in the village, and news of arguments rapidly
circulate round the village, especially amongst the women
who regard it as interesting gossip. The reputation and *mamalu*
of the *matai* can suffer greatly from gossip, especially from the
long lashing tongues of the women, and the *matai* will usually
do his best to come to terms with the '*āiga* to prevent this
embarrassment.

The *fono* has the *fa'asāmoa* right to try and punish a *matai*,
although the Europeans do not generally approve[2] of this or
most other aspects of *fono* justice. If the *matai* is cruel (*sāuā*)
to some member of the '*āiga*, if he tries to keep '*āiga* goods for
himself (*gaoi*), if he persistently neglects his obligations (*fa'-
atamala*), the matter will be treated in the *fono* as a *solitulāfono*,

---

men. These *fono* met regularly usually every week, or monthly in the case of sub-
committees. There were also district *fono*, containing representatives from a number
of villages. Since the 1870s there have also been meetings of national bodies,
containing village representatives (*faipule*)—now the so-called Parliament.

[1] i.e. in the sense of holding the balance of political power—a frequent usage in
the writings of modern political scientists (cf. Rees 1956).

[2] Certainly not constitutionally, although after the Mau, the New Zealand
administration did not interfere greatly with *fa'asāmoa* justice.

a minor crime, similar to theft, trespass or rape in the village, and punishable by a food fine.[1] If a *matai* persists in his offence, or if he commits *soliagasala*, a major crime,[2] he could be deprived of his *mamalu* (prestige) or his title, or his residence rights in the village.

Persistent defiance of the *fono* is usually punished by the removal of *mamalu*. This is done by instructing the *'āiga* not to give the *matai*, *monotaga*, that is the goods and services for ceremonial disbursement, or by banishing the *matai* from the village temporarily (usually six months), and destroying his banana groves or *talo* plots.[3] Usually the *'āiga* themselves will petition the *fono* for the chief's reinstatement, for without him there are only limited opportunities for participation in ceremonial activity. If the *fono* agrees to reinstatement, the *matai* will *ifoga*, that is go through a ritual of crawling in front of the other chiefs and then provide a feast for the *'āiga* and village. In many respects temporary banishment is only a large food fine, since most of the time the *matai* is away he would be preparing for his reinstatement feast, in some hospitable relative's *'āiga*, or in wage labour. And the time of his banishment generally depends on how long it takes him to raise food.

Traditionally in the case of more serious offences, or further offences after temporary banishment, the *fono* could deprive the *matai* of his title, or banish him permanently from the village, destroying all his possessions, or even execute him. Since the German administration,[4] banishment and execution have been specifically prohibited by the Europeans, and although execution is now unknown, permanent banishment is not.

The European judicial system also provides sanctions against the abuse of *matai* power. From the end of the nineteenth century, an untitled person could secure redress against a

[1] *Solitulafono*, minor crimes, were applicable only to offences by one villager against another from the same village. Those offences committed against persons from other villages, or Europeans, were outside the *fono's* jurisdiction, although two village *fono* did occasionally combine to hold a trial where most minor crimes were treated as major crimes.

[2] The most important were murder, manipulating genealogies, etc.

[3] These were regarded as involving a temporary loss, in contrast to the destruction of more permanent crops.　　　　[4] GO 16/9/01, NZO 5/1922.

matai, if he had committed an offence in the European law of the time.[1] In all European laws, chiefs and commoners have been regarded as equals. From 1903 complaints against *matai* could also be taken to the Lands and Titles Court.

Records do not survive to indicate how far these *tulafono pālagi* (European laws) were used. But today the Supreme, Magistrates or Circuit courts[2] rarely handle a complaint against a *matai*. The senior judges are all Europeans residing in Apia and Samoans feel these Europeans do not understand the *matai—'āiga* relationship. The few cases that have gone to court have confirmed this Samoan belief, for European judges may in fact regard Samoan evidence as prevarication, and indeed embodied in the Samoan Act of 1921[3] is the unusual privilege of rejecting evidence, even if it is admissible or sufficient at Common Law. Consequently in cases where *matai* have abused their powers punishments have been innocuous.

On the other hand, a large number of cases have gone to the Lands and Titles Court, where there is only one European judge, and the precedents (and the proceedings) are *fa'asāmoa*. The Lands and Titles Court has always accepted that the *matai* exists to serve his *'āiga*.[4] Consequently a *matai* who has abused his power would normally be severely censured. Since the court's proceedings are widely publicized, disapproval and the consequent loss of prestige is an important deterrent on the abuse of power. But the court is always reluctant to deprive a *matai* of his title, so that the ultimate sanction still lies with the *'āiga* and the village.

Chiefs, then, cannot usually use their position to increase their own wealth. They may however play a very significant

[1] In 1890 Malietoa helped by the consuls drew up a Code of Law. This justice administered by Samoan judges was generally accepted by the Germans (Solf 1907) as a suitable law for the Samoans, and initially by the New Zealand authorities. In 1921 by the Samoa Act, the New Zealand legal structure was transplanted into Samoa, and this has continued, with few modifications, since Independence. The *tulafono pālagi*, the European law, as the Samoans call it, is administered presently mainly by European judges in Apia. The most usual complaints were on grounds of theft (using *'āiga* goods) or assault (forced labour in the *'āiga*). Cf. GCA 2/XVII/A2/V2, 2/IV/5a, NZIT 67/34.

[2] The magistrates court deals with small cases and civil claims, the circuit courts with local magistrates' court work.   [3] S. 248.

[4] Marsack 1961(a): 14.

part in increasing the productivity and wealth of villagers. The most wealthy cash cropping districts, villages, or '*āiga* are those in which the chiefs are the focus of social activity, irrespective of environment or transport conditions. The most spectacular examples are in the island of Savai'i, where chiefs have formed their villages into plantations,[1] with well constructed roads and the most modern equipment. Villagers are either paid a fixed wage for their cash cropping activities, or are allowed to farm individually, paying a rate for the use of village facilities. Again in most cases the chiefs are the driving influence in successful co-operatives which handle cash cropping. Conversely, the poorest villages are those where the chiefs have left the village, where there are only sick or incompetent chiefs, and weak village councils. Most of these villages are in Northern Upolu where environmental conditions are good for cash cropping, where there is adequate labour and good transport, where there is easy access to administration, advice and capital.

Several reasons can be put forward to explain why cash cropping success can be correlated with the existence of a strong *fa'asāmoa* chiefship.

Most significantly, the successful *fa'asamoa* chiefs are not simply an élite group in the usual sociological definition of the term, that is 'persons of relative excellence in a social, political or economic system',[2] but are also 'leaders' in Professor Firth's recent definition,[3] that is persons who also actively direct economic activities. The Samoan chiefs are able to fulfil the vital role of interpreting the economic situation, of dealing with the administration, of introducing new techniques and values, and above all of making policy decisions on critical issues and long-range plans, notably those involving large scale capital assets.

A very important reason why the chiefly leaders are effective in this role is because they are popular.[4] Most people are very glad to have, and to work for, a chief who can fulfil leadership functions. Most people want to participate in the cash economy, but fear or suspect the Europeans who appear to dominate

[1] For example, Vaisala, Salelologa, Lelepa.
[2] Firth 1964(a): 187.   [3] Firth 1964(a): 186–92.
[4] Contrast Dube 1964 who has argued that autocracy hinders development.

it. The leader allays these fears and instils confidence. He symbolizes effectiveness (*mamalu*) and embodies the people's aspirations. Not surprisingly, in some villages chiefs have become charismatic figures. But though powerful, at least in the field of economic decisions, these modern leaders are not the autocrats of the European stereotype. Their power is popular in origin and contingent on increases in the levels of wealth and well-being in the village. A man from Salelologa commented. 'We only follow him (the chief Luamanuvae Eti) because he is helping us to get rich quicker than we could by ourselves, like the people of Vaisala.'[1]

In most countries traditional authorities have not become leaders in cash economy activities, and generally economists and sociologists[2] have claimed that traditional authorities can never effectively stimulate cash production. But in Samoa, at least, effective leadership and traditional authority have been compatible.

A number of reasons can be put forward to explain this situation. First, since the chiefship connotes very high prestige and carries with it very great influence the best men are attracted, including men with experience and education in the outside European world. Since the great traditional titles are still bestowed by rural villages and involve rural residence, many high titleholders have remained cash croppers despite the wage labour attractions of Apia. The existence of transport facilities has also enabled those who are resident in Apia to participate in village affairs. Indeed cash crop production and sales can be greatly increased by a chief who is resident in Apia, able to help in marketing and able to supply knowledge of the latest ideas and market trends. Significantly, no other élite has emerged to challenge the *fa'asāmoa* chiefs. Certainly there have occasionally been non-traditional leaders in village co-operatives, credit unions, etc., including part-Europeans; but generally these people stay only a short time in the village, or are absorbed into the *fa'asāmoa* system by taking a title.

A second reason for the influence of *fa'asāmoa* chiefs results from the fact that they have been able to retain their authority in relation to the administration. It has sometimes been

---

[1] Another village in which chiefs had successfully raised village production.

[2] Cf. Janne 1964, Nayacakalou 1963, 1964.

argued that leaders in under developed countries can operate most effectively, in conjunction with, or as part of, an administrative machinery.[1] But in Samoa, as in some other parts of the world, the incorporation of traditional authorities in the administration has hindered rather than helped the economic development programmes. Both the German and early New Zealand administration[2] attempted to govern and implement development programmes by appointing salaried representatives in the villages (*Pulenu'u*). These attempts to create administrative chiefs failed. Part of the reason for failure was the general opposition to the Apia government in the villages. The *pulenu'u* themselves were failures too. Because the *pulenu'u* was the agent of an alien government, he could not usually command allegiance in the village. Often the *pulenu'u* was too bogged down in a mass of paper work to court public opinion, to attend to his own work, or to increase his prestige in the village. Because the work was onerous and unrewarding, really able and ambitious men preferred to leave the job to others. The Mau rebellion (1925–38) marked the end of the period when the *pulenu'u* was the representative of the administration. After this the *pulenu'u* was appointed in the village, paid only a small honorarium, and was virtually without responsibility to the Apia administration.

After the Mau rebellion the *pulenu'u* because of separation from the administration virtually ceased to exist in some villages. But in other villages he became more important than previously, as a locally elected representative of the people. This was particularly true of the period before Independence when local members of the Legislative Assembly (*faipule*) had few powers and slight influence, and when there were only a handful of local people in the public service. In many villages today the *pulenu'u* acts as a local *fa'asāmoa* leader voicing village grievances and negotiating with the administration on behalf of the village. Often the *pulenu'u* becomes the leader of groups of young and able chiefs and untitled men, in sub-committees of the *fono*. These sub-committees deal with important economic issues such as care of gardens, village

[1] e.g. Bauman 1964.
[2] GCA 1/17/VI/14/XVII/A, NZIT 1/23, 8–11/33/40/45, 48, 49/50–64, 2/1/9/14, 5/2–15, 8/6–12, 25/1–34, 62, 79, 88, 89.

cleanliness, etc., leaving the more lofty and leisurely debates on *fa'asāmoa* to the older chiefs in the main *fono* house.

The third reason for the economic success of *fa'asāmoa* chiefs is that they were able to adapt their traditional roles to modern conditions. In many cases this did not involve a very great change. The traditional role of informal direction of production, of consolidation of resources, of accumulation and distribution of the results of productive effort are relatively easily translated into the roles of a modern manager, especially as production methods have remained largely unchanged. Only a few chiefs remain engrossed in traditional activities and do not take part in cash crop production. For the essence of *fa'asāmoa* activities, ceremonial and political manipulation, in contemporary Samoa necessitates contact with the European world. Cash is the *sine qua non* of successful ceremonial, and negotiation with Europeans is the essence of political activity. The unproductive chiefs are generally those who are sick or old. There is, in fact, a distinct correlation between the distribution of village and '*āiga* wealth and the distribution of debilitating diseases, especially the mosquito borne *mūmū* (Filaria), which affects men particularly.[1]

COMMUNAL DEMANDS

The rights of chiefs are restricted and these chiefs may play a significant role in production. Similarly, communal demands on an individual's goods and services are usually restricted, and communal groups, too, may have important production functions.

Individuals have extensive rights over most goods and services. Communal demands ultimately depend on an individual's willingness to give goods or services, rather than on the pressure of communal demands themselves. If the individual decides to give, there are returns and rewards for disbursement, either in terms of specific goods or more often in terms of status and prestige. These rewards act as a definite incentive to production. There are also definite limits, in theory and practice, on the communal demands themselves.

---

[1] For example, the mosquito is not prevalent in South East and North West Savai'i, probably because of the absence of swamps in this region.

Broadly speaking, there are three types of communal demands on goods and services in contemporary Samoa. Firstly there are the occasional demands for ceremonial (*fa'alavelave*), that is, for feasts and presentations on a household, *'āiga* or village level, especially to welcome visitors, celebrate *rites de passage*, acquisition of title, sporting or scholastic occasions, or to pay for specialist services, or debts. Secondly there are the general demands of kinsfolk for goods and services, or the special demands involved in certain kinship relations, especially the mother's brother-sister's son relationship. Thirdly, there are the non-ceremonial demands for village or district affairs.

There are limits on all kinds of ceremonial demands and occasions. The following is a summary of the ceremonials which took place in Malie in 1964.[1]

The number of *rites de passage* is limited by the biological facts of life. As significant are the economic restrictions, for ceremonial expenditure is, as we have said, of lower priority than subsistence or 'necessity' expenditure. In most *'āiga* there is only a limited amount of money, or time, available for ceremonial purposes. One result of this economic restriction is that in villages, where there has been a rapid population growth, for example on the North West Upolu coast, traditional ceremonials, such as the birth of a younger child, or the *rites de passage* of distant non-resident relatives, are not celebrated at all, and all ceremonial is abbreviated. The people say that it is too expensive to give all their children a birth feast, and that in any case 'it is better to have one memorable feast than many insignificant meals'. In Malie, where the population has doubled since the war, the people say there should be only two *rites de passage* ceremonials in each *'āiga* every three years. Conversely, in more wealthy villages (e.g. Apia) or where the population is smaller (e.g. villages of North West and South East Savai'i), there is much greater participation in *fa'asāmoa rites de passage*, and even the creation of new celebrations, such as birthdays.

Similar comments can be made about other ceremonials, especially receptions for visitors in the village. For example, during the United Nations campaign of economic development

[1] See Table 14.

TABLE 14

Ceremonial exchange

Type of ceremonial	Number in village in period 1959–64	Number of people in giving group in sample exchange	Goods	Cash expenditure per participant[11]
				£. s. d.
A. OUTGOING GOODS				
(a) *Fa'alavelave tele* (Great ceremonial)				
1. Marriage— Titled *'Āiga*				
Malie	1	450	*Oloa (Groom's 'Āiga)*—	1 10 0
Salani	1		15 large pigs, 20 small pigs, 30 large *talo*, 50 *palusami*, 40 *ta'amū*, 25 breadfruit, 220 loaves of bread, 80 2-lb. tins of herring, 100 5-lb. tins of *pisupo* (corned beef), 15 lb. rice, 20 chickens, 15 lbs mutton, 5 lb. butter, 3 5-lb. tins of biscuits, 3 buckets, 4 shirts, 12 *lava* (skirts), 20 yds. material, 4 tins of baby powder.	
2. Death (*Lagi*)— High chief				
Salani	1	780	*Tōga*—23 fine mats, 20 large pigs, 5 small pigs, 30 large *talo*, 15 lb. rice, 200 loaves of bread, 80 2-lb. tins of herring, 50 5-lb. tins of *pisupo*, 50 coconuts, 20 bunches of bananas.	1 18 6
Malie	1			
3. Church opening (Lotofaga)	1	520	*Oloa*—15 large pigs, 20 small pigs, 30 *palusami*, 50 *ta'amū*, 400 loaves of bread, 80 2-lb. tins of herring, 50 2-lb. tins of *pisupo*, 100 5-lb. tins of *pisupo* 20 kegs of *pisupo*, 100 coconuts.	2 0 6
Malie	1			
Salani	1			

Type of ceremonial	Number in village in period 1959–64	Number of people in giving group in sample exchange	Goods	Cash expenditure per participant[11]
				£. s. d.
(b) Fa'alavelave (Ordinary cere- monial)				
1. Marriage— Untitled 'Āiga—Malie Salani	10 8	45	Tōga (Bride's 'Āiga)— 3 fine mats, £25 in cash, 3 buckets, 10 yd. dress material, 6 knives and forks, 2 pots, 4 plates, 5 cups and saucers.	0 9 6
2. Birth—chief eldest son Malie Salani	25 10	58	Oloa (Groom's 'Āiga)— 5 5-lb. tins of pisupo, 3 chickens, 5 lb. mutton flaps, 4 talo, 2 small pigs, 5 lb. rice, 20 loaves of bread, 3 bunches of bananas, 20 coconuts.	0 14 7
3. Birth— Untitled man eldest son Salani Malie	11 22	23	Tōga (Bride's 'Āiga)— 1 fine mat, £8 in cash, 10 yd. dress material.	0 8 0
4. Birth— Untitled man younger daughter Malie Salani	40[1] 10[1]	10	Oloa (Groom's 'Āiga)— 2 2-lb. tins of pisupo, 2 chickens, 2 talo, 2 loaves of bread, 20 coconuts, 2 bunches of bananas, 3 fish.	0 4 0
5. Death[2]— Untitled man eldest son Malie Salani	52 10	10	Tōga—1 fine mat, £5 in cash, 2 talo, 2 bunches of bananas.	0 11 0

TABLE 14 (*contd.*)

Type of ceremonial	Number in village in period 1959–64	Number of people in giving group in sample exchange	Goods	Cash expenditure per participant[11]
				£. s. d.
6. Dedication of church door[3]				
Malie	2	24	*Oloa*—5 2-lb. tins of *pisupo*, 2 2-lb. tins of herrings, 5 loaves of bread, 3 *talo*, 50 coconuts, 2 bunches of bananas.	0 10 6
Salani	2			
7. Accession to Title				
Malie	4	35	*Oloa*—5 2-lb. tins of *pisupo*, 2 2-lb. tins of herrings, 2 lb. rice, 10 loaves of bread, 5 *talo*, 1 small pig, 2 fish, 20 coconuts, 2 bunches of bananas, 5 *talo*.	0 10 3
Salani	3			
8. Cricket celebration[4]				
Malie	15	302	—[5]	—
Salani	15			
9. Scholar's feast[6]				
Malie	5	23	5 2-lb. tins of *pisupo*, 10 loaves of bread, 20 coconuts, 50 bunches of bananas, 5 fish, 20 2 lb. tins of herrings, 3 lb. tins of fruit salad.	1 18 6
Salani	2			
10. Welcome to *Pālagi*—Visitors				
Malie	10	505	5 2-lb. tins of *pisupo*, 20 loaves of bread, 2 lb. potatoes, 1 tin of tomatoes.	0 6 0
Salani	4			

TABLE 14 (*contd.*)

Type of ceremonial	Number in village in period 1959–64	Number of people in giving group in sample exchange	Goods	Cash expenditure per participant[11]
				£. s. d.
B. INCOMING GOODS				
(*a*) *Fa'alavelave tele* (Great ceremonial)				
1. Marriage—				
Titled '*Āiga*				
Malie	1	387	*Tōga* (*Bride's* '*Āiga*)— 10 fine mats, £450 in cash, 15 pieces of *tapa* (bark-cloth), 1 flashlight, 6 knives and forks, 50 yd. dress material, 2 hurricane lamps, 1 small boat.	1 11 6
Salani	1			
2. Death (*Lagi*)—				
High chief				
Salani	1	610	*Oloa*—200 5-lb. tins of *pisupo*, 80 2-lb. tins of herrings, £200 in cash.	1 15 0
Malie	1			
3. Church opening (Lotofaga)	1			
Malie	1	783[7]	*Tōga*—20 fine mats, 20 2-lb. tins of *pisupo*, 100 2-lb. tins of herrings, 10 kegs of *pisupo*, £150 in cash.	1 15 6
Salani	1			
(*b*) *Fa'alavelave* (Ordinary ceremonial)				
1. Marriage—				
Untitled' *Āiga*—Malie	10	38	*Oloa* (*Groom's* '*Āiga*)— 10 1-lb. tins of herrings, 10 1-lb. tins of *pisupo*, 2 small pigs, 5 yd. dress material, 3 shirts, 1 watch, 2 cases, 1 table, £5 in cash, 20 coconuts, 5 bunches of bananas.	0 9 3
Salani	8			

Table 14 (*contd.*)

Type of ceremonial	Number in village in period 1959–64	Number of people in giving group in sample exchange	Goods	Cash expenditure per participant[11]
				£. s. d.
2. Birth—Chief eldest son				
Malie	25	42	*Tōga (Bride's 'Āiga)*—	0 12 6
Salani	10		2 fine mats, £15 in cash, 5 baby dresses, 5 yd. dress material, 1 baby bath, 1 push-chair.	
3. Birth— Untitled man eldest son				
Salani	11	21	*Oloa (Groom's 'Āiga)*—	0 8 3
Malie	22		2 5-lb. tins of *pisupo*, 3 2-lb. tins of herrings, 10 loaves of bread, 2 bottles tomato sauce, 1 small pig, 3 bunches of bananas, 2 *talo*.	
4. Birth— Untitled man younger daughter				
Malie	40[1]	8	*Tōga (Bride's 'Āiga)*—	0 3 6
Salani	10[1]		£1 in cash, 2 baby dresses.	
5. Death[2]— Untitled man				
Malie	52	9	*Oloa*—2 2-lb. tins of	0 9 6
Salani	10		*pisupo*, 2 lb. rice, 2 2-lb. tins of herrings, 5 loaves of bread.	
6. Dedication of church door[3]				
Malie	2	23[8]	£15 in cash	0 13 0
7. Accession to title				
Malie	4	22	£10 in cash, 5 worth of	0 13 6
Salani	3		assorted groceries.	

TABLE 14 (*contd.*)

Type of ceremonial	Number in village in period 1959–64	Number of people in giving group in sample exchange	Goods	Cash expenditure per participant[11]
				£. s. d.
8. Cricket cele-bration[4]				
Malie	15	122	20 2-lb. tins of *pisupo*,	0 15 0
Salani	15		20 tins of herrings, 20 bunches of bananas, 100 coconuts, 2 lb. rice, 50 *talo*.	
9. Scholar's feast[6]				
Malie	5	24[9]	£23 in cash, 1 pen and	1 19 6
Salani	2		pencil set.	
10. Welcome to *Pālagi*—Visitors				
Malie	10	6[10]	1 large jar boiled sweets.	0 1 0
Salani	4			

1. Other births in village (i.e. younger sons and daughters of chiefs, younger sons of untitled men) totalled 50 (Malie) 20 (Salani).
2. Other deaths in the period totalled 52 (Malie) 15 (Salani).
3. Ceremonies connected with the Church occurred approximately twice yearly.
4. Victory over surrounding villages.
5. Victors reward.
6. Winning a place at University or Teachers' Training College.
7. LMS people from other villages.
8. LMS people from other villages.
9. Visitors from outside village.
10. United Nations Experts.
11. Estimate based on approximate cash value.

(1964), certain villages[1] were picked out as models or examples for demonstrations or surveys. When the United Nations experts first came to the villages there were lavish feasts, but after the visits became regular the villages made few preparations. One man commented: 'We like to be hospitable, but we do not like to starve.'

[1] A small number of 'co-operative' villages are usually picked by the local officials where at least the experts will not be physically molested.

10

There are also recognized limits to any individual's cere-monial contribution. As we have said, a person or *'āiga* is only expected to give if he does not jeopardize the 'necessity' requirements of his *'āiga*. Requests are often deflected because of, or on the pretext of, poverty. For a person to participate in a ceremonial a donation has to be given, but this donation need only be a token.[1]

In many cases there are also limits to the amount of goods involved in any exchange. As can be seen in the summary chart[2] all ceremonial exchanges involve the exchange, against one another, of two categories of goods, *tōga* and *'oloa*. Tradition-ally *tōga* were goods made by women, notably finely woven mats (*i'e tōga*) whilst *oloa* were goods manufactured by men, notably garden-land foods. Today *tōga* is usually fine mats and money whilst *'oloa* is usually manufactured goods and local food.

First, the amount of local food in any exchange is restricted to the amount which can be harvested and consumed before perishing, that is, an amount in direct proportion to the size of the labour force or consumer guests, whichever is the lesser. There are also restrictions recognized on the amount of durable European foods (usually canned foods) or cash which should be contributed.

Secondly, there are expected limits on the contribution to various ceremonials which reflect the rank of the persons involved and the type of ceremony itself. Only certain kinds of ceremonial involving the highest ranking individuals warrant what the people call a great feast (*fa'alave tele*)[3] when there is no question of restriction. On most ceremonial occasions broad limits on the volume of wealth to be exchanged are decided by the parties involved beforehand. Contrary to the usual[4] view of Samoan exchanges there is not usually great competition in the disbursement of goods. Two conditions only have to be fulfilled. First, it is felt that everyone present

[1] See Tables 3 and 14.

[2] *Tōga-'Oloa* exchange is discussed more fully in Ch. 9. See Table 14.

[3] The funeral, marriage or accession to title of an *ali'i sili* (high chief) were the only occasions traditionally warranting a great feast. The Independence cele-brations in 1962 were a new addition. Most gargantuan stories of Samoan feasts refer to these occasions. For example, Stace 1956: 60, Copp 1950: 23.

[4] e.g. Watters 1958 calls exchange a potlach.

should be well-fed at all kinds of ceremonial. Secondly, there should be a suitable differential in disbursement reflecting relative rank or prestige. This does not usually increase the volume of goods in an exchange. 'The difference between the greater and the lesser', said one chief, 'is the difference between two pebbles and one pebble as much as the difference between two mountains and one mountain.'

There are also social mechanisms to provide for small contributions, or in cases where lower ranked *'āiga* or villages exceed in disbursement more highly ranked *'āiga* or villages. In such cases it is acceptable for deficiencies to be explained (whether true or not) by some outside restrictive factor, such as the weather or the tins of herrings which fell off the canoe on the way to the feast.

There are returns for any contribution an individual makes. Status and prestige are the most significant of these rewards. Most people are indeed anxious to transfer any goods or labour contribution into a status reward. Secondly, there are the returns in goods. All ceremonials involve the distribution of goods to all persons who contribute to, or attend, the ceremony. Everyone is rewarded with food, and ceremonial foods, especially pig, tinned meats and fish are highly prized as great delicacies. There is usually a surplus of food at ceremonials which is carried back home for those who do not participate. It is said that traditionally people thought staying at home was an inferior and unrewarding part of ceremonial, as food often perished during the journey home, but now that durable tinned foods,[1] cash or utilitarian goods form the bulk of exchange, and people travel by bus rather than on foot, even young men do not mind staying at home, especially if they have interests in cash cropping or wage labour. Some people regard ceremonial simply as an enjoyable means of procuring cash or food.

Contributors usually receive a fair reward or return for their contribution. The redistribution of goods takes place under the direction of the chiefs. The food to be consumed during the ceremonial is shared out amongst all present,

---

[1] Much tinned food leaves the ceremonial unopened. There were even reports of cases of food sent from Apia directly to a participating village without going to the ceremonial village.

but all other goods are redistributed only amongst the group which has contributed goods. In both kinds of redistribution great care is made to see that individuals who have contributed significantly to the ceremonial receive an adequate reward. In some cases this is a status reward, a prestigous piece of food, or predominant position in the food distribution whatever the rank of the individual. For example, young men who do much of the cooking and food preparation often receive such prestigous cuts as the head of the pig[1] and other food and drink, possibly served before the chiefs themselves. Similarly an *'āiga* which has contributed a large amount of food will sometimes be rewarded with a symbol of high prestige such as a fine mat.[2] In general, status rewards occur in exchanges where there is considerable wealth difference between the *'āiga* or villages involved and where the *'āiga* giving wealth has less need or desire for extra goods.[3]

On other occasions, however, especially where there is an insignificant status or wealth differential between the *'āiga*, the reward is expressed quantitatively in goods, especially food. This often reflects the demographic structure of contributing and receiving groups. Families with many members contribute most to ceremonial, and have the greatest capacity to absorb food at the ceremony, or cash and food afterwards.

There are some restrictions on a completely equitable redistribution. Occasionally perishable foods are distributed at the ceremonial to prevent wastage. Cash and tinned goods are sometimes held back by the chief for some future ceremonial or other purpose. However, this is only done after consultation, and in agreement with the other members of the *'āiga*. As we have said, a chief who tries to divert ceremonial goods to personal ends is subjected to very great pressures and sanctions. During marriage ceremonies, also, a large amount of goods, especially cash and utilitarian goods are willingly

---

[1] See Table 8.

[2] The Samoans say '*o le gaogao a ato tele*', 'the emptiness of a big basket'. This is an *upu vivi'i*, a very great compliment for only the most noble give away much food.

[3] The Samoans say '*Fa'atoetoe le mulio le ola*'—'keep the greater part of the food basket'. The story is told of the heroes Ui and Tea who lived in Falealupo (Savai'i) and who were constantly catching fish for their crippled children Gautua and Satai.

diverted to the newly married couple, in order to give them a good start in their married life.

Secondly, the overall pattern of ceremonial activities is reciprocal. The donors of one feast are the recipients of another, bound together in a system of prestation and counter-prestation which extends throughout Samoa.

Thirdly, there are specific rewards in certain cases for individual contributions. In the case of *fa'asāmoa* specialist's services, largely today confined to house builders, there are recognized monetary rewards[1] in addition to the customary feasts during and on the completion of the job. Again, in many *'āiga* it has become customary to pay for individual services from outside the *'āiga*, at specific daily rates.[2] This is not usual for *'āiga* members, but occasionally they will be reimbursed if in participating in ceremonials they lose significant amounts of cash if, for example, they take days off wage labour work, or contribute goods from their trading store.

The second kind of demand on an individual's goods and services, the demand of kinsfolk, is quantitatively much less significant than ceremonial demands. Although in theory goods and services can be solicited (*ole*) from other kinsfolk, as in the Fijian *kerekere*,[3] there are definite limits in practice. Samoans say that soliciting (*ole*) is not always good because it can so easily become *gaoi* (theft). An individual's permission is always required before goods can be taken. If permission is not obtained the act is theft. The amount and type of goods which can be solicited is also restricted. A small and valueless item might be allowed, but after this the donor can, and often will, stop the soliciting. Cash or other valuables, such as fine mats cannot normally be solicited. Again, during preparation for ceremonial when all resources are fully stretched, soliciting is not permitted.[4] Finally, requests are only considered proper

[1] Examples are: Houses, £20–£50 depending on the size of the house and the amount of ornamentation. Canoes (small *paopao*) £10 plus 2 5-lb tins of *pisupo* (beef). Tattooing £20 plus meals. See Ch. 9 for a fuller discussion of specialists.

[2] Examples in Malie were cleaning and clearing land, 4s. 6d. or two meals per day; collecting crops 3s. 6d. or two meals per day; other jobs 3s. per day. The minimum rate in Apia is 12s. 6d. (1964).   [3] Cf Sahlins 1962: 203 ff.

[4] One *'āiga* in Malie had only one person come soliciting in 1964 and this only for coconuts worth about 5s. Five other *'āiga* that were questioned claimed that goods totalling £1 in value were solicited.

if there is genuine need, especially sickness or sudden poverty. If there is insufficient need a request is greed, a heartily detested characteristic.[1] Conversely, any request can be deflected if the potential donor claims that in honouring the request he will place himself in need.[2]

There are also returns and benefits for the donor. Sometimes the man soliciting will give a gift or cash in exchange. If a productive good or resource is obtained or used, part of the output will be returned to the donor. For example, in Malie, in a case where coconuts were solicited, they were paid for, at a price approximately ten per cent below the traders' price. A similar return was given when a canoe was borrowed. If specialist services are acquired by soliciting the specialist will expect to be fed and paid in the normal way. Most significantly the donor himself can solicit at some later date if sickness or some misfortune make this necessary. If he does not, he is still rewarded in terms of prestige. Prestige, rank and soliciting are in fact intimately related. The higher a man's rank the less likely he is to solicit, the more likely he is to be solicited. The desire for prestige by being solicited acted, in fact, as an incentive to individual productivity. Being solicited can be seen in many respects as simply a special form of giving.

There are similar restictions, returns and benefits for donors, in special kinship relations, such as those between the mother's brother and sister's son, relations in which traditionally the sister's son could solicit at will from the mother's brother. In many villages this relationship (*feagaaiga*) is now regarded as an ordinary kinship relationship subject to the rules of soliciting which we have described, although the mother's

---

[1] There are many *upu fa'aulaula* (proverbs of ridicule) referring to greed begging. '*Ga sau fo'i e ati afi lae te'i ua no masi*'. 'He pretended to ask for a light, but he really wanted fermented breadfruit.' It was permitted for a person to go to another's house and ask for a match, but often this was used as a pretext to ask for some more highly prized object such as *masi* (fermented breadfruit). This was thought to be a very poor thing to do. Another proverb says '*A fai ea a'u mou titi se'e se'e*.' Literally 'Am I to become your dirty penis-girdle', that is, are you going to take everything I possess, the penis girdle symbolized complete power (*mālo*) over a person's goods and services. A third proverb referring to greed was '*o le mana ma le ponoi*'—'mouthful after mouthful (until you choke).'

[2] There is a *upu fa'amaulalo* (proverb of sadness) which says '*Ua leo iti le Paia*'—literally, 'The voice of the woman of Paia is weak.' This refers to a story of a woman in Manu'a who died for lack of food. This was felt to be very sad and unnecessary.

brother is still often an important person in providing an *'āiga* to which a sister's son may affiliate. An indication of the change in this kinship relationship and of the decline of specific rights and duties involved in all kinship relations is the general shift from a classificatory to a descriptive terminology and the decline in the use of more special kinship terms.[1]

Even in *'āiga* where the mother's brother—sister's son relationship is unchanged there are returns for the mother's brother's *'āiga*. The sister's son often comes and works in the mother's brother's *'āiga*, at least for a short period and the sister's son's *'āiga* will always help out in cases of need. Sometimes also, a sister's daughter will marry into her mother's brother's *'āiga*, bringing with her a *tōga* dowry of fine mats and money.

The cash economy has only slightly modified the pattern of soliciting. Although cash cannot be solicited, there is a wide range of cash economy goods which can be solicited. However, it is now accepted that a cash payment is proper when soliciting goods purchased in the cash economy. In a few cases this is only a token gesture and not representative of the cash value of the goods, but in most cases soliciting has become virtually a cash sale, with the recipient handing over to the donor a sum of money.[2]

The third kind of demand on an individual's goods and services is for non-ceremonial village or district work (*tautua nu'u, tautua itu*). In both traditional and contemporary Samoa these public works comprise mainly the building and maintaining of roads, water supplies, sanitary facilities and communal buildings, or the clearing and cleaning of land and house sites. Traditionally, service to the village was also thought

---

[1] This is in comparison to the Rev. Pratt's terminology (1911). The Mead (1930) and Holmes (1957: 31) terminologies are less easily compared, since they contain terms unknown in Western Samoa, and possibly peculiar to Manu'a where Mead worked. There are also some possible errors, for example, the calling of the mother's brother (male speaking) —*uso*, a term only applied to siblings of the same sex and generation, or the reference to the mother's sister as *tina*. The main terminology changes from Pratt 1911 are (1). Second ascending generation— *tama/tina o le tama/tina* for *tupuga, tupu'aga*, (2) First ascending generation—*o le tama tuafafine* for *Ilamutu, tuagane o le tina* for *tamafafine*, (3) Ego Generation—*uso*— for all siblings of the same sex, and *o le fānau* for siblings of the opposite sex.

[2] Not the traders' price, but usually substantially lower.

to involve, for all the young men at least, learning village traditions and Samoan customs, but today this is included in the
general schooling which children receive.

As we have shown these activities comprise only a very small
proportion of villagers' time.[1] Labour services are not imposed
on villages, but agreed to by the villager's representatives,
not only the chiefs in the *fono*, but also smaller special committees, which include non-titled persons especially women.
The village women are a most important influence in village
public works, and generally provide significant impetus to
pragmatic and worthwhile development schemes. It is often
the pressures from the women working informally through
their husbands or directly petitioning the *fono*, which makes the
chiefs divert time and money away from ceremonials to the
more practical, if more mundane, tasks of cleaning out latrines,
burning rubbish, etc.

There are also very real benefits from these public works.
The villagers understand that the central administration is
not able to maintain public works, and that the wealth of the
village ultimately depends on these facilities. Consequently,
there is very seldom any reluctance to participate in village
works for the few hours a week involved. Those with valid
objections (sickness, loss of wage labour time) can be excused.

There are also a number of village or district activities for
which contributions of goods or money are required. Some of
these projects are directly connected with public works, with
recognized direct benefits for the health and wealth of the
village. For important projects where capital has to be purchased (e.g. bridges, water supplies, medicines, etc.) a levy decided
on by the village *fono* or women's committee, is raised on every
'*āiga*, or a certain number of cash crop trees are temporarily
appropriated (*sā*) by the village council to provide the money.
Such capital items are an insignificant part of village expenditure and most villages feel them to be very necessary in the
absence of government assistance. But if an '*āiga* does not
want to contribute this is accepted if there appears to be
a valid excuse such as poverty.

Other village projects centre on the Church. Considerable
time and money are spent on church activities, in prayer

[1] See Table 5.

meetings, in cultivating the pastor's land, in cleaning his house, in collecting money for church celebrations, or contributing to central church funds. But both time and money are voluntarily given and form only a small proportion of total time and cash expenditure.[1]

There are also recognized returns and benefits. Church activities are a significant arena in which prestige can be obtained. Generosity to the church is thought to be the mark of a good man and money contributions to the church are constantly being advertised in the village, by word of mouth or on a blackboard. Secondly, the pastors, trained outside the village, often take on the lion's share of education and are sometimes also an important influence in improving health, and the standard of economic activity. Also youth sections of churches, such as the Boys' Brigade, or the Boy Scouts (closely associated in Samoa with the Church) regularly help tidy up the village. Finally, most people (especially the Mormons) believe that their present devotion will be rewarded by a future earthly millennium or a heavenlyparadise.

COMMUNITY DEVELOPMENT PROGRAMMES

Communal rights in an individual's goods and services are limited then, and there are rewards, in a definite sense, for any goods or services sacrificed. The successful organization of cash cropping and ancillary services is based on *fa'asāmoa* communal institutions such as the *'āiga* or village. But there are also communal groups, usually on a village scale, fulfilling important socio-economic functions relating directly or indirectly to cash cropping, often operating under administrative direction or initiative.

During both the German and New Zealand periods, and particularly since the Second World War when the doctrine of 'community development'[2] has become popular in colonial circles, the administration, in conjunction with international bodies, has attempted to utilize traditional communal institutions for specific economic activities or development programmes. It was thought that individuals might derive traditional satisfaction from working in a communal group

[1] See Table 5 for statistical details.
[2] The concept is discussed at length in Ruopp 1953.

towards a common goal, and that this might engender 'the will to improve', 'the desire to pull oneself up by one's boot-laces', 'the desire to have the best kept garden, the shiniest latrine, the fattest bank balance'. [1] Strong arguments were also put forward about the economic advantages of co-ordinated production as well as marketing and consumption. [2]

In recent years the administration has admitted that it considers these community development schemes to be failures. The number of co-operative societies has dwindled, and other groups have failed to live up to the expectations of the glossy and optimistic hand-outs. [3] The admission of failure gave fresh fuel to the critics of communalism both inside the administration and amongst the itinerant experts who periodically reported on Samoa's economic problems. They failed, the critics said, because of the disincentives in the traditional communal organization. [4]

It can be argued, however, that the relative failure of community development schemes stem from inefficiencies and deficiencies in administrative policies rather than from the disincentives inherent in *fa'asāmoa* society. Also it can be said that despite the administrative inefficiencies there remained, in fact, a great interest in community development in many villages, where introduced communal schemes often performed very useful services long after the village or the scheme had been forgotten by the administration.

The main fault of administration schemes is that there is too little liaison between personnel running the scheme and the villagers. Most schemes are foisted on individual villages piecemeal, by personnel who are in the territory only briefly, and have too little regard for local opinion and make too few attempts at explanation. Most significantly it is never explained, or explained adequately, that the philosophy of 'community development' is based on the concept of adapting traditional institutions to modern conditions. Consequently most Samoans regard the community development schemes simply as yet another

[1] NZIT 38/1.
[2] Most communal plans in Samoa hoped to help cash-cropping production though there were a small number of co-operatives (16 per cent of total) which only served consumption purposes. WSDF—Co-operative Registry. See Table 15.
[3] For example, the *South Pacific Commission Quarterly Bulletins*.
[4] e.g. Stace 1954: 1.

TABLE 15

Co-operative Societies in Samoa[5]

| | SOCIETIES REGISTERED | | | | | | SUCCESSFUL SOCIETIES | | | |
	Number[1] registered	Members	Produc-tion type[2]	Savings type[3]	Consumer type	Sub-scription capital	Number of societies	Members	Capital	Capital per capita
						£			£	£
Rural Samoan	42	1,102	38	1	3	10,725	8	290	6,320	21·7
Town	4	2,318	1	—	3	9,500	2	801	1,650	2·1
Non-Samoan[4] rural	2	26	1	—	1	120	0	—	—	—
Totals	48	3,446	40	1	7	£20,345	10	1,091	£7,970	

1. From 1953.
2. Includes also transport and marketing functions.
3. Includes also credit functions.
4. On leasehold settlements at Elisfou and Tafitoala, where part-Samoans, Melanesians and Chinese live.
5. 1963—WSDF—Co-operatives.

European institution, yet another attempt at alien influence or exploitation. Suspicion often breeds opposition or apathy. When the schemes are able to make some headway there is never enough encouragement, advice or capital from poorly organized administrative departments.

The co-operative movement provides a clear example of the effects of these administrative shortcomings. Though there were sporadic attempts to form co-operatives from German times, schemes were first introduced on a large scale by a South Pacific Commission expert in 1952. Unlike many visiting experts this man actually went into the countryside, at lèast around Apia, and consequently a number of village *fono* decided to establish co-operatives. Most, however, suspected that they would surrender a significant part of their authority by forming a co-operative, registered in a government department in Apia and conforming to an externally formulated and unnecessarily involved constitution.[1] Many thought that the capital required for the membership subscription was a thinly disguised attempt to gain government revenue, especially as it was suggested that this money should be invested in European securities or the Post Office. In these villages, the point was not taken, or not made, that the money collected, the supervision from Apia, and even the constitutional apparatus, were designed to help, ensure the success of the venture.

As can be seen in the accompanying table,[2] many of the co-operatives (including the Malie society) went out of business quickly. Part of the reason for this was that the expert himself soon departed from the territory. Although he left behind him elaborate sets of instructions there was only a skeleton organization to carry on. Co-operatives were relegated to an obscure part of the Justice Department, to be managed by a lowly clerk who had many other duties and only a faint knowledge of what was needed. There was then disillusionment and bewilderment in the villages which received no more itinerant advisers. Sometimes the confusion is about economic

---

[1] The basis is in NZO 9/1952. Much of the confusion arose from the inadequate translation into Samoan of European legal concepts.

[2] Of fifty-eight societies registered since 1952, only ten were officially 'active' in 1964. The average life span of defunct societies was $2\frac{1}{2}$ years. See Table 15.

issues, but more often it results from the constitutional procedure to which ideal co-operative societies were supposed to adhere. Confused villagers can obtain very little advice or explanation from the Co-operative Registry, and usually cannot find the relevant official, or files which are stored in an inaccessible attic. Many societies wither away in an atmosphere of such indifference. A few carry on without assistance or advice but often run into financial trouble, mainly debts arising from transport or marketing operations. Generally these debts are simply a result of lack of elementary business skills (e.g. correct book-keeping), which official guidance could easily have corrected. In such cases the co-operative quickly ceases to exist, not usually because of local disappointment or apathy, but because the Justice Department, pressed hard by creditors, speedily winds up the enterprise, without allowing any loans or other measures which often tide the European businesses over hard times.

However, in some cases unknown to the administration, there are village co-operatives[1] at least as successful as those run by Europeans or the closely supervised part-Samoan urban co-operatives. In these co-operatives, some special factor lies behind the success of the venture. In some cases this success can be partly explained by special access to European capital or advice, but often *fa'asāmoa* institutions, an energetic chief or chiefs,[2] or a concentration on traditional cash crop production[3] methods are the reasons for success.

There are also significant though unintended and indirect effects of the co-operative movement. Villages or *'āiga* which did not accept the invitation to form co-operatives, often readily accept the ideas relating to technical innovations or production incentives, which are publicized in the villages by the administration. Improved business methods, particularly, are gladly accepted in many villages, though nobody worries about registration or the involved constitutional procedures laid down in co-operative rules. Co-operative incentives such as profit sharing add further weight to the *fa'asāmoa* tendency

[1] There were five societies officially labelled as 'inactive' which were functioning successfully. All the successful societies were either in Apia or nearby (at Fasito-otua, Falevao, Solosolo, Luatuanu'u, Fagali'i, Motoatua, Faleata), i.e. where there was handy advice and capital. [2] e.g. at Solosolo.
[3] e.g. at Fagali'i.

towards equitable distribution of economic rewards which we have described.

Similar comments can be made about the other introduced communal organizations, particularly the women's organizations.

There were traditionally various groups of women in the village who met occasionally to help in various economic activities including gardening.[1] But the missionaries[2] and later the New Zealand administration, who abhorred the idea of women as agricultural labourers, attempted to interest the ladies in the more 'refined' and conventional European interests of health and children.[3] More significantly the rapid spread of virulent European diseases forced the women to spend large amounts of time in nursing. As poor health conditions have remained in many rural villages, the women still play an important part in the control and treatment of disease. Sometimes the committees work in conjunction with the officials of the Health Department, but most health activities are directed by the women themselves, mainly because they have found that there are many frustrations and difficulties in working with officials who seldom keep up regular contact with the village. The women in most villages supervise the cleaning and clearing of rubbish in the village to prevent mosquito and flies breeding, they check sanitation and treat minor ailments with medicine purchased from funds provided by a levy imposed on all *'āiga*. The women's committees also supervise the nursing of the sick,[4] the isolating of contagious diseases and the transport of serious cases to hospital. In one village[5] the women themselves have established their own hospital supported by charges on patients and their visitors. The women's committee ensure compliance with their direcrections by fining offenders,[6] or persuading the *fono* to do so.

---

[1] *Faletua ma tausi* (wives of titleholders) whose work was mainly confined to weaving. The *aualuma* comprised all the other women of the village.

[2] The missionaries generally thought it was morally wrong for women to work whilst the men 'walked about . . . and dressed their long hair' (Buzacott LMSJ 1836-7, cf. Monfat 1890: 133). The Rev. Hardie also thought gardening made the women promiscuous.

[3] Though this was a traditional activity (Barff and Williams 1830: 100).

[4] Including providing for the cultivation of gardens.   [5] Satupa'itea.

[6] Examples in Malie were: failure to obey isolation instructions, influenza 5*s.*, TB £2, failure to clear away rubbish—2 dozen coconuts.

The result of all this activity has been considerable improvement in village health, especially in minor ailments which often
keep Samoans away from work.[1]

The women also participate collectively in important aspects
of subsistence production, particularly the collection of marine
life from the reef and the planting of vegetable gardens on
house sites, which have greatly improved nutrition. But the
most significant economic activity of the women's committees
has been in the sale of certain village crops and resources,
particularly the production of handicrafts, for the Apia
market and abroad.

Initial impetus to the handicraft industry came from the
New Zealand administration in the 1920s,[2] but the output
was small, being restricted to women working on the government plantation. After the war the Apia merchants[3] went into
the villages to buy handicrafts to sell in the United States.
Many village women's committees responded to this demand,
or began themselves to sell handicrafts along the Apia streets,
especially when the tourist ships arrived.[4] Though the work
is extremely time-consuming and the returns for labour are
low,[5] handicraft income has become a significant part of
earnings in some villages, including Malie,[6] and has recently
prompted the administration to pass legislation designed to
expand the handicraft industry through the women's committees.[7]

The women's committees in some villages have also organized
vegetable growing for sale as export crops in local villages,
or along the Apia streets.[8] These cash crops consist mainly

[1] Particularly boils and ulcers.   [2] NZIT 87/27.

[3] First O. F. Nelson and more recently Aggie Grey who now monopolizes the
trade.

[4] The banana boat comes (1964) every fortnight from New Zealand and there
are occasional calls from cruising liners.

[5] In Malie 0·1s. *per capita* per hour, compared with cash cropping 0·27s.,
vegetables vendors in Apia 1·0s., and wage labourers 1·1s.

[6] Approximately 9 per cent in Malie—see Appendix 2.

[7] WSLA memorandum 1965/2.

[8] Villages in the Lefaga district also Falesi'u and Luatuanu'u in Northern
Upolu sold in Apia. People from Malie and Salani made only occasional visits
to the Apia market. Local village sales were mainly in Savai'i where (November
1964) women's committees in twenty villages had established gardens (particularly
in Palauli, Satupa'itea and Fa'asaleleaga districts). In Iva vegetables were sold
through the Department of Agriculture in New Zealand.

of European vegetables introduced by the administration to improve nutrition. After the Second World War, the women's committees grew and sold these vegetables very cheaply as a public service for many Samoans in Apia who did not have gardens. The women usually left the selling to the young men who relished a trip to town. In the last few years, however, the Apia street market has greatly expanded and many women's committees are making considerable sums of money, not only from Apia Samoans, but particularly from the Apia Europeans who are very anxious to buy fresh fruit and vegetables. The following chart contains a summary of the vegetable vendors in the Apia street market in June and November 1964.[1]

Communal groups, then, and communal incentives, have provided a successful base for cash cropping. Conversely, the individual Samoan cash cropper (i.e. the person who has no connection with an '*āiga* or village) often finds it difficult to make a success of cash cropping. Often there is difficulty in obtaining land, for villagers are very reluctant to allow outsiders to cultivate village lands permanently. There is also usually difficulty in obtaining labour, for villagers greatly prefer working in their own gardens, or relaxing in ceremonial activities in the village, to working for outsiders. The villagers feel no obligation to an outsider, and especially in North West Upolu, plantation labour is held in very low regard, considered to be suitable only for such inferior breeds as Melanesians or Chinese who, until recently, worked on the plantations as indentured labour. If Samoans work at all on the plantations they expect higher wages than most Samoan individual farmers can possibly afford.

Without kin group, land or labour, the Samoan plantation owner is forced to seek capital to run his plantation. Cash is needed to purchase or lease the more expensive government or freehold land, to tempt labour if labour can be found,[2] or to replace labour-intensive cultivation methods with modern machinery.

There are many difficulties in capitalization. The Samoan

---

[1] See Table 16.
[2] Indentured labour was prohibited by the New Zealand administration. Most labourers prefer to work in Apia. See Ch. 7.

TABLE 16

Sales and hours in the Apia street market[1]

		per cent of total vendors
1. Sex	Male	63
	Female	37
2. Age	Under 20	23
	20–30	28
	30–40	26
	+40	23
3. Village of residence	Apia	6
	Non-Samoan Settlements[2]	19
	North West Upolu[3]	30
	North East Upolu[4]	20
	South Upolu[5]	18
	Aleipata	6
	Savai'i	1
4. Total number of vendors[1]		98

5. Type of goods	amount sold
	£. s. d.
Talo[8]	226 16 0
Ta'amū	191 0 3
Bananas	103 13 0
Coconuts	24 8 0
Beans	7 11 0
Pumpkin	7 5 0
Pawpaw	6 14 0
Cacao	5 1 0
Pineapples	5 17 0
Fish[9]	4 4 0
Cabbages	2 12 0
Cucumbers	2 12 0
Tomatoes	2 2 0
Lūao[10]	1 15 0
Mangoes	1 6 0
Water Melon	1 4 0
Yams[7]	1 0 0
Miscellaneous[11]	1 16 0
6. Total	596 16 3

11

TABLE 16 (*contd.*)

		per cent of total vendors
7. Working hours per week	0–2	1
	2–4	1
	4–8	61
	8–16	17
	16–24	17
	24–32	1
	32–40	2
8. Total hours	903	
9. Total vendors		98

1. A vendor is the person said to be in charge of the stall. There were also often other helpers, usually children, who relieved and sometimes ran the stall.
2. Mainly the settlements at Elisefou, Solomona, the homes of former Melanesian plantation workers and their descendants.
3. West from the Apia town boundary to Mulifanua.
4. East from the Apia town boundary to Uafato.
5. Mulifanua to Lepa inclusive.
6. The sample was conducted in the Apia market during the weeks 17–23 September, 4–10 November 1964. There was only 5 per cent variation in the number of vendors in the two sample weeks. The sample contains all the vegetable sellers in Apia, and also a fish seller.
7. 4–10 November 1964.
8. Including *talo* leaves.
9. Including oysters.
10. Ready-made dish containing coconut cream and *talo* leaves.
11. Starch, eggplant, avocados, limes, crustacea, breadfruit, coconut switch brooms.

individual cash cropper is equated by possible European sources of credit with the village Samoan and hence regarded as a credit risk even if he can raise the normal security required.[1] Also few Samoans have access to the few administrative sources of capital which do exist. However, even if suitable capital can be acquired there are the constant problems of maintenance and unsuitability of plant.

The individual cash cropper is also deprived of *fa'asāmoa* incentives and the satisfactions and benefits of village life.

[1] Credit is discussed more fully in Ch. 8.

Life as an individual cash cropper is lonely, especially for the bachelor or the aged person. Many find unbearable the con- tinual round of hard work and frugality, unrelieved by the leaven of ceremonial and village courtesies, the life on which some part-European and Euronesian farmers seem to thrive. People say in the village that when a man has had six months in the 'bush', that is away from village life, he will want sixty years in the village.

There is very little chance for the Samoan individual farmer to gain access to the charmed circle of European planters. In most cases these European planters are part-Samoans who have since the German period carefully main- tained their distance from village Samoans. The European planter's life is never *fa'asāmoa* style ceremonial, but a round of afternoon teas, cocktail parties and elegant dinners, when imported foods and drinks are consumed in the polite surround- ings suggested by the glossy American magazines and films which are the planters' delight. The rural Samoan is regarded by many of these European planters as an inferior person a 'kanaka', 'animal' or 'pig'.

Also, separation from village society increasingly lowers the reputation of the farmer in village society itself. At first, the renegade is tolerated and even admired by some, but continual reluctance to participate in village affairs leads to gossip and ridicule. The farmer is thought to be *fafasa* (not all there), 'a man who goes to the bush to masturbate', a man who concocts evil schemes possibly in conjunction with evil spirits (*aitu*), or attempts to encroach on village land. Often, too, the individual farmer will be equated with, and referred to, as a *pālagi* (European) even if the European planters have rejected the farmer completely. Once regarded as a *pālagi* (European) there will be no doubt in villagers' minds that the farmer is up to no good, and relations with the village are almost always very strained.

The absence of communal assistance has more direct and deleterious effects on individual Samoan plantations. The administration public works department provides only a very sketchy service in most areas outside the Apia town boundary. Individual cash croppers have to attend themselves to the many details of road, water and possibly power maintenance, usually without technical knowledge or necessary labour. Such maintenance often raises insuperable problems. There are stories of individual cash croppers without power or water, overgrown with weeds and creepers, living a hermit existence on roots and berries. Sickness is also an intolerable burden for the individual cash cropper, who has no alternative source of labour to carry on the enterprise or even to provide subsistence foods.

Because of these difficulties Samoans do not often become individual cash croppers, and if they do, they do not usually last long, soon returning to the village, at least on ceremonial occasions, or leaving for the bright lights of Apia. There are, admittedly, some exceptional individuals who have carried on for a period of years. For example, a young Samoan with an American university degree grows bananas and *talo* for the market on a thousand acres of land leased from Salani village. This young man possesses many advantages which most Samoan individual cash croppers do not have. He has adequate technical and marketing knowledge, secure land tenure and adequate land,[1] a good house, good contacts with the administration, where his brother is a high official, and good contacts with the European world generally, a world in which, with his overseas experience, he moves easily. He has, consequently, no capital problems and he can afford to raise labour. But despite these advantages the young man confided that he made very little after he has paid all his outgoings. Significantly, he finds the loneliness of the plantation very trying and does not intend to stay permanently.

In addition to the two types of cash cropper we have described, that is the *fa'asāmoa* cash cropper, farming entirely within the *'āiga* or village, and the individual cash cropper who completely severs his ties with the village there is a third, intermediate kind, the individual *fa'asāmoa* farmer—i.e. a man who farms away from the village, but retains some ties with village society, usually acknowledging an affiliation to an *'āiga*, and participating in its ceremonial activities.

In this kind of cash cropping the general pattern is that the man earns his money and spends his working life on his

---

[1] The land was originally leased to a brother from former German plantations land. The lease had the administration's blessing.

individual farm, and spends his leisure and cash seeking status in village society.

There are a number of economic advantages in this co-existence of *fa'asāmoa* and introduced institutions. This kind of farmer is regarded as a local person and can easily obtain local land and labour for a nominal price, under the general conditions applying to *fa'asāmoa* rents and wages which we have described. He also benefits from general communal assistance in public works and health.

The individual *fa'asāmoa* farmer is, however, an ephemeral social phenomena. He works on his plantation to earn money to gain status in the village. Accession to title is often accompanied by a complete return to village society, the farmer leaving or leasing his plantation to a younger relative and involving himself completely in *'āiga* or village affairs. Occasionally the chief continues to develop his plantation, using his status to secure additional land or labour, and possibly attempts to secure capital to enlarge his holding by working through Samoan representatives in the administration. In two cases chiefs have not only expanded their cash cropping activities but have also started cattle ranching for which, in South Upolu and parts of Savai'i, there are suitable and previously unused submontane pastures in the village hinterland. When the chiefs remain on their plantations there is not usually any change in the relationships with the village. Extra cash earned is usually spent on acquiring higher status through ceremonial disbursement, though plantation chiefs cannot take such an active part in the everyday running of village affairs.

7

VILLAGE WAGE LABOUR IN TOWN

THE most important way of earning cash in contemporary Samoa is to sell village resources. A second, and increasingly important way is to sell village labour in the wage labour market.

Wage labour dates from the first days of European contact, when the Samoans signed aboard visiting whalers.[1] Other opportunities occurred when the large German trading firm of J. C. Godeffroy[2] made Apia their Pacific headquarters in 1857 in order to buy and grow tropical products and sell European goods. By 1874[3] there were many job opportunities in the Godeffroy trading empire, or providing for the entertainment of the 250 permanently resident Europeans and the large floating population of traders and mariners. In the late nineteenth century and in the twentieth century job opportunities rose or fell with trading conditions, with fluctuations in exports of tropical produce, and subsequent changes in local purchasing power. There were, therefore, few jobs when Godeffroys collapsed in the recession of the 1890s or during the great depression of the 1930s. There were many more jobs during the Second World War when the prodigal American marines were garrisoned in Samoa, or after the war when cash crop prices boomed. By 1964 nearly 30 per cent of the Samoan working force were wage labour employees, and approximately 40 per cent of Samoan income was derived from wages.[4] The following table indicates the occupational structure.[5]

In this chapter we will explore the relationships between *fa'asāmoa* social institutions and the institutions and values associated with wage labour, analysing the ways in which *fa'asāmoa* institutions contributed to productivity and economic

---

[1] Murray 1876: 42. [2] Kirchoff 1880, F. Spoehr 1936.
[3] NZAJ 1874/1/3B/10, GBMPR 6/30.
[4] Estimate in WSDF Statistics Department. [5] See Table 17.

TABLE 17

Occupations of Samoans[1] 1961–4

Occupation[2]	Number of Samoans	Proportion[5] of employed Samoans	Malie village[8]	
			Numbers	per cent
		%		
1. Village Agriculture[3]	17,461	73	481	91·5
2. Professions	1,478	6	2	0·5
Mission Personnel[4]	600	2	1	0·25
Teachers[4]	724	2	1	0·25
3. Commerce	1,365	6	4	1·0
Shop Assistants	673	2	—	—
4. Manufacture and Construction	1,216	5	9	2·0
5. Plantation Agriculture	872	3	—	—
6. Entertainment and Service	624	2	2	0·5
Domestics[4]	442	1	2	0·5
7. Government and Administration[7]	600	2	21	4·0
8. Transport and Communication	501	2	5	1·0
9. Unemployed[6]	345	1	—	—
Total	24,463		624	

1. That is persons not registered on the Roll of Individual (formerly European) Voters or their descendants. This table is based on materials collected in the 1961 Census, and other data in the Statistics Department Apia, relating to occupational changes since 1961. Apart from village agriculture all other categories are projections for 1964, or in the case of Malie results of a fieldwork survey May–June 1964.
2. Categories as defined in Western Samoa Population Census 1961: Section 9. Categories are in descending order of numerical significance.
3. Includes only adult males.
4. Sub-category of the above main category. Groups comprising over 1 per cent of all employed Samoans are included. Only those personnel who are paid are included.
5. To nearest 1 per cent.
6. Apia only.
7. Except for teachers and doctors.
8. Salani Village had only four wage employees resident in the village, three were with the Government Banana Board, one with an Apia transport firm.

development through production methods, incentives and organization.

FA'ASĀMOA AND GROWTH OF THE LABOUR FORCE

Fa'asāmoa society affects the labour force both quantitatively and qualitatively. In the first place, *fa'asāmoa* institutions are largely responsible for the large size of the labour force, which provides a pool of labour, under-employed in cash cropping, and readily available for wage labour.

The demographic history of Samoa has never been adequately described or analysed. Most accounts[1] portray a dramatic decline in the nineteenth-century population and an 'explosion' in the twentieth century in accordance with the general belief that native populations always dwindle away when confronted with European vices and diseases, and expand when 'pax Europa' is established and European medicines distributed.

The evidence for these theories from Samoa, however, is extremely dubious. First, the figures for the nineteenth-century decline in population are extracted from the compounded estimates of sailors, some of whom merely counted wisps of smoke as they passed in their men-o-war; from consuls, whose sources are never named; and missionaries who counted heads or houses near their stations. Of these, only the mission censuses can be taken seriously, though in some cases even these may be over-estimated resulting from the frequent mission habit of multiplying converts to satisfy the demands of their home societies.[2] With one exception[3] the mission figures show a steady increase from 24,000 in 1837 to 33,478 in 1906, the date of the first German census which distinguished Samoans as a separate category.

The evidence for the 'decimation of disease' is based on the same dubious sources as the population estimates, and whilst it is certain that introduced diseases killed some people, especially babies, there is seldom any certainty of how many people

[1] For example, United Nations 1948, McArthur 1956.

[2] LMSB11JAF6.

[3] The 1837 figure was constructed from a count of houses made by Rev. Mills (LMSB11F4JC). The exception is Stair's figure of 40,000 for 1845. I could find no record of this census in the LMS archives and possibly it was only a compilation of estimates. For a summary of other figures see McArthur 1956.

were killed, especially outside Apia and the mission outposts.[1] Certainly there is no evidence of fatalities comparable to the pandemic of 1918 which is usually taken as the analogy for all epidemics. The missionary Dr. George Turner who lived in Samoa from 1842 to 1884 even comments that the Samoan generally had a good resistance to fatal disease.[2] The Samoans may well have developed this resistance before the Europeans arrived, through long contacts with other islands (e.g. Tonga, Tahiti) where European diseases were introduced earlier, or from sick sailors who were abandoned by their ships.

After the 1918 pandemic, mortality from disease certainly decreased, though inaccurate census figures may mask higher mortality rates than the administrations claim. But there is some doubt whether the administrations' health and sanitation programmes were the main reason for this decrease. Medical facilities, through conscious policy or lack of funds, were concentrated in Apia and benefited the people of North West Upolu most. Throughout the twentieth century there are many reports of epidemics of introduced diseases, or unidentified *fiva*, especially in rural areas.[3] The decrease in mortality was largely a decrease in infant mortality, mainly the result of improved nutrition and better infant care introduced into the villages by the Samoan women's committees, with only occasional assistance from the administration.

Nor did the nineteenth-century wars of succession, for which the Europeans provided arms and advice, noticeably affect mortality rates. Although in the nineteenth century some European military tactics were introduced, especially the use of lethal weapons, *fa'asāmoa* military tactics predominated. *Fa'asāmoa* wars were not usually violent, but were polite and highly formalized ceremonies, extensions of debates over the succession to high titles, which were fought when discussion broke down or when one group felt able to raise enough allies to overwhelm its opponents. Battles, like the political discussions which preceded them, were also generally polite and courtly.[4]

[1] Most reports are vague on the number of deaths, e.g. Turner 1861 (epidemics up to 1858), LMSB12F6JC (1839 'flu epidemic), LMSB20F6JA/B (1847 'flu epidemic). One exception is McDonald's report of the 1849 whooping-cough epidemic (LMSB21F5JE).   [2] Turner 1884: 136.   [3] NZIT 8/29, IT 1/32.
[4] For accounts of Samoan wars see Pritchard 1866: 56, Stair 1897: 246. Turner 1884: 194, LMSB11JAF4.

The meeting of 'hostile' armies was a time of feasts and *'ava* (kava) at which speeches of mutual respect as well as war challenges were exchanged. Often because of rain or night-fall it was agreed to postpone the conflict, in which case the troops would sleep peacefully next to one another until the signal was given for hostilities to begin.

If the armies met at all in battle, it was in brief skirmishes and lightning raids from fortified positions. More usually one side would quickly acknowledge the other side's superiority by flight, whereupon the victorious side (*mālō*) would destroy a number of *fale* (houses) or gardens, or simply slash a banana tree or eat a dead foe, all symbols of overwhelming victory.[1] Wars were, in fact, won or lost before the battle. The victorious side (*mālō*) was usually the side with the greatest number of allied villages, alliances which had been carefully constructed by strategic gifts and marriages over a number of years. The battle was, in a sense, only a symbolic expression of existing political facts.

After the war the *mālō* were expected to be, and were usually, merciful. The Samoans say 'The courage of warriors may disappear, but the clemency of authority remains and is remembered when destruction is forgotten.'[2] Sometimes men would be killed or taken as slaves, or women made con-cubines, but property was the most usual demand of victory. Even then, the defeated party (*to'ilalo*) would be only occasion-ally visited by the *mālō* and then only deprived of moveable property.

Other European 'vices' such as alcohol, which included a wide range of liquors, methylated spirits, toilet waters, etc., killed or prostrated only the occasional person as they do today.

The slow rise of the nineteenth-century population was, according to an informant, due partly to the *fa'asāmoa* custom of infanticide. If a child was unwanted for any reason it was neglected until it died either from denial of the breast (which might be given to a suckling pig or puppy), or from lack of

---

[1] Cannibalism was never a feature of *fa'asāmoa* war. According to the people of Malie, cannibalism was abolished by Malietoa Poluleuliaga (sixteen generations ago) who hated the habit after nearly eating his own son.

[2] *E gase toa, 'ae ole pule. Ee mānatua pule 'ae lē manatua fa'alaeō.*

food. The people say that this was done when times became hard in the late nineteenth century and that the custom stopped when better cash earning opportunities became available. The missionaries who abhorred infanticide claimed that they had stamped it out before 1850,[1] and the custom is not mentioned elsewhere.

Secondly, and much more significantly, *fa'asāmoa* institutions promoted fertility, the major cause of the population explosion of the twentieth century.

Some of the reasons which favoured high fertility rates were biological. Samoans reach physical puberty early in life and have relatively high reproductive powers. Diseases which limit fertility, particularly venereal diseases,[2] have only recently become important.

Far more important are the sociological reasons, particularly the early age and universality of *fa'asāmoa* marriage and the importance of procreation in it. Only morons or invalids are permanently celibate. Even widowhood is a temporary state, the levirate or sororate being common. Unmarried persons usually have a sexual partner.

But marriage, the social recognition of sexual union, is the preferred state. It is the adult role expected of all males and females soon after they have undergone the rites of puberty.[3] Sex and procreation are only condoned as part of, or preliminary to, marriage, and a couple who consorted together habitually are expected to be formally married according to *fa'asā-moa* custom, pay a fine to the village council of chiefs (*fono*), or leave the village.

There are other pressures forcing a couple to marry. Most parents, especially in chiefly *'āiga*, want their children to marry

[1] Turner 1884: 79.

[2] The spread of venereal disease (syphilis) has coincided with the eradication of yaws which probably gave an immunity.

[3] For both sexes at about age 14–15. Boys were traditionally tattooed (circumcision was much earlier) which entitled them to drink *'ava* and take part in the dances. Many boys are still tattooed, though adulthood may be recognized only by admission to the *'ava* circle, or simply by stopping calling them boy (*tama*). Girls would not entertain a 'boy' as a lover. Girls soon after the regular appearance of menses would go under the care of a female relative usually within the *'āiga potopoto*. After some instruction in sexual matters, a small feast would be made, after which the girl would no longer be called *'teine'* (young girl). Marriage was called *uluga 'āiga*, a strong foundation for life.

so that the '*āiga* can acquire valuable *fa'asāmoa* property, especially fine mats, and possibly rank or political allies.

There are few obstacles to marriage. Except in high, chiefly '*āiga*, courtship, betrothal and marriage ceremonies are not elaborate, involving only small feasts and gift exchanges. Couples can always elope to another village where they have '*āiga*. There are few categories of prohibited marriage. It is preferred that a person does not marry inside his '*āiga potopoto*, nor any first cousin, nor inside the village. But marriages between cousins and members of the same '*āiga potopoto* do occasionally take place, the couple usually moving to a new village, whilst intravillage marriage in both Malie and Salani accounts for a quarter of all marriages. Changes in property are in no way contingent on marriage. Land and the means of self-sufficiency are readily available in all villages, for all young couples, though time may be needed to assemble marriage gifts. There are no objections to plural marriages. Traditionally many chiefs had more than one wife, to increase the size of their following or to cement political alliances. Also 'une polygamie successive',[1] as Père Violette has called it, was very common. After the birth of a child the wife would often return to her own '*āiga*, and her sister would come, sometimes with *tōga* dowry, to take her place.

Generally speaking, in recent years the pressures for marriage have increased and the obstacles decreased. The missionaries insisted that pregnant girls should be quickly married, that any sexual activity should be regularized by marriage, and that people should stay married. The administrations introduced concepts of illegitimacy and difficulties of securing divorce.[2] Many villagers now feel that marriage should precede intercourse and that people should separate or divorce only to contract another marriage. The accumulation of marriage gifts does not now retard marriage as administrations have attempted to restrict, and periodically have prohibited, gift exchanges.[3] Today many parents in addition to, or instead

[1] Monfat 1890: 9 ff. Cf. Rev. Chisholm noted 'a lad of 12 with three wives' (LMSB17F7JC).

[2] e.g. N.Z. Samoa Act, pts. IX, X. There are very few legal divorces in rural villages.

[3] e.g. during German times GCA 1/17b/V3/40, 1927–36 NZO 1927/2. Attempts have recently been made to discourage the size of gift exchanges.

of, wanting *fa'asāmoa* rank and property, want to share in *pālagi* status and wealth by marrying their children into a family of European status[1] or to a person who has made good in Apia or abroad.

Polygamy is still common though the old forms have disappeared. Polygamy today is largely the result of wage-labour migration. Most male migrants marry before they leave the village, and then establish new domestic relationships in Apia or abroad. I knew one man who had five wives and families, one in his home village where he held a title, one in Apia where he worked, and one in New Zealand and in American Samoa and Hawaii which he had visited for extended working holidays.

The administrations did make some attempt to restrict the number of marriages by prohibiting on occasions marriages with 'Europeans' and plural marriages, by establishing minimum ages, and by limiting the number of licensed marriage officers.[2] Such attempts were almost completely unsuccessful, partly because there were restricted means of enforcing such legislation,[3] and partly because *fa'asāmoa* marriages had a certain validity in court procedures if not in statute. In any case the New Zealanders particularly had an ambivalent attitude to Samoan fecundity. For population increase was a certain sign for the Mandates Commission or Trusteeship Council that care was being taken of 'native welfare'.

The most important reason for marriage, however, and the most important reason for the high birth rate is the desire to have a large number of children. Fertility is of prime importance in the Samoan value system. A successful man and a man with many children are addressed in the same complimentary terms—'*o le pa'ū a le popouli*', the ripe coconut which falls and sprouts. *Tamāo'āiga* is to be both wealthy and to have many children. On the other hand, the immature person is *mu'amu'a*,

---

[1] 'Europeans' in German times were any people who could speak fluent German (GCAO 2/8/12). Under the New Zealand administration, Europeans were those who were not of Samoan status, i.e. originally full Samoans (NZ Samoa Act 1921, s. 3), but recently (NZO 1934/1, 1963/14) anyone with Samoan blood who did not wish to be registered as a European or as an individual voter on the electoral roll.

[2] N.Z. Samoa Act 1921, pt. X.

[3] Until very recently registration has been inadequate. It is estimated that 40 per cent of present day marriages are *de facto* or *fa'asāmoa*. *De facto* marriages in Samoa have the same legal status as *de facto* marriages in English law.

the partly ripe coconut which cannot produce new trees and old people are *afega*, the dying leaves of the coconut frond which have no part in regeneration. Fertility is assumed to be a characteristic of gods, revered ancestors and Old Testament patriarchs whose prodigious reproductions account for the greater part of most legends, traditions and public bible readings. During pregnancy the woman is coddled and protected, surrounded by *tapu* and laden with gifts from her husband's *'āiga*. Conversely, barrenness is considered as a curse, the butt of ridicule in song and legend. The barren woman is *fa'amotu 'āiga*—the person who breaks or degrades her *'āiga* and traditionally she was expected to leave her husband and find him a new mate, though today a barren wife usually adopts children.

Children are also desired because they secure an individual's position in two significant dimensions of his social universe, on the one hand by placing him in a lineal continuum containing gods, ancestors, those living and those as yet unborn, on the other by sealing the affinal ties which marriage has initiated. Children are also often adopted between *'āiga* connected by marriage, descent or friendship.

Children also bring wealth and rank to the *'āiga*. As we have said, the prestige of the *'āiga*, the acquisition of rank and title, is closely related to cash-cropping productive capacity for ceremonial distribution which in turn largely depends on manpower. As well, children are increasingly desired for their cash earning ability in the wage earning market. One man in Malie said: 'If I have only two boys they will have to work in the garden (that is cash cropping), but the rest of my boys and girls can go to Apia, Pago (that is American Samoa), New Zealand or Hawaii, and they will send me back money. So now you know why I have eighteen children.'

Village income from migrants is as large as the income[1] from coconuts, the most important cash crop. In Malie and Salani some families are completely supported by migrant remittances.

Because children are important, procreative activity is also

---

[1] See Appendix 2. In 1963 an estimated £250,000 was sent back from New Zealand alone. There were (1964) approximately 20,000 Western Samoans in American Samoa, Hawaii, United States and New Zealand.

important, especially inside the marital relationship. The only periods of temporary celibacy for a woman, during menstruation or after pregnancy, do not significantly affect reproduction. Virginity is only insisted on for daughters of high chiefs (*tāupou*) who play a significant role in '*ava* ritual and intervillage diplomacy. Procreation is the main reason for the wife's presence, and traditionally if, through absence or infertility, she could not conceive she would be replaced. Wives rejected because of infertility joined the *aualuma* (young unmarried girls) partly to instruct the young girls or men in sexual matters[1]. It is thought proper for a man to have constant intercourse. Premarital sexual adventures are considered to prepare him for the serious business of marital procreation, and there is usually an intermediary (*soa*) to instruct and encourage his courtship.

European values have generally added to the importance of fecundity in village life. In many villages the missions, Protestant and Mormon equally as much as Roman Catholic, condemned the traditional birth control of abortion and firmly resisted the introduction of European birth control. The administrations[2] generally gave legislative support to these views. Today the hardest thing to buy in Samoa are contraceptives which are obtainable only on rarely given prescriptions from the main hospital in Apia. In Apia village there is some demand for birth control, mainly from part Samoans, some of whom bring in their own supplies from New Zealand. Some of the men in Apia practise 'coitus interruptus'. In Malie and Salani, however, many people think contraceptives are *agasala* (evil, sinful), 'used by prostitutes' and there is little demand for them.

EUROPEAN INFLUENCES ON THE LABOUR FORCE

Although large, the Samoan labour force is relatively un-skilled. Until recently the majority of Samoans have been employed mainly as labourers or in the most menial tasks

[1] cf. Kramer 1902 v. 1: 476, Pritchard 1866: 133, Walpole 1849 v. 2: 53, G. Brown 1910: 43. This group freely available to all comers gave early travellers an impression of Samoan license.

[2] Both the Germans and New Zealanders thought high birth rates were a sign of the success of their administrations (e.g. GCA 17/A).

in shops and offices[1] in Apia. The Europeans have tended to attribute this lowly position in the labour structure and any production deficiencies in the labour force to *fa'asāmoa* customs which they say encourage indolence, discourage regular and continuous labour, and lead to an insensitivity to monetary reward and to unsuitability for European technology.

These assumptions may be challenged on several grounds. First of all, it is doubtful whether the Samoan labour force is as unproductive as Europeans claim. Certainly Europeans' opinions are held without any accurate knowledge of Samoan labour perfomance, as in most labour situations there is very little contact between European employers and Samoan employees. Certainly there are no scientific work studies or accurate assessments of wage labour output. Unlike cash cropping where there is a definite measurable output for any input of labour or capital, wage labour output cannot easily be quantified. Wages are of little use as indicators since they tend, in Samoa, to be flat rates which do not reflect differential achievements, time or skill. Calculations using time measurements also present many difficulties. In the first place it is very difficult to establish what is an optimum time for any task, because of lack of comparative data in Samoa or other underdeveloped countries.

There are admittedly some observable deficiencies in Samoan labour production, some irregularity in work activity (arriving late, sleeping during the job), incompetence (breaking tools, not following out instructions), or dishonesty. But it does not necessarily follow that *fa'asāmoa* institutions are responsible for these deficiencies. Samoans themselves explain production deficiencies in terms of disincentives in the wage labour situation, particularly low wages and bad working conditions. These criticisms have some validity. There are no trade unions in Samoa and there is very little legislation relating to labour.[2] Consequently, low wages and bad working conditions are common. The average wage for Samoan unskilled

---

[1] For a brief survey see Duncan 1953, Clare 1962. The following data is based on fieldwork mainly amongst wage labourers from Malie and Apia nu'u, totalling in all some 200 persons.

[2] The Labour Ordinance of 1960 (NZO 3/1960) dealt only with problems of gathering statistics and a workers' compensation which did not have a wide application (WSLA Memo 1964).

labour in 1964 was 12s. 6d. a day, a wage rate that has only risen slowly in the last hundred years and has lagged far behind rises in the cost of living. Wages in government jobs and in merchants' offices and shops are similarly low. The administration, operating on a small budget, has been forced to restrict wages, whilst the merchants are glad to follow this lead. Many Samoans in offices and shops work in cramped and insanitary conditions without adequate ventilation or toilet facilities, whilst work on the wharves or in the road gangs is very dangerous.

Bad labour relations are also a contributing factor to bad working conditions and low productivity. The European employers feel Samoans are not contributing significantly to output, and employers are not, therefore, prepared to raise wages or improve conditions. Most employers do not think. as some aggrieved Samoans claim, that Samoan labour is cheap, and where possible most Europeans try to replace Samoan labour with machinery. In the case of public servants low wages are explained as the result of revenue deficiencies, which most Europeans feel to result in turn from the incompetence of Samoan cash croppers.[1] Samoans, on the other hand, feel they are being exploited, and do not work as hard as they might. The vicious circle is perpetuated because there are few channels for negotiation or discussion. Some employers feel, in fact, that the Samoans, because of their supposed limited needs and wants, do not want higher wages, and most Samoans do not realize that the employers are interested in, and prepared to reward, increased Samoan productivity.

Neither Europeans nor Samoans feel the other has any desire to improve these labour relations. Europeans point to the absence of trade union movements amongst the Samoans. But this is, partly at least, the result of an administration policy which has excluded from the territory overseas people connected with the trade union movement, in the belief that such persons will sow the seeds of a communist revolution amongst the Samoans.[2] The administration prohibition certainly did have some support from a number of chiefly factions who saw in an urban political organization a potential rival to their own power. This support,

---

[1] Most government revenue comes from cash crop duties.

[2] Radical unions in New Zealand (e.g. the Watersiders (dock workers)) did have an interest in Island conditions.

though never very extensive, as chiefly participation in radical anti-administrative political movements has indicated, did enable the administration to pass on the responsibility for excluding the trade unionists.

Bad labour relations not only result in labour apathy, but also lead to incompetence and dishonesty. There are many instances of Samoans deliberately breaking or stealing tools as a form of protest, or to take what they consider to be their fair share of employers' wealth.

Incompetence can also be explained to a large extent by the administration's educational system. There are very few ways in which Samoans can obtain the necessary wage labour skills. Technical and commercial training facilities were only slowly introduced and have remained inadequate to meet the demands of the local wage labour market and of the Samoans themselves. The ordinary school system does not make a significant contribution. Only a small proportion of children are able to go to the few secondary schools where there are relevant courses.[1]

FA'ASĀMOA AND WAGE LABOUR ACTIVITY

Fa'asāmoa institutions, on the other hand, do contribute to wage labour productivity. Skills learnt in the village, for example, digging, copying figures, cooking etc., are important in the labouring, clerical and domestic jobs which the Samoans take up. Much more significant are the effects of *fa'asāmoa* production incentives. Most Samoans retain their connection with the village and most Samoans use the rewards of wage labour, either cash or prestige, in *fa'asāmoa* institutions in much the same way as a cash cropper uses his cash rewards.

For the purposes of analysing the nature of these production incentives, five kinds of wage labour in contemporary Samoa can be distinguished; village employees, daily commuters, temporary and permanent absentees and *pālagis*. The following tables indicate the sizes of these groups in Malie and Salani in 1964 and also the nature of population movement in and out of the villages.[2]

[1] Less than 3 per cent of the school population were at secondary schools in 1963 and most of these were part-Europeans (WSDF Education Department).
[2] See Table 18.

The village employees are those people who live and work in the village. In general, these are government employees, remnants of successive waves of decentralization in administration policy. In every village since German times[1] there has been a *pulenu'u* (village mayor), and in one village in every district,[2] there have been judges[3] (*fa'amasino*), messengers (*failoutusi*),[3] assistants (*leoleo*), garden inspectors (*pulefa'atoaga*), Samoan doctors (*fōma'i*), nurses, teachers (*faiā'oga*) and members of parliament (*faipule*).[4] In addition to government employees in every village there are also Samoan missionaries (*faife'au*), who attend to religious needs, and sometimes run the local school and dispensary as well.

In general, these village employees are completely involved in village affairs and fit the duties of their jobs to the demands of village life. For example, the *pulenu'u* are officially the representatives of the administration in the village, responsible for all communications to and from the administration, and for the implementing of any official ordinances or directives issued by the administration.[5] But all *pulenu'u* are chiefs and they behave as chiefs. Any directives from the administration are dealt with in the *fono* in the normal *fa'asāmoa* way. Demands on *pulenu'u* time always take second place to village affairs. *Pulenu'u* may use their position not to carry out administrative instructions, but as a lever to increase their own *fa'asāmoa* status, and there are records of the use of administrative money for ceremonials. The *pulenu'u* will normally only introduce measures which he knows will be popular.

Similar comments can be made about other government employees in the village. The judges, assistants and garden inspectors are also chiefs. In all their duties they follow the direction of the village *fono* and usually devote most of their time to improving their *fa'asāmoa* status.

There are often, too, chiefs amongst the Samoan doctors and

[1] Notes and case studies from the German administration are in GCA 2/XVII/ B4/V2, B1/VI/25 ff., 1/17b/13 ff., V3/53. At one time the Germans had 400 employees in the villages.

[2] The size of the districts varied for different purposes and under different administrations. There are forty-one Faipule districts. For most other purposes the Islands were divided into approximately twenty districts. See NZAJ A/4 1930.

[3] Until 1958.

[4] For a full account see, WS District and Village Affairs 1950.

[5] GCA 1/176/V3, NZ Instructions to Officials 1922.

TABLE 18 (a)

Permanent[1] population movement, Salani, Malie, Apia, 1964

	OUTGOING			INCOMING		
	Salani	Malie	Apia	Salani	Malie	Apia
Basic figures						
Total number	30	39	151	9	75	212
Percentage of village population	7	4	9	2	8	13
Percentage males	62	42	51	30	52	51
Average age	26.8	24.8	25	32.2	25	25.2
Destination and source of migration (percentage of total migrants)						
Bush Hinterland	2	10	—	—	2	—
Apia and Environs[2]	46	8	4	10	5	2
Elswehere Upolu	10	5	8	43	52	62
Savai'i	—	—	2	47	41	32
United States and Tutuila	6	33	24	—	—	2
New Zealand	34	44	58	—	—	—
Reasons for migration (percentage of total migrants)						
Work	55	80	78	—	42	70
Education	20	6	8	—	12	7
Marriage	17	8	8	80	23	11
Adoption	3	2	2	10	15	2
Malaga[3]	7	3	3	10	8	10

1. Those people leaving or arriving in the village for a period exceeding one month during 1964.
2. Within ten miles of Apia.
3. Visiting on *fa'asāmoa* business, particularly *rites de passage*.

teachers. These people also usually adapt their duties to village life, even if they are sent, as often happens, to villages other than those in which they hold a title. It is accepted that a title gives a man the right to participate in any village *fono*, in any part of Samoa, provided that he intends to remain in the village for at least a year.[1] Often, however, Samoan doctors

---

[1] In Apia nu'u there were thirty-five chiefs from other villages who participated in the Apia *fono*.

TABLE 18 (*b*)

Wage Labour and Migration in Malie and Salani 1964

Type of migrant	Malie number	Malie proportion of total migrants	Salani number	Salani proportion of total migrants
		%		%
Village employees	9	6	6	10
Daily commuters	52	32	2	3
Temporary absentees				
(*a*) Weekly migrants	12	7	2	3
(*b*) Monthly migrants	37	23	29	49
Permanent absentees	39	25	20	33
Pālagi	11	7	1	2
Totals	161		60	

and teachers and most of the mission employees[1] are young, untitled people who through their scholastic ability have won places or obtained certificates from the Suva medical school, the Apia teachers training college, a secondary school, or the mission seminaries. These untitled people are often sent to villages far from their home village, so that the European medicine, education or religion which they come to teach or preach will not be influenced by traditional custom. But despite this policy the doctors, teachers and pastors are usually quickly absorbed into the social life of the village, through marriage,[2] accession to title, or simply participation in ceremonial activity. Samoans generally find it very difficult to stand aloof from village life. People who cut themselves off from the village are always labelled as peculiar, or ridiculous, or—worse—'people who try to wash off their brown skins', that is, people who try to become Europeans.

Participation in village life inevitably affects the duties of doctors, teachers or mission employees. Schedules of work have to be adapted to the ceremonial calendar for example. But this participation does not usually adversely affect the

---

[1] Most missions forbade their pastors to hold titles.

[2] Roman Catholic pastors, catechists—*fesoasoani*, as they were called, were permitted to marry.

promotion of health and education programmes or the inculcation of Christian beliefs. Indeed, an attachment to *fa'asāmoa* society and an ackowledgement of *fa'asāmoa* beliefs is in many ways an advantage. For example, many Samoans still believe that ultimately spirits (*aitu*) cause disease, and there has always been a wide range of local physical cures which people feel will immediately cure some diseases, although many European medicines have been accepted by Samoans. The Samoan doctor usually accepts these traditional cures. Often he himself feels doubts about the efficiency of European medicine as a result of many European cures or drugs which have failed to work in a tropical environment. But in any case he does well to honour some of the *fa'asāmoa* cures whatever he thinks, to ensure acceptance of his person and his profession by the villagers. Firstly, people feel secure when the doctor is a Samoan, a person they feel sure will help them, and not a European (*pālagi*), a person who may well try to hurt them. Secondly, tolerance towards *fa'asāmoa* custom makes the doctor acceptable to the traditional healers (*foma'i*), men and women who are still active and influential in some villages.

Conversely, the doctor who cuts himself off from *fa'asāmoa* society is at a considerable disadvantage in his profession. He is regarded by the villagers as an outsider, even as a European. People may feel that he is trying to make them sick rather than cure them, and any death or severe illness following treatment may be attributed to some European poison in the medicine. Often doctors who cut themselves off from village life are shunned by the villagers, and if they are not actually turned out of the village, they usually leave disillusioned.

Similar comments can be made about teachers and mission employees. In many village schools, the three Rs are taught in the vernacular in a relaxed atmosphere without regular hours. Teaching is complemented and illustrated with *fa'asāmoa* lore. In village churches Christianity is accepted, though in preaching and prayer, God, Christ and the saints take on the attributes and characteristics of traditional *atua* (high gods) and the devil comes to resemble the *aitu* (evil spirits). Moral injunctions are backed with biblical reference and *fa'asāmoa* proverbs. Generally successful teachers and pastors recognize and abide by these adaptions of *fa'asāmoa*, whatever their personal beliefs, whilst unsuccessful teachers and pastors are often those who try to substitute European ideas completely for Samoan norms.

The main reason for the absorption of village employees in village life and the adaption of work patterns, ideologies and incentives to *fa'asāmoa* ends is undoubtedly social pressure in the village, and the strong desire of most Samoans for *fa'asāmoa* status in the village. Another important reason for this situation, however, is the failure of European organizations which employ the Samoans to provide adequate incentives for, or control over, their employees.

Wages, as we have commented, are very low for all government and mission officials, and are in some cases non-existent. In 1964 four fifths of all Samoans earned less than £200 per annum, and only 2 per cent over £600.[1] All village employees are forced to make gardens for subsistence or cash sales, or to rely on the generosity of others to eke out their miserable stipends. This forces employees further into the nexus of village life and institutions.

More significantly the actual control over employee's work remains in the village rather than in the town. The absence, or low level, of wages partly explains this pattern. Withdrawal of wages cannot normally be a controlling sanction, if there are no, or very small wages. Nor can dismissal be used as a sanction. Whatever the regulations say,[2] dismissal by the administration is only valid if the villagers approve. No man in the village will take on a vacant job without some village support, or leave it unless this is locally approved by the village *fono*. An unwanted replacement is stoned or ignored until he is forced to leave. Even if the new nominee is able to muster a significant proportion of local support, the incumbent always retains some support and a feud is the result. The administration, always most anxious to avoid trouble in the villages, especially feuds, therefore usually consults village or district opinion in making an appointment. Job holders are elected in much the same way as title holders, either by village councils or specially convened district councils.

The missions are similarly placed, though an unwanted

---

[1] The comparative percentages for Europeans are 35 per cent and 31 per cent. The figures for Malie were 75 per cent and 0 per cent.

[2] For example, NZ Instructions to Officials 1922.

pastor is usually removed from the village with subtle insult, rather than flying basalt. Even excommunication cannot influence the village, for the village may then form a splinter church. The missions are never anxious to lose adherents, and know from experience that even a single village splinter can act as a focus for dissatisfied coreligionists in other villages. Consequently, pastors are also usually elected by local church councils, consisting of deacons who are also chiefs.

Finally, administration departments themselves often communicate little and care less for their representatives in the field. Sometimes this is the aftermath of government reorganization or centralization policies,[1] when the administration does not wish to offend the villagers by withdrawing officials. More often it is the result of departmental apathy or inefficiency. In such cases village employees are left high and dry, virtually without a master. The *pulenu'u*, for example, after the decline of the Native Department and District Affairs Boards have come under the Head of State's secretary who attends to them in between checking floral arrangements at Government House.

Apart from village employees there are the temporary absentees, that is, those who work outside the village but return at least once a month. A significant number (around 1,500) of these temporary absentees are daily commuters. In areas such as Savai'i or South Upolu people often go to work on nearby plantations, but most commuters go to work in Apia from villages within a fifteen mile radius of the town.[2] In Malie, for example (9 miles from Apia), forty people (10 per cent of the adult working force) make the journey to town by bus every day and the proportion increases to over 20 per cent in villages nearer Apia.[3]

Daily commuting is considered to be a very advantageous form of earning cash. It is felt to combine the best of both Samoan and Europeans worlds. As one man put it, 'You can have the village and the town. You can enjoy all the pleasures of *fa'asāmoa* and walk about in the European world with the money and the European things which make you a big man in

[1] Particularly when a Labour Government was in power in New Zealand 1935–49.
[2] Where people came from further afield this can be usually explained in terms of poor village resources (e.g. Fagaloa, Mulifanua).
[3] Cf. Pirie 1964: 145 who made a survey in 1956 of commuters.

the village.' On the other hand, by living in the village, a man can participate in village life, keep his finger on the pulse of village affairs and in particular constantly emphasize his claims to prestige and power, a prestige that is daily demonstrated in the village by his arrival and departure to and from the sophisticated outside world. Most commuters also combine wage labour with the production of food goods which can be used to advantage in ceremonial activity.

It is also in many ways cheaper for a wage labourer to remain in the village than for him to live in the town. The wage labourer in town usually has to pay rent and always has to pay for subsistence food. Pressure of population in Apia make both these costs high relative to the size of income. After the urban wage labourer has paid for his outgoings, he has much less left than the village cash cropper. The wage labourer resident in the village on the other hand does not usually have rent to pay. He obtains land through his *'āiga* connections for a relatively small outlay of labour or cash. From this land the wage labourer can obtain subsistence food either through the work of older people, women or children, who can seldom find work in the Apia labour market, or by working the gardens at *fa'asamoa* working times, that is in the cool part of the day, in the early morning or late evening, before and after exertions in European jobs.

It is thought to be more comfortable to live in a village. Most Samoans in Apia are forced to live in squalid huts around dank swamps or in the airless mosquito infested forests of the lower foothills. Most Apia houses have very poor sanitary facilities, usually poorer than those in the village and there is no beach and little bush to use. There are very few septic tanks and a single water tap may serve several hundred people. Certainly many town houses have electricity unlike most village *fale* but this is usually a single light bulb replacing the Coleman lamp of the village. Electrical equipment is more a status symbol than a comfort, for the power supply is very irregular, sometimes going off for weeks at a time, whilst poor wiring leads to many fires and shocks.

Transport is admittedly an additional cost for the village wage labourer. But transport in the commuting zone is convenient and cheap. During rush hours (6.30—8 a.m.), (3.30—

5 p.m.) a bus[1] hurtles through Malie village every few minutes and the nine miles of twisting broken road to town takes an average of 25 minutes, when an axle or an arm is not broken by the severe jolting. The fare is officially (1964) 1s., but the rate is usually much lower, ranging from a free ride, if a relative is driving, to about 6d. plus a coconut if the driver is unknown to the passenger. In addition there are a large number of vehicles,[2] taxis, trucks, motor cycles, passing through the village offering a ride free or at a rate similar to the bus.

There are admittedly some drawbacks in commuting. First, the commuter, like any other villager, is expected to participate in village activities and generally commuters want to take a full part in village life. Like the cash cropper their ceremonial obligations can be avoided but at the cost of prestige. The commuter is expected as important ceremonials arise to find any and every means to get time off work. The only occasion when ceremonial obligations can be deflected and prestige retained is if the employee in taking time off runs a serious risk of losing his job. In general, however, there is not usually a great conflict between ceremonial and job obligations. Ceremonials, as we have said, occur only occasionally and many employers are prepared to grant a reasonable amount of leave for certain ceremonials, especially funerals. In the few cases where there is trouble the argument over ceremonial leave is generally only a symptom of more deep-seated troubles in labour relations. If leave cannot be obtained, the wage labourer will probably be sacked or leave, either for a more congenial job or to return to village cash cropping. A commuter who is deeply involved in village affairs rarely risks his prestige by staying in a job that cannot be adapted to *fa'asāmoa* demands.

Some dissatisfaction is felt by some young people who consider it difficult to enjoy all the sophisticated pleasures of urban life whilst living in the village. There is very little time during working hours to go to the cinema, the dances, the ice-cream parlours, the beer clubs or the shops. If a person stays on

---

[1] Samoan buses consist usually of a truck chassis on to which a wooden super-structure has been nailed by local craftsmen.

[2] In 1962 2,186 were registered and many more were unregistered (WSDF Police and Prisons).

late after work or comes in on Saturday nights there are few buses back to the village and there is always a danger of breaking the rules of the village or household curfew (as early as 7 p.m.) after which only people of evil intent wander about at their own risk. Others feel that to live in the village taints the aura of romance and excitement which surrounds urban living. 'The village', said a young man from Malie, 'is for the old and the dying, or for those pigs who swill away their lives on orange beer (*fa'amafu*).'[1] Recreational reasons are not the only motives for the young person's dissatisfaction with village life. Wages are thought to be large in the towns and many young men dream of becoming wealthy through wage labour. Many think that by leaving the village they can get rich quickly.

In general there is very little objection to young people going to live in the town. Residence away from the village is accepted by many as a desirable part of the life cycle. A chief in Malie said: 'You must plant your coconuts away from the house, and only bring them in when they are ripe.' Many people also think that youth, with its socially disruptive passions, is best spent away.[2] Both young and old feel that valuable experience, prestige and capital can be gained from the outside world and most feel that contact will not be lost in the process, that the migrants will eventually come home to the village. In fact, for most migrants, *fa'asāmoa* and the village did remain the most significant end in life, the end which determined the nature of their participation in the cash economy.

Four kinds of relationships between migrants and villagers can be discerned for analytical purposes. First, there are a small number of migrants who live in the town during the week, returning to the village at the week-ends. In general these migrants live in villages with poor communications with Apia, villages such as Salani where the bus journey to Apia involves a four-hour drive over a twisting mountain track, or where the job involves special hours, night shifts or duties in remote areas of the island. The social activities of the weekly

---

[1] Made from orange cordial to which any intoxicating liquor is added.

[2] Many inter-'*āiga* and intervillage feuds and fights began with some impetuous youth seducing a girl.

migrant are similar to those of the daily commuter except that the weekly migrant naturally bears fewer of the burdens of everyday duties. The weekly migrants participate fully in ceremonial life, seeking prestige and responding to production incentives in much the same way as the cash cropper or the daily commuter.

The second, statistically more significant type of migrant is made up of those who stay away from the village for longer periods, usually a month. This group comprises, in the main, the young people who seek the bright lights and entertainment of the cities, but still want the prestige and power of *fa'asāmoa* status. The regular return to the village is regarded as a central part of *tautua*, the service in the *'āiga* necessary to secure, support, or enhance a title. For untitled people *tautua* involves helping in the gardens or with the village chores during one week-end a month. Unless it is a funeral of a parent, child or sibling, attendance at ceremonials is not considered to be necessary for the monthly migrant if the ceremonial occurs during the week but attendance at any week-end ceremonials is thought to be desirable, though this can be worked in with *tautua* duties.

Migrant chiefs are also expected to return approximately once a month to help with village affairs. Very often these chiefs, especially from remote villages, are the informal representatives of the village in the town, dealing with specific problems arising usually from relations with the Apia merchants. Monthly visits are used by these chiefs to report on urban activities, and by the villagers to bring up new problems for the urban chiefs to deal with.

The period of absence of the monthly migrant from the village is determined not by years but with reference to the focal points of the *fa'asāmoa* social structure. Both young men and women often return to the village when they marry, for it is very difficult to bring up a large family in the town. In fact, urban migration can be seen as part of the pattern of courtship in contemporary Samoa. Since marriage partners are usually obtained from outside the village young people are able to meet more suitable people of the opposite sex in the town, at work, dances, socials, clubs, ice-cream parlours, etc. 'In the village', one young man from Malie said, 'you know what all the girls are like. They are either family or friends you have played with since you were a kid.'

A second critical time when many young men return to the village is when they are elected to a title. As we have said, very often residence is insisted on by those who award a title and is necessary to provide the constant demonstrations of wealth or ability which help keep prestige high. A title does not necessarily mean that the man will stop being a wage labourer. Wage labour provides cash which is transformed into prestige through disbursement or leads to prestige directly. Consequently on accession to a title many monthly migrants become daily commuters, if transport or job permit.

A third critical time for return to the village is when through death or disease or some other misfortune the migrant's labour is needed in the 'āiga. Generally, this is either a temporary return to the village over the crisis period, or a prelude to accession to title and marriage when residence becomes permanent.

A special case where migrants are only temporarily absent from the village but participate fully in village affairs are the villages in Apia town itself. Originally, Apia was only a section (*pitonu'u*) of a larger village Sagauga, itself one of six villages[1] which stretch along a three-mile bay. As the Apia township expanded with the establishment of European suburbs and clusters of migrants huts, these villages were absorbed physically. The Apia villages found it very profitable to sell most of their garden land, though all the villages retain some garden land in the less valuable foothills behind the town. The sale of Apia land slowed down in the early twentieth century but by this time most of the foreshore and coastal plain around the town had been sold. These sales to Europeans, in contrast to the sales in rural Samoa, were almost without exception approved by the 1893 International Land Commission. The proceeds of these sales were quickly spent and the villagers became wage labourers. There are also in Apia newly created Samoan villages without significant garden land, usually formed by groups who have left their home villages because of population

[1] Sagauga contained also the *pitonu'u* of Matautu and Tanugamanono. The other villages were Fuaiupolu (*pitonu'u* Matafagatele, Vaiala, Magiagi), Vaimoso, Lepea, Vailoa, Vaiusu. Platt LMSJ 3/10/1835.

pressures on land due to land scarcity,[1] disaster,[2] or administrative purchase.[3] But although these Apia villages have very little land and most people work, village life, and *fa'asāmoa* customs are not greatly affected. The chiefly system, the desire for titles and the exercise of chiefly prerogatives, the round of ceremonial remain the keystone of the social structure and economic life.

The temporary absentees are regarded by Samoans as persons who live in the village, socially indistinguishable from any other villagers. Those who stay away from the village for periods longer than one month but retain some connection are usually still regarded as 'people of the village' (*tagata nu'u*) but are said to reside outside the village. This kind of migrant, whom we shall call a semi-permanent absentee, still often participates in village life. Many such people hold a village title, particularly the high honorific *Ao* titles which do not require village residence. In fact, a large proportion of the more permanent absentees leave the village not to seek cash alone, but in order to further their *fa'asāmoa* status. Status comes partly from proximity to the European world, but the highest status, especially titles, can be acquired or enhanced by gaining positions in the centralized native government established by the Europeans from the late nineteenth century, or by acquiring the support of one or other European faction in the *fa'asāmoa* political struggles over high titles.

This chiefly migration began in 1867 when the then *Tafa'ifā* (king) holder Malietoa and his *'āiga* moved from Malie to Mulinu'u in Apia Bay, to be nearer European sources of advice and arms for use in the chiefly wars then in progress. Within a short time the rival high chiefs, with their *tulāfale* (orator chief) advisers and assistants from the rival *tūmua* (traditional capital villages) and their families were also established in Apia. In 1873 the consuls, missionaries and traders set up what they thought would be a native government run on European models of a bicameral legislature. Although this body never got beyond *fa'asāmoa* ceremonial arguments, more lower-ranked chiefs and their *'āiga* came to Apia to take part

---

[1] e.g. Manono and Apolima.
[2] e.g. The villages in the wake of the 1905 volcanic eruption.
[3] e.g. Mulifanua, after the building of the Faleolo airport.

in the *Faipule* (lower house) or to work as unpaid public servants, jobs which like any other white collar jobs, quickly acquired a high prestige. Despite challenges from other *tūmua*,[1] Mulinu'u remained the political capital, and after the reconstitution of native government by the European Powers in 1890 Apia became the permanent residence of many high chiefs.

Migration slackened when the German and New Zealand administration centralized governmental functions and ran 'native affairs' with only a small, mainly European staff. The chiefs remained in Apia, which became a focus of anti-European political groups, particularly the Mau,[2] run by a coterie of high chiefs in conjunction with part-European merchants. Migration of chiefs quickened again in the period after the Second World War to fill jobs in the public service when, in 1947, New Zealand decided to make Samoa independent and to 'Samoanize' the public service.

Despite more or less permanent residence in Apia the connections between the absentee chiefs and the villagers remain strong. First, the appointment to the titles remain in the hands of groups of orator chiefs in the villages. More significantly, to hold any title the chiefs have to contribute considerable sums of money or goods to provide feasts at regular intervals in the villages, or to advise on large village projects or serious village problems, and to entertain villagers when they are in town. Very often, if the chief does not go into the village, the village will come to him and his house and land in Apia will be transformed into a section of the village, with many people coming and going on some piece of business real or imagined. Most urban chiefs are glad to retain their village connection. They soon lose interest in the bright lights of Apia or are rejected by European society and they long for the congeniality of the village. Being host to the village adds to the lustre of their prestige. The absentee chief also represents the village in dealings with the European world and in some cases becomes the elected representative (*faipule*) of the village or district in the Legislative Assembly. Finally, although the absentee chief is generally away from the village, it is expected that

---

[1] e.g. the establishment of a rival government by Tamasese with German backing in Leulumoega 1884–7.

[2] The Mau made their headquarters in another Apia village, Vaimoso.

all titleholders should return to the village occasionally, at least once a year, or on the occasion of a very important ceremonial.

Holding a village title and providing feasts is the most important means of remaining within the ambit of *fa'asāmoa* society without residing in a village. But there are other recognized means of retaining a place in the social structure without a title or residence. The most significant of these is to send money back to the village either to the *'āiga*, to the village chiefs, or to the church pastor. Samoans say this 'keeps the place (*nofo*) warm' as well as being a proper thing to do. Money is generally considered to be a payment in lieu of the monthly services of *tautua*. Most migrant money comes from abroad, rather than from Apia where migrants can normally return to the village to do their stint. It is estimated that as much money comes into Samoa from overseas migrants as from the most important cash crop, copra, and certainly this is true of the fieldwork villages.[1] As in the case of *tautua*, such money is a monthly contribution, usually sent through the ordinary mail. The amount varies to some extent with the income of the migrant, the size of his salary, and any extenuating circumstances,[2] but a minimum of approximately £10, or $30 a month is thought to be proper. In general, most migrants willingly send the money. It is only a small proportion of their total income,[3] and is considered by the migrants to be a small outlay to secure a place and possibly a title in the village, when their exertions in New Zealand or the United States are over. The absentee migrant who wants to enhance his position in village society can also supplement his money remittances by sending letters containing news and by an occasional visit.

Although sending money is the most favoured method by which overseas Samoans retain a place in village society, the social relationship can be preserved for many years, even for a lifetime, provided the migrant acquires enough cash or status in the town. Cash is usually used to provide for a feast or a

[1] See Appendix 2.

[2] For example, sickness.

[3] In a sample of 400 migrants in New Zealand in 1962 the average wage was £100 per month though wages were not as high in America. Samoa, cf. United States' Department of Labour 1957.

church donation,[1] to acquire an ordinary title if the migrant wants to remain in the village, or an *Ao* title if he wishes to remain in the town. In general much more cash is needed for a title than when a cash cropper aspires to a title. A probationary period (approximately three months) in the village is also expected, so that the village can assess the trustworthiness and character of the candidate.

Status itself can also be used to reactivate ties with the village. Prestige attaches to all persons who go into the outside world. One chief in Malie said: 'When you go into the European world you breathe European air and when you come back to the village you are a bigger man and you blow tough.' The further the migrant goes into the outside world the more prestige he acquires. The migrant who goes to Pago (American Samoa) has more prestige than the migrant who only reaches Apia but less than the migrant who goes to New Zealand, less still than the migrant who reaches the United States which is for most Samoans the ultimate symbol of sophistication and desirable living. Prestige attaches to anybody who makes money, but also to certain people who earn low salaries from occupations which do not involve manual labour. At the top of the list are the administrative employees.[2] Administrative work, even lowly jobs, is felt to be work fitted only for chiefs. Second come doctors and teachers; these are people who have acquired mastery over what are considered to be important activities whose benefits are greatly desired by many Samoans. Thirdly come the employees of large firms who are in constant contact with prestigious items such as money and sophisticated consumer goods. Fourth come those persons connected with the transport industries, that is bus, launch and taxi drivers, and particularly anyone connected with the new airline. The remaining occupations, that is mainly labouring and domestic jobs, although not prestigious are not looked down on. They are considered to be steps to higher things or simply short-term expedients to obtain cash.

[1] It is claimed in Malie that a man who has been away a lifetime would need about £500.

[2] No attempt is made here to grade occupations quantitatively on a scale. First there are the difficulties of assigning values to preferences (Yaukey 1955). More precisely, in the sample surveys conducted in the villages the people would only specify a preference for broad occupational groups, and then would only say whether they thought these groups prestigious or not.

13

Administrative employees, doctors, and teachers usually acquire a title with only a small outlay of cash, and usually without a probationary period in the village. As one descends the occupational scale, more cash has to be spent on the acquisition of status, though the amount of cash is offset to some extent by the amount of prestige attaching to the migrant from the place where he has worked. Consequently those who return to the village from the United States or New Zealand have very little difficulty in obtaining titles.

Finally, the migrant can retain his place in village society by affiliating to, or participating in, the activities of groups of relatives in the town. Both in Apia and New Zealand the most important social units often reflect the common origin of members. Usually these groups are segments of a village or '*āiga*. There are many advantages for the migrants in an affiliation to a town '*āiga*. It provides congenial living amongst well known faces. More significantly it often provides access to accommodation or employment, both very important in an environment of unemployment and high rents. As in the village it provides help and succour when there is sickness, trouble with the police or financial misfortune—a very valuable service in the absence of good medical or legal facilities in the predominantly European towns. The affiliation makes the migrant feel himself to be a part of village society. It enables him to remain *au fait* with village news and affairs. It enables him to demonstrate virtues of wealth, hard work, or simply the high status of living in the town to kinsfolk who are constantly returning and writing to the village. In this way a young man can be kept before the notice of those who select title holders. The church also provides a means of retaining contact with the village, especially through the donation of funds which are returned to the village. The links with the '*āiga* or the church are important because non-traditional groups are weakly developed and European groups resist the participation of Samoans in their activities. In Apia and overseas most social activity outside the '*āiga* and the church is in informal institutions (pubs, dances, cinemas) where strong social links are not formed.

It is true that most overseas Samoans have not returned to Samoa even for a short stay. In most cases, however, this does not reflect a desire to stay away. The size of fares, family and mortgage commitments make a return very difficult in the short term. Migrants say that they want to go to Samoa to enjoy status or title which, they say, takes at least ten years wage labour. Most Samoans also feel that they should only return when they have 'established' their children, that is, seen them through school and into marriage or a job. These ambitions are usually only achieved when the migrant parents have reached their fifties. Most migrants have come to New Zealand and Hawaii since the war and are very much younger than fifty, so that one would not yet expect any significant return migration.

Most Samoans see wage labour migration in the context of *fa'asāmoa* village society and *fa'asāmoa* incentives remain of paramount importance in the structure of economic action. There are a small number of migrants who sever their ties completely with the village, or abandon *fa'asāmoa* completely. These migrants can be divided for analytical purposes into two types. The first consists of those who sever their ties with village society but do not completely abandon *fa'asāmoa*. Sometimes the severing of ties with the village can be explained by a special reason which prevents participation in village life, for example, a disgrace, descent from a family which has migrated from other parts of Polynesia, or Melanesia, or the European pressures to abandon the village background which develop when a Samoan marries a part-European. These migrants usually abandon some of the outward trappings of *fa'asāmoa* life. They wear trousers, they live in wooden houses, they eat European foods, and they do not hold registered titles.

The migrants retain, however, important *fa'asāmoa* social traits. Their speech is always Samoan and their basic values and social activities are very similar to village Samoans. Although formal titles do not enter into the social structure, this is mainly because the Registrar of Lands and Titles does not recognize these migrant groups as villages which can legally possess titles. There are leaders amongst these people who have all the prerogatives of chiefs and even meet in regular councils like the village *fono* to decide on *fa'asāmoa* matters in their residential unit.

Within these groups the pattern of production incentives is

for the most part indistinguishable from the rural villages. There is, in fact, a tendency for this group to be unstable as a social entity and sooner or later to form ties with a village. These ties are occasionally formed when a person renews his own links with the village, possibly expiating or outliving his disgrace, or having a change of heart about the lowly status of his rural relatives. More often ties are formed by marriage. Marriage sometimes leads to complete reabsorption in village life, the acquisition of land, and the acceptance of a title. Always marriage means an involvement in the continuing round of ceremonials which marriage initiates.

Again the *fa'asāmoa* characteristics of this migrant group and the developing links with the villagers can be partly explained by the affective and social attractions of *fa'asāmoa* society, even for those who are neither Samoan or Polynesian. But an equally important part of the explanation are the discouragements which arise from attempts to contact and communicate with the Europeans and part Europeans. Many overseas Europeans and local part Europeans tolerate a handful of high ranking Samoans or Samoans who stay 'in their place', i.e. in the village. But they intensely dislike and actively discriminate against Samoans and other Polynesians or Melanesians who aspire to urban residence. There is little the Europeans can do to stop Samoans acquiring the outward signs and symbols of European life if Samoans have the money to purchase goods. But Europeans can, and do, restrict other forms of communication. There is pressure to exclude non-Europeans from European housing areas, though the Europeans or part Europeans explain their prejudice as being due to the fact that Samoans are slum dwellers. Samoans are not included in the round of parties which are the focus of European life. They are excluded from the more élite clubs or ignored in conversation at the bar or around the billiard table. Although there is considerable sexual contact between the European men and the Samoan prostitutes, club attendants, secretaries, and house girls, there is very little marriage, which Europeans regard as a 'disgrace', as 'going native'.

There is a very small group of Samoans who abandon completely all connections with the village and *fa'asāmoa*. These migrants live in European areas, eat European foods, wear

European clothes and mix only with Europeans. Samoans say they are *pālagi* (European). There are a small number of *pālagi* migrants in Apia, but most live in New Zealand, Hawaii or the United States. Even here the *pālagi* state is often ephemeral—the local island church or community beckons in a largely European society which is not prepared to accept the Samoan on equal terms.[1] There is a definite tendency for the *pālagi* migrant to re-establish contact with the *fa'asāmoa* world at least by joining the local community or by sending letters home.

SOCIO-ECONOMIC EFFECTS OF MIGRATION

Fa'asāmoa, then, remains a significant part of the Samoan wage labour world providing the main incentive and social framework for migration. This migration does not usually have adverse effects on *fa'asāmoa* society or economic conditions generally. Administrators in Samoa, relying mainly on information from other parts of the world,[2] have argued that urban migration will lead eventually to the destruction of traditional life and to village poverty. It is argued that when the young men migrate in sufficient numbers village life crumbles away and the villages are left to the old and sick who live in squalor amidst neglected gardens waiting only for migrants' remittances with which to buy tinned food. It is also argued that the national economy is adversely affected by the migration overseas of what is thought to be the most able and highly skilled sector of the population.[3] Finally it is argued that migration also leads to social and economic problems in the towns, both locally and overseas where there are insufficient jobs, and there is overcrowding, and inadequate sanitary facilities.

These theories, however, have to be considerably modified in the Samoan situation. Certainly migration, consisting largely of the economically active sector of the population, did deplete the village labour force to some extent. For example, in both Salani and Malie approximately two-thirds of the

---

[1] Despite Harré's arguments about racial tolerance in New Zealand (1963), there is considerable evidence of bad and worsening race relations in New Zealand as far as Samoans are concerned (e.g. many of the articles in Thompson 1963) and Hawaii (Hirsh 1956, Knaeffler 1965).

[2] e.g. Schapera 1947 was read by senior officials.   [3] See Stace 1956.

population is under fifteen or over forty-five, compared with the national average of one half. As migration generally runs in *'āiga* (in Salani and Malie migrants were from one-third of all *'āiga*), there are some *'āiga* without working adults, male or female, and others with only one or two young men to tend family gardens. But in these *'āiga*, cash crop production is only slightly below the village average.[1] Gardens and village facilities generally are not in bad condition. For the absentees return to the village at least once a month to help with the gardens and, if necessary, the upkeep of village facilities. Much more significantly the migrants bring or send back much more cash than can be earned from cash cropping. In Malie and Salani the average total cash income in *'āiga* with wage labour migrants is higher, usually far higher, than the *'āiga* without migrants. In Malie, one *'āiga* received over £100 per annum *per capita* from migrants' remittances. Some of the village stores, as well as important capital (trucks, fertilizers etc.) were purchased with cash sent home by migrants. In cases of *'āiga* need (for example, a death or a pressing debt) the migrants will quickly and generously respond. Many migrants also bring back valuable skills to the village. The best gardens in Malie and Salani are run by chiefs who have worked in the Department of Agriculture. The most efficient trading stores are run by men who leave the shops shut during the day, or the wife in charge, to work with one of the big firms in town. There are also the non-monetary benefits, especially the prestige that accrues to those who have relatives immersed in the vibrant outside world. Consequently, most people are not sorry, but indeed anxious for their sons and daughters to go out and become wage labourers. 'This is our best export crop', said one chief. When the administration suggests restricting migration to the towns[2] there is always a vigorous protest from the villagers.

Similarly, overseas migration does not usually have an adverse effect on the local economy. It is not only the better educated and more highly skilled Samoans who migrate

[1] See Appendix 2.

[2] This was first suggested in the 1930s, cf. Keesing 1934:336. Since the war restriction has been stimulated by Fijian experiments with a commutation tax system.

to New Zealand. As the accompanying table indicates, only a third of a sample of migrants to New Zealand in 1962[1] had some secondary school education or could be classed as skilled labour[2] (that is, an occupation which requires some

TABLE 19

Employment[1] of migrants to New Zealand, 1962

	SAMOA	NEW ZEALAND
	Percentage of total migrants	
Nurses	2	4
Teachers	4	1
Skilled labour	6	4
Government, clerical	11	1
Shops	4	1
Unskilled factory	—	39
Labourers	5	25
Domestic servants	1	16
Agriculture[2]	20	—
Female domestic duties	41	1
Full-time school	6	8

1. Last occupation Samoa, first occupation New Zealand, based on a sample of 400 migrants.
2. Includes in Samoa men engaged in subsistence agriculture.

Source—New Zealand Department of Labour.

specialized preparatory training). And many of these could not find a job in Samoa whatever their qualifications, or only a job where their skills had little application. For example, one man with a school certificate runs messages in a government department. There is no room in the agricultural department for graduates of the agricultural college. Many girls with a secondary education are unemployed and nearly three-quarters of the skilled labour migrating in 1962 to New Zealand were women. Most overseas migrants prefer unskilled labour in New Zealand, to the poor pay and prospects of skilled employment in Samoa.

[1] By comparison only 10 per cent of Malie adults had some secondary school education. The following comment on migrants in New Zealand is based on a sample survey of 400 migrants living mainly in Auckland and Wellington.

[2] See Table 19.

A large number of overseas migrants are superfluous in the local labour market and some are also social misfits. As in other parts of the world,[1] some migrants want to leave because they feel insecure within their own society, rather than for any economic reason. Consequently, even if migrants are able, many local Samoans feel their migration is a good thing. The chiefs are relieved that a potentially dangerous political opposition can so easily be disposed of. Many of the migrants have connections with the European community, or entertain European ideas such as American views of democracy or Marxist ideals which involve the dismantling of the chiefly system. One chiefly politician explained, 'Overseas migration is a safety valve, it allows the young men to let off steam. Let them explode in the New Zealand pubs and come back when and if they feel more quiet.' Some local people share the chiefs' dislike of overseas migrants. Like some vague yet attractive force of evil it is thought these young men will lead the Samoans to disaster as surely as the Europeans will. Certainly people think the migrants are clever, but they are also felt to be undisciplined, men who like the Europeans they emulate easily get drunk and brawl. As a consequence of all this, no effort was made by the Samoan authorities to persuade the New Zealand or American Governments to restrict the outflow of skilled labour, a pressure to which these overseas governments would have readily responded. Indeed, there are violent objections by the Samoan Government whenever restrictions are suggested to them.[2]

Migration also affects the labour force in the receiving as well as in the source areas. Jobs have always been short in Apia relative to migrant demands. Jobs have become harder[3] to get as private European capital has moved out especially since Independence (1962) and since United Nations specialized agencies have introduced plans involving the intensive use of capital rather than labour. But the high level of unemployment is not usually reflected in low levels of living. Many of the unemployed work in the Apia villages' garden land behind

[1] Cf. Musgrave 1963, Appleyard 1965.

[2] For example, in June 1964 when the American Samoan authorities attempted to introduce entry restrictions. The local chiefs called this an 'iron curtain'.

[3] The number of jobs declined by approximately 10 per cent in the period 1951–61 (WSDF Statistics Department).

the town. Many are fed and, if necessary, receive money from their home villages. Abroad, in New Zealand, in American Samoa (where the Americans have established new industries), in Hawaii and the west coast of the United States, there is a great demand for labour, particularly for unskilled labour which the local population dislikes.

Similarly, social conditions are not as bad as the critics of migration have claimed. In Apia there is overcrowding in some houses and much poor sanitation,[1] whilst in New Zealand many Samoans live in old, crowded and insanitary houses. But there is the same number of people to a *fale* in Apia village as in Salani or Malie (5) and the sanitation is little worse in Apia and much better in New Zealand than in the villages. In general Apia and New Zealand Samoans are healthier than village people, mainly because drugs and medical attention can be more easily obtained, and higher incomes and better retail facilities permit more nutritious diets.

[1] In my survey of Apia village only 20 per cent of houses had flush toilets.

8

VILLAGE CAPITAL FORMATION

In previous chapters we have discussed two means by which Samoans earned cash, that is through the sale of resources and labour, and we have tried to show that *fa'asāmoa* society could be an asset rather than a liability in increasing productivity. An important contributory factor to cash crop or wage labour productivity was capital formation. In this chapter we will examine contemporary capital formation in rural Samoa.

Economists and anthropologists have not always agreed on what they mean by capital formation which has had a wide range of theoretical interpretation,[1] but the notion of deferment of present consumption for future productivity is central to most modern usages.[2] Strictly speaking all the factors of production[3] can be capital in this sense; resources have inherent productivity and labour must be applied to resources for production to take place. Labour also embodies future productivity, especially in the skills of the labour force. But an analytical distinction at least can be made between the ultimate sources of production (the resource base, the labour force, etc.) and the goods or skills which lead directly to future productivity—these goods we shall call technological capital. Secondly there are those goods, generally money in the market economy, which command purchasing power over other, possibly productive goods —these goods which lead indirectly to future productivity we shall call wealth capital. Thirdly, there are the skills and abilities of people which affect productivity. We shall call these skills human capital. The two important elements in

---

[1] For modern reviews see Lachmann 1956.

[2] Though the analytical distinction between productive and non-productive goods goes back to Adam Smith. For modern discussions with special reference to underdeveloped countries see Frankel 1954: 69 ff., Firth and Yamey 1964: 18 ff. Capital in this sense is rather similar to Steiner's 1954 'positive translation', i.e. the retention of resources in the productive process. Cf. Salisbury 1962: 122 ff.

[3] Conversely Professor Hayek regards capital as resources (1940: 54).

this human capital are first the accumulation of productive or potentially productive knowledge, including literacy, general knowledge, technical and entrepreneurial skills, and secondly improved health and nutrition.[1] A high level of all kinds of capital formation has been regarded by many post-war economists to be the most important dynamic to economic development in underdeveloped countries.[2] Wealth and technological capital particularly are needed initially to build the economy's infra-structure (that is, its power and communications system) as well as for the modernization of agriculture and establishment of factories. Because these capital needs are so great in underdeveloped areas, and because local resources are so small, much of the capital must be found externally. But it is also agreed that levels of domestic capital formation, both wealth capital, such as savings, and particularly investment in technological capital must be as high as possible if production is to be sustained after the initial capital injection and become eventually self-generating, if the economy is to 'take off' in Rostow's phrase.[3] Productive knowledge, like physical capital, has also been regarded as a mechanism for triggering sustained growth. Knowledge, especially productive knowledge, not only facilitates technological capital formation but also engenders a 'development mentality', a 'view beyond the village', a sophistication and objectivity which stimulates the people to want to help themselves, or at least makes them more receptive to the administration's programmes. Health and productive knowledge also contribute directly to output through the labour force.

Although there are no precise statistics available in Samoa on levels of domestic capital formation it has generally been assumed that capital formation is comparatively low relative to development needs.[4] The empirical evidence, however,

[1] On the concept of human capital see Debeauvais 1962, Lewis 1961.

[2] The emphasis on massive injections of capital as the panacea for underdevelopment, for breaking the vicious circle of low investment and low productivity began with the work of Rosenstein-Rodan and was more fully developed by Nurkse, Scitovsky, Lewis 1955: 274 and in the United Nations Report (United Nations 1951). Since then 'non-conventional inputs', human capital, entrepreneurship etc. have come to be regarded as more important. See Singer 1961.

[3] Rostow 1960.

[4] Estimated to be less than 5 per cent of national income. See Fairbairn 1963 for a summary.

suggests that capital formation is relatively well developed in the villages. Secondly the important constraints on capital formation are external to the *fa'asāmoa* social structure.

FA'ASĀMOA WEALTH AND TECHNOLOGICAL CAPITAL

First, wealth capital in our definition, exists in *fa'asāmoa* society. Certain goods, especially fine mats and other items used in ceremonial gift exchanges including food, can be regarded as stores of future purchasing power, since they lead to future consumption. Many of these exchange goods can be accumulated, being durable and easily stored. Admittedly the purchasing power of fresh food in the humid climate is of relatively short duration. But many food goods are preserved by deliberate conservation in the use of resources, and some by special preservation after use. For instance, most agricultural products are conserved in that the utilization of most resources is carefully controlled by *tapu* (*sā*) or secular regulations imposed by the village *fono*. Wild yams in the bush, certain coconut groves, *talo* beds, fishing grounds, animals on the hoof are specifically kept for future use in subsistence or ceremonial consumption or against possible future food shortages due to hurricane or drought. Great efforts are made to prevent pests destroying food or crops. Certain foods are also preserved. Traditionally fish, birds and turtles were smoked or dried, and today bananas, talo and especially bread fruit are stored in baskets or fermented in pits lined with coconut leaves covered in with stones. Often breadfruit pits are opened in a few weeks, but they can be, and sometimes are, left for years. In recent years in many villages the people have begun to eat rice because it is easily kept. While some of these food goods are used for consumption rather than in productive activity, many food goods can also be used to acquire technological capital, either directly or through specialist services. Wealth capital projects involve a good deal of village time also. In Malie and Salani approximately one half of all the debating time[1] in the village *fono* or sub-committees is spent discussing economic plans concerned with conservation or preservation and much more time is devoted to the subject in informal family conclaves.

[1] See Table 5.

There is also an extensive range of *fa'asāmoa* technological capital[1] relative to available resources and subsistence needs. Traditionally although there were only two horticultural implements, the hardwood digging and planting sticks (*'oso*), there were many other tools used in a wide range of productive activity, including stone axes, chisels, gouges, knives, and scrapers. There were also many devices for hunting. There were baited or decoy spring traps to catch rats, wildfowl, and in the Savai'i hills, pigs. In certain parts flying fox were caught in a fowling net, and pigeons were often caught in this way or with hooks from a tree platform. Threads of coconut were used in slip-knot snares to catch birds, especially the parakeet and seagull (*fua'ō*). Although some of this equipment is no longer frequently used much is still used occasionally.[2] Where items have been replaced this has often been because there is a more useful European substitute. For example, steel tools were quickly realized to be far more effective than stone or wooden tools, and within twenty years of the arrival of the missionaries, steel tools had replaced *fa'asāmoa* instruments.[3] These European tools have been absorbed into the *fa'asāmoa* economy and used in much the same way as *fa'asāmoa* tools.

Traditionally the most highly developed capital was fishing equipment.[4] There were cords, slip-knot snares to catch sea centipedes, fresh-water crayfish or sea eels, and large nooses of three-ply sennit cord, used with decoys, spears, and clubs, to noose sharks. There were weirs or dams made of coconut or banana leaf or stones to trap shoals of fish on the outgoing tide. Hardwood fish spears were often used, and bows and arrows were occasionally used from canoes or from the reef. There were many types of nets; various sizes of dip nets for fishing in the lagoon, for catching flying fish at night, for shrimping, casting nets with sinkers and floats, various types of seine nets, set for use inside and outside the reef. There were many types of small traps to catch small fish, sea crayfish, crabs, etc., and large bamboo traps to catch sea eels, using baits and lures. Fish are caught by the mouth with forked

---

[1] See particularly Buck 1930, also Kramer 1902 v. 2: 203 ff., Demandt 1913.
[2] See Appendix 1.
[3] Wilkes 1847 v. 2: 66, 123 GB FO 58/63/252, LMSB11F85A.
[4] The best account is Demandt 1913.

sticks, with wooden, shell and bone hooks. Trawling hooks and spinning lures were used extensively to catch bonito. Narcotics were used to stun fish in small pools. Finally there were five types of fishing canoe, small dug-outs (*paopao*) with two out-rigger booms and paddles for fishing inside the reef, larger dug-outs (*soatau*) with more outriggers and sometimes sails for fishing outside the reef, and plank canoes (*va'aalo*) for deep water especially bonito fishing.

It is true that apart from the small nets and the *paopao*, *fa'asāmoa* fishing equipment is not extensively used in villages today. As in the case of tools, this is due partly to the replace-ment of *fa'asāmoa* goods with more effective European sub-stitutes. Steel fish-hooks, hemp lines and clinker-built boats were all in frequent use in the villages before 1850. The change is also due to increasing taste for European substitutes for *fa'asāmoa* fish foods, especially tinned fish.[1] Effort is consequently put into cash-earning activities rather than fishing.

Again efficient production techniques, i.e. skills which lead to future productivity, were present in traditional society and these *fa'asāmoa* techniques are an effective method of grow-ing cash crops, yielding a product which is acceptable in the market and which, by European as well as Samoan stand-ards, represents an adequate output for any input of land or labour.

Traditionally there were two important means by which agricultural production was increased; first by the extension of land use and secondly by increasing fertility. Both kinds of production increases were carefully planned and executed, and there was a vast corpus of practical knowledge of means to increase fertility. These *fa'asāmoa* methods have been applied successfully in cash cropping. There has been very little ex-tension of coconut land since the Germans made every *'āiga* plant coconut trees at the turn of the century,[2] although there

[1] See Table 1.

[2] GCA 2/XVII/V5, GO 5/4/1900. For example, in Malie the boundaries for 1924 can be seen in Map 1924 (Table 13) which was the only cadastral map of a village made by the New Zealand authorities before the Mau. Also in aerial photographs (Maps 1956) the remains of low stone walls can be detected (though these are difficult to find on the ground) which people say were built traditionally at the edge of the coconut groves to prevent pigs reaching the *talo oloa*, the open space behind the village where *talo* is grown.

is constant planting of new trees in existing groves to replace dying trees.[1]

Much more significant are the attempts to increase output by increasing present fertility. Planting of all cash crops is done carefully in most *'āiga*. For example, fallen nuts are collected[2] by the young men or children, placed in a heap in a shaded part of the grove and left until the young leaves are the length of a man's arm, after which they are placed in a shallow hole. Only the strongest shoots are planted in suitable soils.[3] Around the sapling, stones or other materials are built into a low wall to keep out marauding pigs or wandering children until the sapling is strong. Similar comments could be made about the cultivation of the other important cash crops, bananas and cacao.[4]

Most *'āiga* keep the weeds and vines down in the groves by cutting them back at least once a month. There are also attempts to control pests such as the Rhinoceros beetle or the banana bunchytop virus. The villagers say that since the Rhino beetle[5] was introduced there have been weekly searching parties (consisting often of boys and girls) to find the larvae of the beetle and destroy it. Beetle-searching is the business of the village council (*fono*) and fines are exacted on *'āiga* which do not search. Many people also let their pigs root about in the groves as they believe that the pigs destroy the larvae.[6]

There are also measures to conserve both the use of fruit and fronds.[7] *Tapu* (*sā*) are placed on trees by the village

[1] The Samoans say that a coconut tree is like a man (*o le tagata niu*), i.e. it is able to bear fruit for approximately fifty years.

[2] Sometimes a nut will be left to grow where it falls, especially if it has strong-looking leaves. The Samoans say that it will make a strong tree if it is able to start life without any protection.

[3] There is a considerable body of knowledge concerning soil fertility. Various plants and the height to which they grow is used as an index of the fertility of a particular piece of ground.

[4] Both were introduced, but several species of bananas were grown traditionally. Cacao is generally treated like coconuts though it is recognized that the trees need wetter soils.

[5] About 1902—the searchings were ordered by the German Govenment (GO 21/1/11). The New Zealand Government also made strenuous attempts to expand beetle searching, even offering a silver cup to the village who collected the most larvae (NZIT 24/2).

[6] I could, however, find no correlation between pigs and the observed incidence of Rhinoceros beetle, though beetle searching seemed to be effective.

[7] The removal of too many fronds kills the tree.

council (*fono*). Traditionally it was believed that a thief would risk a horrible death by touching the tree, the type of death depending on the *tapu* (*sā*) sign placed on the tree. These signs are still placed on the tree,[1] and though the most important sanctions are today secular (fines from the *fono*[2]) there are few people who would tempt fate by touching a *tapu* tree.

The preferred method of harvesting crops is simply to pick them up from the ground when they have fallen. Early observers[3] attributed these harvesting methods to native laziness or hedonism but in fact ripe coconuts gathered on the ground make good copra, better copra than unripe nuts picked from the trees.[4] These nuts are husked in the gardens or in the village by the young men, by dashing the nut on a steel spike stuck in the ground. Most crops are carried back to the village often by young women, in baskets at either end of a pole, or simply tied to the pole. In the village crops may be stored on poles or in storage bins, but usually copra or cacao is made immediately, or the bananas dispatched. Thus far people say that all methods are *fa'asāmoa* and traditional, though some methods are demonstrably introduced.[5] Opinions are divided, however, on the making of copra by sundrying or roasting, or cacao by fermentation. Some people say that these methods were introduced by the Germans,[6] but many think that Samoans traditionally made copra or even cacao, or that a Samoan invented the idea.

A number of '*āiga* do not make copra or cacao but simply sell or barter the unprocessed nuts or beans to the trader. Although time and effort are saved in this transaction, and it is important during ceremonials when time is at a premium,

---

[1] For example, plaited coconut leaves in the form of various fishes (e.g. shark) placed on the trunk would result in death from that fish. If clam shells were left at the base of the tree the thief would get tuberculosis or some other form of *fiva* (fever). A spear in the ground meant ulcers, a plaited coconut leaf square, death by lightning, a basket filled with ashes meant that a rat would eat the man's fine mats (*i'e tōga*).

[2] Small food fines in *talo*, or up to a £1 in cash, larger food fines (including pigs) and up to £5 in cash for persistent offenders.

[3] e.g. Turner 1861: 277, LMSB11F5JA.

[4] Though there are always some nuts which will make good copra on the trees and nuts left on the ground for any length of time may begin to germinate.

[5] e.g. the method of carrying nuts on poles (from the Chinese), the steel spike method of husking, the beetle searching.

[6] It is reputed to have been introduced by the managing director of the German firm of Godeffroys around 1865.

the trader only pays approximately one-half of the price he would pay for the meat of a processed nut or bean. Most people preferring the extra cash to the extra leisure, still process their goods. Copra is usually made by the young men splitting the nut with a bush-knife and by drying the meat in the shell or in small pieces. Great care is taken during the three days of drying. The meat is placed by the old women on a clean dry surface, sometimes a platform especially built for the purpose. It is watched constantly by anybody who is sitting in the *fale* (house) or nearby, to keep away wandering dogs, pigs or children, or to bring it in should it begin to rain. At night the meat is brought into the house and carefully packed away in tins or other suitable containers.

Many '*āiga* also try to use mechanical driers to process copra. In some '*āiga* these are simply open fires or ramshackle tin huts where the coconut flesh is roasted using husks and shells as fuel. But attempts are made to regulate the heat so as not to scorch or discolour the meat. A few '*āiga* have more sophisticated hot air driers (i.e. where the meat does not come into contact with the smoke), but most '*āiga* do not have enough money or know-how to build one of these.

The major difference between traditional cultivation and present day cash production is the insignificance of supernatural explanation or garden magic today. According to early observers, garden magic did not dominate traditional agriculture but what were considered to be tutelary deities were regularly propitiated.[1] These practices and beliefs were to ensure ultimate success, and to avoid in particular the inexplicable natural tragedies which occasionally befall man and his crops. Immediate success, the actual growing of the crop, was based on the solidly pragmatic lore which we have described. Today the government, the overseas merchant, and a vague belief in chance have replaced the tutelary deities in the general schema of economic explanation, though the Christian God is felt by some to have a vague influence on agriculture. Today only a few features of garden magic remain, all without productive significance.

Fa'asāmoa production methods have generally a much higher

---

[1] Particularly *O le sa*, incarnate in birds see Stair 1897: 42, Turner 1884: 47. The usual method of propitiation was a feast or an '*ava* offering.

rate of productivity or production efficiency (i.e. a high output of goods relative to inputs of resources, labour or capital) than is usually realized,[1] a rate which is satisfactory to Samoans and in certain respects as high as rates of productivity found on European plantations in Samoa.

As with the notion of consumption efficiency,[2] the difficulty in measuring production quantities is to attribute values to goods or services which lack specific money values. But it is possible to work out some productivity ratios in terms of physical quantities, for example the ratios between output and area of land used, or number of trees, or input of man-hours, the usual ratio in economist's productivity analysis—though here too the usefulness of these ratios is diminished by the difficulties of accounting for differentials of soil fertility, or skills and efforts which may vary greatly between production situations.

For example in Malie the yield of copra is as high as 1,400 lb. per acre per annum in one *'āiga*, but the average is 875 lb. per acre.[3] This figure compares very favourably with the yields given for European plantations in Samoa,[4] especially when it is realized that the European plantations are situated on the best soils in Samoa, and that much skilled labour and capital is applied in the groves. The cash return to Samoan growers per acre is, however, considerably lower than on the European plantations (£20—£8 (Malie)). However a large part of every acre in the villages is used for subsistence. In a survey in Malie and Salani of the consumption of coconuts over a four-month period in 1964 only approximately 40 per cent of nuts were bartered or sold to the traders. Also most Samoan cash croppers do not have the use of modern hot-air driers to produce premium grade copra and some prefer to sell unprocessed nuts to traders at well below official prices.

The output per man-hour[5] is 3 lb. of copra per hour *per capita* or a cash return of approximately 5*d.* per hour *per capita*.

---

[1] See Stace 1956.   [2] See p. 41.

[3] Based on a sample survey of the production of ten *'āiga* (200 people) over a four month period, May–September 1964.

[4] Stace 1956: 15. The argument has been put forward that Samoan groves produced such a high rate of nuts because the trees were crowded. This is unlikely to be true since crowded groves (particularly since rats live there easily) are known to produce fewer nuts than uncrowded groves.

[5] i.e. all time spent on copra production by men, women and children including the time spent on discussing and organizing copra production in the *'āiga* or

This rate is almost exactly the same as the average *per capita* unskilled wage rate for a family in Apia village.[1] Similar comments can be made about productivity rates in other cash crop activities in Malie and Salani[2]; indeed rates in Salani, where production methods are most traditional, are generally higher than in Malie.

The value of any return to the Samoan cash cropper is also greatly enhanced by the fact that the labour and resources used in cash crop production have few alternative uses, or can be dovetailed into any other demands for time in the cash economy. That is to say, resources, labour (and also capital), were cheap in terms of cash.

Women, children and old people play a very important part in cash cropping,[3] helping to gather and process nuts and beans, helping with weeding, selling *talo* and vegetables on the Apia streets, etc. These people can very rarely obtain a job in the wage labour market and, other than leisure have very few alternative uses for their time. Certainly young men, actually or potentially wage labourers, do the more arduous tasks especially in banana and *talo* cultivation, as well as the heavy jobs of cleaning and clearing land, maintaining tracks, etc. But these tasks are usually done in the cool of the day, before or after wage labour if the young man is a commuter, or on any Saturday which he has available. The amount of labour which it is considered only young men can perform is relatively small, approximately one day a month. In most villages in Samoa, as we have said, there are wage labourers who return home to work once a month or when a marriage, death, birth, etc., in the village enables the man to combine work with the duties and pleasures of ceremonial.

Similarly the land used in cash cropping in the twentieth century has had few alternative uses. Until 1893[4] when there

---

fono, but excluding the time minding the copra as it dried, since it was rare for the watcher to have to interrupt her activity other than giving a shout to wandering dogs, pigs or children.

[1] The average wage in Apia village for an unskilled man was 2*s*. 6*d*. per hour and the average size of these families was seven.   [2] See Table 5.

[3] See Table 5. The tables only give adult man-hours, but the children contribute approximately 20 per cent of all cash-work activity.

[4] The restrictions imposed by the Samoan Government of 1873 (that the council of chiefs validate all sales) was ineffective (GBPR 6/25).

was virtually unrestricted sale of land to Europeans, land had a definite and relatively high market value. Many Samoans then preferred to sell land rather than grow cash crops.[1] But after the International Commission's prohibition on freehold purchase (1893), and especially after the New Zealand administration's prohibition of leases as well, there was relatively little alienation of Samoan land and there has never been extensive exchange of land amongst Samoans.[2] Consequently in Samoa today land can be said to have very little exchange value. In many villages if the *'āiga* do not use the land for cash crops it would probably lie unused. Admittedly in villages near Apia where land is scarce because of population pressure or plantation encroachment, land does usually have a potential alternative use at least in the subsistence sector of the economy. But even here the preference for cash to purchase European goods rather than subsistence equivalents, means that subsistence land use is not often actually preferred to cash land use.

The further development of capital formation, and particularly technological capital, is restricted not because the Samoan is shortsighted in economic activity but because he has little need to be farsighted. In some areas, hurricanes spoil tree crops occasionally,[3] but roots grow well in the volcanic soils and there are always the resources of the sea. Again there has never been a shortage of land. The weak development of horticultural implements, in part at least, may be because most subsistence crops require little attention.

Similar comments can be made about the cash economy. In contemporary Samoa there has always been ample productive cash crop land guaranteed in perpetuity from 1893, by the administration. As we have said, the most important cash crops need little attention. Samoans say, 'Give a coconut a day and it will give you a lifetime'. The security of livelihood on the land and restricted needs of important cash crops means that the Samoan has less need to acquire wealth capital for future productive needs or technological capital to make a present living. In a definite sense the Samoan's capital is

---

[1] GBFO 58/137/52.   [2] See Ch. 5.

[3] There are hurricanes approximately every six years, but Samoans say that only once in a lifetime does a hurricane devastate the land. Up to 1964 there had been only two devastating hurricanes, though there have been two very bad hurricanes since 1964.

his land. Significantly those with a restricted access to, or rights, in land, such as the villages where land has been sold, or Polynesians from other islands, or the European and Asiatic immigrants, did accumulate more wealth capital or learn special skills, or if they did acquire land, use more technological capital.

SAVINGS AND INVESTMENT

Even though the accumulation of wealth or technological capital is not a necessity Samoans participate busily in both activities.

It has often been claimed that in underdeveloped countries, including Samoa, traditional institutions inhibit or prevent the accumulation of savings. During the German and New Zealand administrations[1] native society was blamed for the failure of any savings schemes.[2] In support of this thesis a recent survey by South Pacific Commission experts[3] has claimed that less than 10 per cent of the population have Post Office savings bank accounts, that only 2 per cent use their accounts regularly or had more than £3 in credit and that savings bank deposits were declining.

This thesis is, however, a misrepresentation of the Samoa savings situation. First, the figures themselves are misleading.[4] The decline in deposits in the period mentioned was only small (under 5 per cent) and before 1954 and after 1957 deposits have risen steadily, even spectacularly. By the end of 1963[5] there were 70 per cent more depositors in the Post Office savings bank than in 1957 and *per capita* savings compared favourably with other under-developed countries. The following table indicates the patterns of savings in 1964.[6] Although departmental files do not distinguish between Samoan and European depositors, most of the new accounts were from Savai'i where most of the population is Samoan. Certainly there are fewer accounts in Malie and Salani where there is only one account to every forty-five and seventy persons respectively. But this

---

[1] NZIT 1/17/8—the Post Office Savings Bank was opened in 1920; before then money was deposited with the Native Department.

[2] NZIT 1/17/8.   [3] Stace 1956.

[4] The following information has been extracted from Departmental files (WSDF Post Office).

[5] There were then 18,270 accounts.   [6] See Table 20.

TABLE 20

Savings and investment in Malie and Salani, 1964

	POST OFFICE SAVINGS					TRADING BANK		SAVINGS BANK		SAVINGS WITH APIA MERCHANTS	
	Number of accounts	Proportion of 'Aiga	Persons per account	Total in accounts	Average per person	Number of accounts	Amount	Number of accounts	Amount	Number of accounts	Amount
		%		£	£		£		£		£
Malie	15	28	70	7,115	8	2	600	5	50	5	320
Salani	9	29	47	1,330	4	—	—	1	20	2	140
Western Samoa	18,270[5]	—[1]	—[1]	356,204	19	2,012[6]	1,032,000[2]	350[7]	4,000[3]	—[1]	—[1]

	SECURITIES		CO-OPERATIVE SOCIETIES		CREDIT UNIONS		DEPOSITS WITH MISSIONS		EXPORT[4] CROP LEVIES	HOARDINGS	
	Number of 'Aiga with securities	Amount	Number with savings	Amount	Number with savings	Amount	Number with savings	Amount		Number of 'Aiga	Amount
		£		£		£		£	£		£
Malie	2	150[9]	3	50	2	15	2	55	5,650	All	4,250
Salani	1	50[9]	—	—	1	5	1	32	2,500	All	1,220
Western Samoa	—[1]	—[1,11]	—[1]	10,050[8]	—[1]	1,250[10]	—[1]	—[1]	530,000[4]	—[1]	400,000[3,12]

TOTAL SAVINGS

	Amount per capita	Amount
Malie	£13	£5,247
Salani	£18	£18,170
Western Samoa	—[1]	—[1]

NOTES TO TABLE 20

1. No available figures, or insufficient evidence for an estimate.
2. 13 May 1964. Time and demand deposits. There are no details on the proportion of funds or accounts held by Samoans.
3. Estimate 13 May 1964, Bank of Western Samoa, Files.
4. Banana and Copra Reserve Funds—WSDF, Banana Board, Copra Board. The village share is calculated by their share of banana and copra production.
5. WSDF—Post Office.
6. Bank of Western Samoa, Files, June 1964.
7. Bank of Western Samoa, Files, June 1964.
8. WSDF Co-operative Registry.
9. 1964—Western Samoa Government Stock.
10. WSDF—Credit Union Registry.
11. In 1963 £71,000 was remitted overseas—WSDF, Economic Development Secretariat.
12. Estimate made by subtracting money in circulation from money issued —Bank of Western Samoa, Files, 1964.

does not mean that there is proportionately as little savings. Savings accounts are held for convenience in these villages by the *'āiga* and the accounts are much larger than the national average of approximately £20. In Malie the average account size is £474 and in Salani £147, and accounts are regularly used.

As significantly there are alternative savings facilities which absorb far more cash than the Post Office savings bank. First, during the German and early New Zealand administrations money was deposited with the Department of Native Affairs for safe keeping, and most missions also accepted funds.[1] Again, many villagers and urban Samoans have had trading bank accounts since the early twentieth century, and especially since the Second World War. In the period 1959 to 1964 the number of accounts at the Bank of Western Samoa has tripled.[2] At the end of 1964 twenty-five new accounts were being opened every week almost entirely by Samoans. When the trading bank established savings bank facilities in 1964 many people opened accounts. Considerable sums of money are also deposited in co-operative thrift societies, in credit unions, in the merchants' savings schemes[3] and particularly in the compulsory savings held by the Banana and Copra Boards. Lesser

[1] NZIT 69/87.   [2] 849 to 2549—BWS Files.
[3] Three-quarters of the purchase price of expensive items was required by most firms.

amounts are deposited with insurance companies and building societies.

Finally, in the countryside a great deal of money is saved without any reference to European institutions. These hoardings, as we shall call these savings, are often deposited with the village *fono* (for a specific village project), the village women's committee, the village pastor or with individual chiefs. These *'āiga* or village savings are kept in strong-boxes or stored away with *fa'asāmoa* valuables, often under piles of fine mats. Also every *'āiga* and many individuals have their own little black box, piggy bank, or purse where money is stored away. Although estimates can only be made of the extent of national hoarding it is undoubtedly considerable. The bank is constantly importing coin to make up for the withdrawal of coins in circulation whilst note issue always far exceeds note circulation.[1] Certainly in Malie hoardings are worth more than £3 10s. per person. In fact, when all forms of savings, at least in Malie and Salani, are added up, the total is at least three times as high as the administration's estimate and high in comparison with most under-developed countries.

The extent of savings in introduced institutions has been underestimated in modern Samoa, and the existence of large *fa'asāmoa* savings has been ignored. The reasons for any restrictions in the levels of savings, especially in European institutions, have also been misinterpreted. We have already pointed out that there is no inherent incompatibility between the values and institutions of native society and the accumulation of cash or goods in the cash economy, partly because communal demands are restricted, and partly because attitudes and behaviour in the kin economy are separated from attitudes and behaviour in the cash economy. The main reasons for restrictions in savings have little to do with native society.

Apart from the inadequacy of educational facilities, an important reason for restricted savings is the inadequacy of banking facilities. Banking and savings facilities have always been concentrated in Apia. Branch offices of the Post Office savings bank and trading bank have only recently been

---

[1] In the period 1960–4, £560,000 of notes were issued. The average note circulation in 1964 was about £120,000 (BWS Files). The bank estimates that allowing for note depreciation about £250,000 of notes and £150,000 in coin is hoarded.

established in other areas and are only open for very restricted hours. A new mobile unit introduced by the Bank of Western Samoa has had great mechanical troubles and has not yet become an important instrument of savings.

There is some reluctance amongst villagers to use existing facilities, but not simply because of a weak desire to save. In some cases suspicions are simply misunderstandings, as in the case where a man regularly takes all his savings out of the bank to count them. But there are real defects, too, in the banking system. Deposits with the Department of Native Affairs ceased when a notorious administration officer embezzled native funds. Under the New Zealand administration particularly, there was a great reluctance to use the Department of Native Affairs because it was firmly believed that the Administration was merely trying to deprive Samoans of their rightful rewards. The Post Office savings bank, the trading bank, insurance companies, etc., are also felt to be European devices for exploitation, especially since all monies are invested overseas. Again, especially in the case of the Post Office savings bank there are too frequent and widely publicized defalcations.

Savings, of course, are not true capital unless invested in capital goods. And uninvested savings do not help, indeed hinder, economic development by withdrawing potential purchasing power of capital. Economists and administrators in Samoa have often claimed that Samoans are prevented by *fa'asāmoa* values and institutions from investing savings or other funds. This claim is used to rationalize the administration's overseas investment of native savings. 'The Samoan is not a capitalist,' said one administrator, 'he doesn't realize that money has value; it is something to spend on eating and boozing, or the relatives. He doesn't think of the future, only *fa'asāmoa*. He doesn't realize that he would be better off if he used his money to buy tools or fertilizers or invest it in some securities. He sells the future for the present.'

This assumption is in many respects a misconception. First, there is much inexpensive, but economically significant, technological capital in all villages. Working tools, hammers, axes, shovels, steel fish hooks, etc., are possessed by all *'āiga* in Malie and Salani.[1] And the villagers regard such items as

_____
[1] See Appendix 1.

necessity goods to be purchased and maintained as a first priority. Admittedly, there is a shortage of certain equipment, for example, spades and wheeled equipment. But this is largely because *fa'asāmoa* equipment or methods can do as well. Hardwood digging sticks are more useful for people who do not wear shoes or who only wear Jandals (a rubber Roman sandle made in Hong Kong). Human carriage is appropriate where loads are light and where the jungle has few paths and fewer roads.

Again many villages or *'āiga* possess more important and expensive technological capital usually bought without outside assistance. In 1964 all villages had copra driers, many had cocoa kilns or fermentation vats.[1] Fencing, drainage, and the use of fertilizer and pesticides greatly increased in the post-war period despite official indifference to requests for assistance in the form of tariff reductions, etc. Some villages bought tractors and trucks.[2] As we shall shortly see, village traders and entrepreneurs often have extensive capital equipment such as bakery ovens, refrigerators and warehouses.

There was also a great expansion in the post-war period in what is sometimes called 'social overhead' capital, that is, transport and power systems. Several villages have established and maintain their own electrical plant.[3] All villages extended or improved main roads or built access roads using local labour and makeshift materials sometimes without supervision. By 1964 only two villages[4] were without road connections to the outside world and all villages had access roads to their gardens. Many villages on their own initiative have built storage sheds for cash crops, or wharves and jetties where water transport is more convenient or profitable than road transport. Many villages have bought battery radio sets to enable them to hear of banana shipping movements and one village is installing a radio telephone to facilitate marketing.

Most of this technological capital is financed from hoardings, usually from village or *'āiga* funds. One reason for this is that it is difficult to make withdrawals from the Post Office savings

[1] WSDF Agriculture Department.
[2] 334 were registered in 1964 (WSDF Police).
[3] e.g. Sala'ilua, Samata.
[4] Tafua, Uafato. In the period 1956–63 official road mileage increased from 98 miles to 201 miles (WSDF Public Works).

bank. Often people also feel that Post Office savings should be kept for a 'stormy day', that is, in reserve for some future disaster. Most people keep running hoards, constantly withdrawing and replacing funds. There are many reasons why people spend their hoardings. Spending minimizes the risk of theft and stops the declining purchasing power of money which all villagers complain about. More significantly, people realize that unspent hoardings have no productive use. 'I leave the money in my house,' said one man, 'and it gets cold.' In Malie it is estimated that approximately 30 per cent of all hoardings are used for the purchase of technological capital. Other hoardings cannot be used for capital expansion because these funds are usually earmarked for subsistence contingencies.

Although the limited use of hoardings for productive purposes is one reason for restrictions in capital formation, a more important reason is that very little assistance in capital formation can be obtained from outside the village. Until very recently there have been very restricted official sources of credit. There are records in German times of small sporadic loans from the administration to Samoans, but these seem to be largely bribes for the good behaviour of high chiefs.[1] Although the Samoa Act of 1921[2] provided for Government loans to Samoans there was very little change in the early days of the New Zealand administration and all official lending ceased with the outbreak of the Mau rebellion (1925–36). The question of credit for the villages was raised again when the copra industry was organized officially after the Second World War and when a copra reserve fund was established. But the idea was dismissed on the grounds that the copra industry needed protection from overseas market conditions before capitalization, that the Samoans had no securities to offer (despite the existence of the copra fund itself and hoardings), and would probably spend any credit on ceremonial.[3] Some administration officials even argued that Samoans do not want credit, or technological capital, since Samoans feel that this is an alien invasion into the privacy of *fa'asāmoa*. Whilst it is true that some chiefs are suspicious of European credit, and the influence the lender acquires thereby, this feeling

[1] GCA XVII/AI/V3/36.   [2] Section 23.
[3] NZIT 87/7.

is largely the result, as we shall see, of the unscrupulous behaviour of some European moneylenders rather than any distaste for capitalization. Indeed the various government departments are daily overwhelmed with requests from villages for various capital projects.

The administration also explain their policy by claiming that credit and capital assistance to villages is in the form of expert advice or technological capital itself rather than in the form of cash. Villagers, they say, are not able or knowledgeable enough to convert cash into productive capital. This is not even a true representation of administrative practice. Relevant expert advice and suitable technological capital are almost as scarce as government cash. There are severe deficiencies in standards of advice[1] and the amount of technological capital, and very great deficiencies in the deployment of it. Again as in the case of cash, Samoans cannot easily gain access to this capital. Government departments or at least the influential people in these departments, are Europeans or part-Europeans with whom villagers have little contact or rapport. When meetings do occur they are usually held in an atmosphere of distrust and suspicion which seldom has productive results.

The following table indicates the sources of credit in Malie and Salani in 1964.[2]

TABLE 21

Sources of loans (cash and credit)
in Malie and Salani, 1964

	MALIE		SALANI	
SOURCE	Amount	Proportion of total borrowing	Amount	Proportion of total borrowing
	£	%	£	%
Credit Union	5	—	—	—
Relatives	618	24	230	22
Traders	1,850	75	750	78
Total	2,473		980	

[1] See Ch. 1.   [2] See Table 21.

The credit unions,[1] which have been established in recent years mainly by the Roman Catholic followers of Father Garvey of Fiji, were taken over officially by the Justice Department in 1960. But the scheme in 1964 was only of minor importance. Only 172 Samoans belong to the twelve existing credit unions, eleven of which are located in or near Apia.[2] The available capital from subscriptions or permitted borrowings totals less than £1,500, and most loans are for insignificant unproductive purposes. For instance, in the village of Solosolo in 1964, money was spent on repairing a school roof, mending a truck tyre, allowing a man to get new batteries for a radio, for another to buy an eye-shade, for another to buy a bottle of motor oil, but most of the funds seem to have gone on regularly transporting the Treasurer to deposit the union's funds in Apia. An important reason for the weak development of credit unions, as in the case of co-operatives, is that Samoans are suspicious of all European schemes, especially when the administration from Apia takes over. Most people do not understand the complex legal regulations surrounding the unions. Many people do not like the investment of their subscriptions by the Justice Department. Many people are disappointed that more money is not available from official sources even when adequate securities can be found.[3] Most people imagined at first that their credit unions would, in some mysterious way, usher in a new age of prosperity. Societies are called 'paradise' (*parataiso*) or 'riches' (*fa'a moni*). When paradise or wealth does not materialize people lose interest. As a result of all this, although visiting experts put considerable pressures on villages to establish credit unions, the village *fono* generally rejected these overtures.

A third official source of credit is through loans approved by the Justice Department, generally from the trading bank or big firms, to purchase land or capital equipment. But either these agencies will not lend to Samoans or will lend on most disadvantageous terms. For instance in 1962 only 64 out of the 210 approved loans went to Samoans. The bank will only give a mortgage or lend money to Samoans who can

---

[1] WSDF Justice Department for the following.
[2] The exception was the Monono credit union.
[3] Borrowings could be no more than 50 per cent of subscriptions and deposits.

offer freehold land or a regular job with a salary over £500 as a security. Some firms will not lend to Samoans at all, whatever security they have. Those who do make loans charge high interest rates (10 per cent or more) or insist on difficult terms such as complete repayment within six months. Some firms use loans as a lever to secure a monopoly over a cash cropper's produce, sometimes at fixed, sub-market values, or to insist that traders buy all their goods from the firm at hyper-wholesale prices. This procedure, though within the law, has been criticized by the administration but the firms explain that such apparently harsh terms are necessary to insure against the supposed risk of non payment of debts. In fact, there have been very few (under 5 per cent) cases of Samoans defaulting on the original debt, though many cases where the trader's debt to the Apia merchant is a continuing one, necessitated by the trader's need to do business, and his legal obligations to do it with the Apia merchant who lent him the money in the first place. The only exceptions are the loans from the missions or Public Trustee. The missions, for example, do not usually take any interest. But in 1962 there was only one mission (Mormon) loan and only two small mortgages from the Public Trustee.

Because of official indifference Samoans are forced to look for other credit facilities, all of which have their restrictions and special problems.

First, there is the *fa'asāmoa* solution of borrowing from the local *'āiga* or from the far flung *'āiga* overseas. Borrowing from relatives has some advantages. Although, as we have seen, all borrowings have to be returned, these loans can be spread out over a period of time. There is no, or little interest on cash borrowed, which can be returned in goods or services, or if the lender prefers transformed into a *mea alofa* (gift) for which the donor only receives prestige or status. Court action, though not complaints to the village *fono*, when a person fails to repay a debt to his relative are rare. There are, however, disadvantages which make *'āiga* credit of lesser significance in the structure of Samoan credit.[1] Relatives in the village, like the aspiring borrower, are usually looking for cash or transforming it into prestige-bearing goods rather than lending

[1] See Table 21.

it or giving it away to acquire prestige. Money-lending is also a lowly valued activity, associated with Europeans generally and particularly with the Chinese, who live in the back streets of Apia. It is thought to be an activity that always involves an element of dishonesty, and can involve the worst of *fa'asāmoa* sins, an attempt to deceive and exploit relatives. The relatives who have more money live abroad, and although, as we have seen,[1] they are usually quite willing to lend or give money, the borrower has to go to the trouble of writing a long explanatory letter or sending a token gift. Then he has to wait a month for the return air-mail letter. Finally, all Samoans know that there is a chance that money will be extracted from the letter by an overzealous customs man, or a light-fingered person at the airport, or at the Post Office.

Consequently borrowing at high interest rates from part European village traders or Chinese money-lenders in Apia flourishes despite official prohibition. Many of these traders and money-lenders are considered credit-worthy by the trading bank and are able to borrow money at around 6 per cent interest rate, which is promptly lent to Samoans at interest rates of between 15 and 80 per cent. Again many Samoans, especially those dependent upon a fluctuating cash crop income, are forced to pledge their new seasons crops to traders and storekeepers at even higher interest rates. The result of this credit dependence on high interest unofficial sources is indebtedness, defaulting, and possibly the origin of the myth that the Samoans are not credit-worthy.

The reliance on the traders for credit also restricts the kind of capital a Samoan is able to acquire. The traders, or at least the back-street or village traders who always give credit, concentrate on the sale of consumer luxuries. Much capital equipment, especially the more expensive technological capital, can only be acquired from the larger merchants or the Government who are very much more reluctant to give credit. This credit situation has two significant and detrimental effects on capital formation. First, potential deposits on capital purchases are frozen and potential cash crop production to pay for purchases is curtailed when these purchases are not made. In Malie, one reason for the large size of hoardings in most

[1] See Ch. 7.

'*āiga* is that much money is earmarked for future capital purchases which are currently prevented by tight credit. Potential restriction on cash production is less significant as there are usually other reasons for continuing cash production. Secondly, potential deposit savings are occasionally diverted into ceremonial expenditure. This is partly because credit on ceremonial goods is easily acquired from the back-street merchants or village traders. It is also because high status through the ceremonial distribution of goods is the ultimate ambition of most Samoans. Capital formation to obtain more goods is to a considerable extent simply an intermediate step in attaining status. Many Samoans feel that if capital formation is not possible any savings should be used directly to secure status through ceremonial disbursement. 'If I cannot get a ladder to pick all the bread-fruit on the tree, I will stand and pluck the lower branches,' as one chief put it.

Conversely, the economic success of Europeans or part-Europeans can be explained in terms of the easy credit terms and constantly available advice and assistance that exists as part of the social relationships between Europeans.

A final reason for the low level of expensive technological capital is the unsuitability of much equipment for island conditions and the inadequate repair facilities. Tractors for instance are not very useful on the fragmented Samoan soils and this is an important reason why there are few of them. Again, many fertilizers do not work in village conditions. European fishing tackle is not suited to the sudden offshore drops found in both Upolu and Savai'i. But much more important is the paucity of servicing and repair facilities, especially for moving equipment. Even the most common spare parts for tractors or outboard motors have to come from Australia or New Zealand, and in all areas delivery can take over a year. The story is told of a chief in Malie who ordered a spare part for an outboard motor attached to his canoe. The part arrived five years later, by which time the chief had died, the canoe had rotted on the beach, and the parts of the out-board motor had been re-used for a hundred different purposes in the village. The part was eventually worn by the chief's grand-daughter as a pendant round her neck.

Similarly Samoans understand well the profitability of

investment of wealth and capital to realize interest. This is one reason why interest accounts in the Post Office, and recently the Savings Bank, have been popular means of savings, though the Samoans think that interest rates are too low (2–2$\frac{1}{2}$ per cent) as it is known that these funds are reinvested in overseas securities at much higher rates of interest. But less than one half of Samoan savings, at least in Malie,[1] are in interest-bearing accounts; there is only a very small Samoan investment in high interest overseas securities; and a very large amount of savings obtain no interest.

The concentration of savings in low interest accounts and the absence of high interest investment to a large extent reflects the availability of savings institutions. Some Samoans think the Post Office savings bank or the trading bank savings accounts are the only means of saving. Both institutions are not anxious to publicize each other, or any other, competitive facility. Many Samoans, however, know of higher interest rates in trading bank deposit accounts, and particularly in Government securities, stocks and shares overseas. In Malie and Salani such knowledge was transmitted to the community by two chiefs who had returned from New Zealand where they had taken night courses in accountancy. Others obtained this knowledge through their involvement in the co-operative movement and one '*āiga* found out about investment by reading a second-hand paperback novel about the big business world of America. But although many people know about high interest savings facilities, most do not know that small investors can enter the market or how to go about investing their money. Investment activities, either in Apia or overseas, are considered to be part of a European world in which Samoans are not well received, or in which Samoans can easily be fleeced. Investment in Apia is associated with the lawyers or the bank officials all of whom are considered to be the merchants' creatures. There is very little contact between these people and the villagers. The few Samoans who have attempted investment say that bank officials will not see them, or quickly reject any ideas of assisting them with investments, even when they have accounts and are willing to pay for assistance. The lawyers are greatly mistrusted, both because they are considered

15   [1] See Table 20.

to be helping the merchants to make a profit, and because they have been associated with a number of unsuccessful defences of Samoan murderers.

A clear example of the great interest of Samoans in high interest investment when easy investment opportunities are available, was the Western Samoan Government loan floated in July and August 1964. This $5\frac{1}{4}$ per cent ten-year stock was the first loan ever to be advertised in the villages (through the press) and special facilities were laid on in Apia for investors. Although the minimum subscription was £50, and all multiples were of £50, the loan was oversubscribed. It was said that every village in Samoa contributed. The overwhelmed officials explained that the great response was the result of Samoan patriotism, rather than fiscal interest, for this was the first Government stock issued in Independent Samoa. However, most people in Malie and Salani who contributed to a subscription said they were more interested in making money. Many in fact thought the loan was a New Zealand not a Samoan affair, since the stock was suggested, underwritten, and managed by official New Zealand agencies.

There are also a number of explanations for the large amount of money apparently saved without interest. First, no interest is given to villagers for the considerable funds in the copra and banana reserves (over £600,000 in 1964), or in the co-operative or credit union funds or sometimes in unofficial mission or government savings schemes. Interest on cash crop funds is ploughed back into reserves, though in the case of the Copra Board only after deducting running expenses which are not, like most Government departments, drawn from Treasury funds. Similarly, interest on co-operative and credit union funds are generally absorbed in running expenses and liabilities.

Secondly, hoarded money does produce some monetary returns. Most hoarded money does not lie idle for long. Apart from expenditure on, or reserves for, technological capital or ceremonial, a proportion of hoarded money is used for gambling, in *fa'asāmoa* or introduced games, or overseas lotteries. Samoans certainly enjoy gambling but most confess that the real reason for the habit is that they want to make money more quickly than can be made from cash cropping, wage labour or capital formation. Gambling is a carefully calculated risk. Most are only prepared to play a fixed proportion (about 10 per cent) of hoardings and other forms of savings are left untouched. The most popular gambles are in small scale village games[1] where odds are thought to be high, where all stakes are known to stay in the village without any middleman profit. The recognized drawback to village games is that the small size of village incomes limits the size of stakes and prizes. Consequently many villagers also like to gamble occasionally in Apia, on important inter-village rugby or cricket matches, at the races, or to send money to relatives in New Zealand to purchase tickets in the national New Zealand lottery, the Golden Kiwi. Gambling outside the village accounts in Malie for less than 10 per cent of all gambles. Villagers explain that since the odds are much longer than in village games a small stake has relatively as much chance of success as a large stake.

HUMAN CAPITAL

There are, then, important means of technological and wealth capital formation relative to local needs in modern Samoa. Restrictions in savings and investment can largely be explained by factors outside the village, particularly administrative indifference, incompetence, and insensitivity to local problems, rather than by obstacles in *fa'asāmoa* society. Similar comments can be made about human capital formation.

Fa'asāmoa values and institutions are not usually a significant obstacle to the acquisition of productive knowledge. Samoan thinking is not generally, and certainly not in economic activity, irrational It is true that traditionally Samoans saw supernatural forces behind most natural processes. But to a large extent these forces were regarded as ultimate rather than immediate causal factors, or as means of explanation when there was no obvious empirical alternative. For instance, agriculture was seen to be in the hands of a number of tutelary dieties. The most important of these *O le sa*, incarnate in an owl, was considered to be responsible for the rain, and for the success of crops, and there were numerous *tapu* and prohibitions

---

[1] Notably cricket, billiards, and particularly cards and dice games. The *fa'asāmoa* game of *lafoga* played with coconut discs was also played.

designed to ensure his full co-operation. But there was also an extensive body of knowledge, a solidly pragmatic lore to ensure that economic activity was in fact successful. Names and properties of trees, plants and soil types, marine life, were well known. Great care was taken in planting to make the most of edaphic and micro-climatic conditions. Conservation was well understood. There was similarly an extensive lore in other branches of economic activity.

Traditionally there were also means for teaching and developing these practical skills. General knowledge and especially gardening skills were either taught informally in the '*āiga*, or more formally after puberty in the young men's ('*aumāga*) groups. There were no regular lessons in these groups, instruction was practical, and on the job, and seems from all accounts to have been effective.[1] More specialized training was given in special institutions, resembling medieval guilds,[2] which taught 'apprentices' a wide range of skills involving the manufacture of technological capital. 'Guild' training operated within the context of the '*āiga* system. According to informants in Malie, in each village there would be at least one '*āiga* whose chief was an expert house builder, canoe builder, or manufacturer of fishing equipment, and in some villages each '*āiga* was defined by an occupational specialization or expertise.[3] In these specialist '*āiga* there were several apprentices, either sons of the house or young men with special aptitudes who affiliated and often married into the '*āiga*. As in the young persons' groups instruction was practical. Although all guilds, and indeed all '*āiga*, had tutelary deities, these took care of ultimate destinies rather than immediate economic problems.

In modern times traditional lore has declined. The missions especially were anxious, wherever possible, to replace local magical knowledge with European scientific knowledge, and the administrations often consider the introduction of scientific knowledge to be part of their civilizing mission. Possibly these activities have had some benefits; Ma'ia'i[4] has suggested that a constant reading of the gospel has given Samoans a strong sense of causality. But often the Europeans in removing magical influences discouraged traditional practical lore as

---

[1] e.g. LMSB11F5.   [2] e.g. Buck 1930: 6.
[3] See Ch. 9.   [4] 1960: 199.

well. The decline of this pragmatic traditional lore has had bad rather than beneficial consequences particularly in agriculture. The decline of traditional cultivation methods (especially the conservation *tapu*) has been an important contributing factor to the serious conservational problems found in some villages. The decline in canoe building has contributed to the shortage of fresh fish and consequently to the problem of malnutrition. The replacement of traditional houses where air circulated freely, with unventilated wooden or lime wall houses has contributed to the problem of endemic respiratory disease.

The conclusions of the psychological tests regarding the illogicality or prelogicality of Samoan thinking, are also extremely dubious, not only because they were given to small, quite unrepresentative, samples but also because they were saturated with European influences which made results in a Samoan environment invalid. For example, some of the tests[1] involved the manipulation of unfamiliar shapes or the interpretation of ink blots (Rorschach) or the standard Thematic Apperception Test pictures. To many Samoans, Rorschach tests were only mirth-provoking meaningless ink blots whilst the TAT pictures were curious representations of strange Europeans or unfamiliar countrysides which evoked no *fa'asāmoa* sensation and only confirmed the Samoan's impression of the peculiarity of the *pālagi*. The rather hard-headed Samoans are reluctant anyway to disclose any fantasies they might have. For many people think fantasies are the pastime of the idle or the mentally defective.

There is much evidence to suggest that increasingly Samoans do desire knowledge, especially productive knowledge. Any villager, male or female when asked for their greatest ambition for themselves or their children will always reply, 'a good education'. When the first schools were established by the missions there was intense competition for places. The New Zealand administrators were astounded[2] at the. crowds that turned up when they opened the administration schools after the First World War. When New Zealand, League of Nations, or United Nations experts came to inspect the territory they were overwhelmed with petitions for more and better education and

[1] e.g. Cook 1942(a), (b).   [2] NZIT 13/1/7.

violent objections to any restrictions on education such as the introduction of compulsory school fees. The Samoans say they want their children to go to school not only to learn but also so that they will know how to become rich and not be exploited by the Europeans. It is generally believed that the key to the European's success is his superior training. 'The Europeans', said one Samoan, 'are no better than us but they have learnt more, they know the magic of money, and when we find out the secret we will have as much of the good things as they have. We will be able to stop them strangling us.'

Particularly since the Second World War the demand for education has increased and education has become an important reason for urban migration. In Malie and Salani every second young person in 1964 left the village to go to school in Apia or overseas and all primary school children in the village expressed a desire to go to secondary school. Since the war the competition for places in higher educational establishments has become very great. Obtaining a place in a secondary school or equivalent institution is highly regarded in the village and thought to be worth a feast comparable in importance to the feasts given for the birth of a first child. Those who obtain entrance to the teachers' training college, to the Suva medical school or to a New Zealand or American university qualify for a large village feast.

The desire for knowledge also has an advantageous effect on primary school education in the village. Because there is a desire for knowledge people go out of their way to see that village activities do not interfere unduly with the children's schooling. Attendances are low in some areas certainly, but there are reasons other than the distractions of the village for this. To a large extent the low attendance figures reflect, as we shall see shortly, the unsuitability of curricula and the low standards of teaching and teaching equipment. In many areas the low attendance figures also reflect the European teachers' poor adjustment of timetables to the seasonal cycle of economic activity, and their failure to adapt to the demands made on younger labourers by migration or commuting to the towns. Again, whilst it may be difficult to study in the village, because of noise, poor lighting, etc., whenever books come into the village they are eagerly read and passed from hand to hand until they fall to pieces. People read avidly whatever book they can get their hands on.

Far more relevant to the low levels of productive knowledge than any obstacles in native society are the deficiencies in mission and administrative programmes in both basic education (that is, literacy, the three Rs, basic general knowledge, scientific principles, etc.), and particularly in vocational or practical education (that is the teaching of subjects relating to cash economy activities).

The missions were almost always the pioneers in the educational field and by 1964, despite losing much ground to the administration, still controlled most pre-school education and had a very great influence on primary and secondary education.[1]

The major defect in basic education in mission schools is the heavy bias towards those biblical subjects which help the mission's main task of propagating the gospel, or subsidiary tasks of training pastors, but which do not have a great deal of relevance to the modern world. Again the standard of teaching is not high, being in the hands of slightly trained Samoans or missionaries who are not usually trained teachers. There is also, apart from the Mormon mission, a great shortage of funds and so teaching materials, school buildings, etc., as well as the teaching are of a low standard.

But there are also some significant by-products of mission education, often overlooked by critics.[2] First, the missions are largely responsible for the relatively high level of literacy found throughout Samoa. Secondly, the mission schools alone provide pre-school education in the general absence of parental ability to help in this respect. Thirdly, and most significantly, the missionaries usually thought the economic development of the native people to be a part of their task of propagating the gospel and spreading enlightenment. From the first missionaries, instruction has been given in practical subjects. Many of the early missionaries were in a definite sense only artisans with strong convictions. In all missions the virtues of thrift and industry have been inculcated, whilst in the self-supporting

---

[1] In 1963 (WSDF Education) approximately 36 per cent of primary school (including intermediate) and 60 per cent of secondary school pupils went to mission schools.   [2] There is a good summary in Ma'ia'i 1960.

Roman Catholic estates training is given in all aspects of plantation management. Everywhere advice and protection against exploiting Europeans is available.

There are also serious defects in administrative educational programmes which have remained largely unchanged since 1945. The first major deficiency, despite the prominent place of education in total expenditure, has been the small size of government spending both in comparison with spending in other countries, and in view of the need for teachers, schools and teaching materials.[1] A second major deficiency lay in the content of basic education in the administration's schools. Broadly speaking, the curricula has reflected the administration's belief that the best foundation for economic development is a European style education similar to that found in the metropolitan country. But often European curricula have little relevance to village life and are consequently a hindrance rather than a help to educational development. For instance, it is difficult for children to learn much, or sustain an interest in learning, when the readers used tell stories of robins in the snow or train trips to London.

Although a European type education is considered to be essential the administration find it easier with a predominantly native staff to use the vernacular as the primary vehicle of instruction for basic education. The use of the vernacular aggravates the difficulties which the European style curricula creates. The literature in the vernacular is very restricted. Much of the literature, because of the missions' predominance in vernacular publishing, is religious in nature and the non-religious materials are restricted to a few uninspiring 'potted' classics, such as *Treasure Island, King Solomon's Mines*,[2] etc.

A third major deficiency is the low calibre of teaching staff. Most teachers have a very limited competence and there are many reports of teachers who are literally only two or three pages ahead of pupils. There are a number of reasons for these poor standards. Bad teachers are the product of poor secondary education and particularly of poor training facilities and low wages. Teachers enter the profession at a lower wage than a labourer. As a consequence the Education Department

---

[1] £8 per head of population compared with £45 in New Zealand (1963).
[2] Ma'ia'i 1957, 1958(a), (b).

cannot attract able personnel, and there is a constant danger of losing trained personnel. Staff shortages force the administration both to employ personnel who might normally have been rejected and to overwork staff. The problem is aggravated by the fact that overseas personnel cannot be found to fill key positions or train staff.

Consequently, although the Samoan learns to read and write in government and mission schools he learns little else which has meaning in his daily life or which stimulates or helps him in learning after he leaves school. The effect of basic education on most people is ephemeral and a few years after leaving school many people cannot manage even simple textbooks or manuals in the vernacular let alone specialist works in English.

The most significant reason for the low levels of productive knowledge are the deficiencies in vocational or practical education, that is in the training of specific skills for activities in the cash economy.

First, agricultural education does not occupy a prominent position in school curricula at any level, least of all at the primary level which contains most of the student population. There are a few small, mainly mission institutions devoted entirely to the teaching of technical subjects but most have only been established since the Second World War. Programmes of agricultural extension (demonstrations, model and experimental farms, etc.), though much publicized,[1] are available to only a small proportion of farmers. Similarly, there are few facilities for commercial training. The official courses and night classes can cater for only a handful of pupils. The missions have started commercial classes and a trade school but these have been forced to close through lack of funds. People receive technical or commercial training on the job, informally in the offices and workshops of Apia and the standard of such training, if it is available, is not high. The whole field of adult education is also seriously deficient, particularly in subjects which have a direct relevance to economic development. There is little attempt to adjust the content and techniques of the few programmes there are to village conditions. Too often the subject of courses (flower arrangement, table

---

[1] For example in the South Pacific Commission Publications: (WSDF Education Department).

setting, etc.) has little relevance to village life or to economic development. Meanwhile programmes which do have some relevance to development, especially community development programmes, fail, as we have pointed out, mainly because of the shortage of competent personnel and their unfamiliarity and lack of rapport with village society.

The absence of facilities for practical education has other effects on economic development. Though it might be true, as it is sometimes argued,[1] that a European-based 'humanist' education (as non-practical education programmes are euphemistically called) produces a dynamic desire in the people to improve themselves, 'to pull themselves up by their bootstraps', such an education also produces consequences which are detrimental to economic development. For example in Samoa, if it produces anything such a humanist education produces a distaste for rural or manual activity and a desire and aptitude for white-collar jobs. The basis of the economy, the agricultural sector, receives too few able people. There are other detrimental effects. In the minds of the well educated Samoan the 'humanist' education produces a conflict. In most cases there is an antipathy to *fa'asāmoa*, a desire to become a European and in many cases to migrate abroad. For example, one out of four of all scholarship students sent to New Zealand since 1945 have abandoned Samoa to return to New Zealand and many of those who are still studying in New Zealand try every means possible to extend their grants.[2] Some have stayed as long as fifteen years. Occasionally European values are rejected, often when antagonisms develop between white teachers and Samoan pupils. In these cases a person returns to the village and refuses to have anything to do with the European world.

The Samoan, then, has very limited access to practical knowledge. Practical knowledge in itself has only limited economic value unless there are also means whereby this knowledge can be applied. In Samoa a further serious deficiency is that the few Samoans who are able to acquire practical knowledge have too few chances to use this knowledge. There is no room, for instance, in the agricultural department for graduates of the agricultural college. A return to village cash cropping is also made difficult since there

[1] Evans, 1962.   [2] WSDF Public Service Commissioner.

are no means of obtaining capital to run a plantation or because European superiors look down on a man who 'goes native again'. There are few jobs in Apia for those with special industrial skills, for example carpenters, especially if these people do not have enough capital to buy tools for themselves. People with school certificates sometimes have to take jobs running messages or making tea.

Education, though the most important, is not the only means of diffusion of knowledge in modern Samoa. Another contributing factor to the low levels of productive knowledge, especially basic knowledge, is the weak development of the informal channels of communication. Mass media are weakly developed. In 1964 there was a radio station which transmitted approximately fifty hours of scheduled broadcasting per week including four hours of school broadcasting to an estimated 6,000 receiving sets and 60,000 audience.[1] But nearly half the programmes are in English, which because the vernacular is the primary vehicle of instruction, is not well understood especially in rural areas. Most of the radio sets are in the towns where there is electricity, and are owned predominantly by Europeans or part Europeans who demand English programmes There are other reasons for the predominance of English programmes, such as low costs and the unfamiliarity of overseas or local European radio officers with village society. Again, apart from short daily broadcasts to schools, national programmes consist of non-productive knowledge, largely music or soap opera. The number and circulation of newspapers is restricted and their content consists largely of non-productive consumption knowledge. The weekly *Samoa Bulletin* and the *Samoana*, published in both English and Samoan by commercial interests have a combined circulation[2] of approximately 9,000 but consist mainly of advertisements and comics. The other papers, with very small circulations, are the monthly *Gazette* of Government announcements (*Savali*) and the various mission papers containing church news and sermons.

Another serious deficiency, in the general absence of adult education programmes, is the sparsity of literature available to those who want to obtain general or technical knowledge. Apart from the book box system operated in the schools and

---

[1] WSDF Broadcasting.   [2] WSDF Statistics.

the public library in Apia there are no lending libraries in the territory. The mobile unit from the public library seems to be constantly in mechanical trouble. There is only one book shop run by the Methodist Mission, selling mainly religious books and classics. In other shops, war and western comics predominate. Films, though reaching a wide audience through mobile projectors (estimated 300,000 per annum)[1] consist entirely of consumption knowledge of a very low standard. The merchants who control most of the mass media claim that the reason for the poor quality is that the Samoans themselves demand and enjoy it. This assumption, however, has never been tested and the merchants will not risk what they call 'highbrow' films or books. For most villagers film-going is an exciting social pastime, a chance for young men to meet young girls, for older people to gossip or doze, while reading is a pleasurable and relaxing recreation. To a large extent it is the actual film-going or reading rather than the material in them that is important. For example, when the Health Department brought out a film on the life cycle of the mosquito, there was as packed a house as when Dracula showed the week before, and the older chiefs and their wives who normally slept through the film were wide awake, even taking notes, on the subject which affected village welfare. Many villagers in fact complain about the standards of films which they say are boring, immoral or unchristian. One man said he only goes to the films to see what swines (*pua'a*) the Europeans are to each other and in particular to 'coloured people', the Red Indians, the Japanese soldiers, etc. Another man thought the films were a deliberate European device to implant feelings of European superiority in the Samoan mind and he was agitating to ban mobile film units from the villages.

The most important way in which knowledge is spread is through the circulation of the population. Passengers, letters, and drivers on buses and boats running to or from Apia into the rural hinterland carry news from the town and abroad. In more isolated areas *fa'asāmoa* mechanisms, such as the *malaga*, the ceremonial travelling party, are important means of communication. Recently the Health Department has successfully used the *malaga* to spread information.

[1] WSDF Statistics.

The informal diffusion of knowledge in Samoa, then, does not contribute positively to levels of productive knowledge. Indeed it can be argued that the consumption knowledge which predominates has adverse effects. The glossy magazines, the comics, the motion pictures all exude an impression of affluence, of high consumption levels, acquired without apparent effort. This helps to stimulate demands for luxury wants and dulls demand for utilitarian goods or knowledge, as well as over-emphasizing spending and leisure and under-emphasizing saving and work.

Health can be regarded in a similar way. Traditionally[1] many Samoans thought that some diseases were supernaturally caused and cured, directly by a spirit or ghost (*aitu*) or through the instigation of another human being. These beliefs and practices did not, however, always lower standards of health. First, there were recognizable psychological therapeutic benefits from magical treatment. More significantly only a few serious diseases were explained completely in magical terms and in all diseases physical cures were used as well as magical cures. There was an extensive range of local pharmaceuticals, many of which had been empirically tested and known to produce the desired results. Medicinal herbs were imported from as far away as Tonga. Massage (*lomi*) was extensively used for the relief of pain and masseurs were highly skilled and greatly respected full-time specialists. Surgery was occasionally used. In certain diseases known to be epidemic, sick persons were isolated, and possessions and sometimes the person pushed out to sea in a canoe or boat. In recent years the category of magical diseases has shrunk or has been absorbed into European medical categories, most significantly germs being equated with spirits.

Even where magical categories remain they are not usually antithetical to modern health programmes. For germ theory and magical explanations are not explanations of the same type. First, magical explanation is not primarily a theory of immediate causation, as in fact germ theory is, but of ultimate causation, of not how a man contracted such and such a disease, but why he did and at that particular moment. Secondly, magical explanations and cures are concerned primarily with the social

[1] The best account is in Kramer 1902 v. 2.

consequences of diseases, not its physical causes. If a man becomes seriously ill, especially if he is a young man his sickness may seriously disrupt the normal pattern of social activity. Consequently the explanation of his misfortune is in terms of the forces (usually *aitu* spirits) which are considered to disrupt society. For example, blindness in youth has even today a magical explanation, but blindness in old age, that is when the disease has fewer social consequences, when disruption due to disease or death is expected, has no magical explanation. Serious illness is also socially part of the rites surrounding death. Many of the gifts brought to a sick man are redistributed when, or if, he dies. Death is the only time when the spirit world is thought to significantly affect or control the person.

Because magical explanations and germ theory are explanations of a different kind they are not contradictory or incompatible. In Malie, European germ theory is accepted and cures are eagerly demanded. The people say that what they want is good health so that they can make money quickly and that all they are interested in is the quickest cure for any malady. The people queue for hours outside the district hospital or village dispensaries for drugs, particularly penicillin, which are known to relieve troublesome and debilitating symptoms, especially staphlococcal infections. But although European physical cures are accepted the people still often explain the ultimate causes and social consequences of disease in terms of their own social idiom.

A more important reason for the failure of health programmes and bad health are deficiencies in the medical programmes themselves. An important factor contributing to poor health is the weak development of public health and sanitation facilities. Equally significant are the shortages of adequately trained staff, and shortages of drugs and equipment. The content of health programmes is also often unsuitable for village conditions. Too often inadequate explanations are given of why a measure should be introduced in a village. For example, in explaining why privies are necessary, too often vague 'sanitary' reasons are given. As a consequence, the people do not build the privies or else build them to please the administration and do not use them.

The more important reason for the failure of health programmes is the resistance in the villages to the health workers. This is largely due to mutual misunderstanding and mistrust. Outsiders are suspected because they are assumed to be agents of the Government prying into village life for some nefarious purpose. Local savants resent the outsiders' knowledge and standing, and attempt, often successfully, to alienate the village. They and the villagers often consider, or claim, that their own cures are often better for certain diseases. Too often health workers are contemptuous of the beneficial psychotherapeutic aspects of traditional medicine and the considerable physical properties of the local pharmacopoeia. Again overzealous health workers rouse opposition by trying to prohibit insanitary and deeply ingrained habits like tobacco chewing, whilst possibly continuing to smoke themselves. This estrangement means that there is an unwillingness to confide in outsiders and even a fear of them. For European, or part-European doctors are thought, like the traditional spirits, to cause more diseases than they cure. And in a sense, for certain diseases this belief is not without foundation. The European doctor who insists on the lonely isolation of a tubercular patient, for example, in a bare white-washed room far from the familiarity of friends and family, causes tremendous psychological stress and undoubtedly many unsuccessful cures. Finally, because outside health workers do not generally understand native society, they can rarely really use the intricate, highly charged undercurrents of village politics in putting programmes across.

The employment of local Samoan doctors and nurses has been more successful. This scheme was begun in the early New Zealand administration because of the difficulties of securing adequately trained European staff. Selected villagers are sent to the medical school at Suva for a three year course and nurses are trained locally at the Apia hospital. But the administration has never backed the scheme fully or attempted to extend it. The main reason is that the administration fear that the pressures of *fa'asāmoa* will prevent the doctors or nurses carrying out their medical duties properly. But *fa'asāmoa* does not usually have adverse effects on the Samoan doctors' or nurses' duties. The doctor is usually greatly admired, even venerated for his knowledge and given the respect due to a high title. He occupies in the village a similar position to the village pastor, and indeed the dispensaries and hospitals which the villages build often resemble churches. Also, like the pastor, whatever respect the doctor receives, his authority in all matters is always subordinate to the chiefs in the village. The chiefs cannot officially appoint or dismiss the doctor but they can make life unbearable, even physically dangerous for him. The chiefs' demands are not usually great. A doctor receives house and food, but there is no demand for a goods or cash payment. The only services the doctor is expected to provide are his medical services. The chiefs do not interfere in medical matters provided the doctor does not violate any deeply held *fa'asāmoa* principles. It is thought to be a doctor's job simply to cure illnesses with drugs. The ultimate cause of the illness or any social consequences of disease are beyond his scope. In his physical cures, whatever the medical necessities, the doctor cannot transgress the *fa'asāmoa* rules of rank and respect. For example, chiefs cannot be told to vacate houses, however insanitary, or miss important ceremonial whatever diseases they have, or suffer such indignities as a bowel wash.

Relatives are not usually a problem either. It is usually recognized that a doctor should be able to levy a fine on a relative or secretly carry out the job himself. 'The doctor', said one man, 'is not my brother today, he is the doctor, when he comes home at night he is my brother.' Many local doctors in fact use *fa'asāmoa* institutions, for example family gatherings and prayer meetings, to put across health propaganda and many use their *'āiga* as an example to introduce new ideas into the village and to allay fears in other *'āiga*.

Provided the doctor makes the gesture of respecting the chiefs he can succeed in introducing most drugs into the village and more significantly he can command a confidence that remains whether the drugs have any effect or not. If a drug succeeds, the doctor is greatly praised. When it does not the people will explain away the illness in terms of factors outside the doctor's control, the malevolent *aitu* (spirits), fickle fate, the immorality or carelessness of the patient, faults or mistakes made by the European manufacturers of the drug. Confidence in the doctor generally increases as the doctor moves closer to *fa'asāmoa* norms, as he participates in ceremonial or marries, or accepts a chief's title. There are only slight restrictions on the degree of involvement. The doctor is expected to be a man of learning, devoted to healing, and unmindful of ambition for himself or his relatives or the acquisition and display of wealth. When a doctor strives for *fa'asāmoa* status too stridently or helps relatives too obviously in ceremonial disbursement, whispers will start in the village that the doctor is using his position and perhaps medical funds for personal or *'āiga* aggrandizement. The doctor's medical popularity will then wane and pressure will be put on him to relinquish his job. Consequently most local doctors, if they accept a title, usually accepted an honorific *Ao* title which absolves them from familial duties and the chicanery and manoeuvrings of local politics.

Conversely, the doctor who spurns *fa'asāmoa* is seldom successful. If he is not actually run out of the village or stoned in his house, few people will come to him for treatment, ostentatiously going to Apia or to a doctor in another village. When people do go to him and are cured they will claim that they would have got well anyway, or if they are not cured there will be dark mutterings of poisoning or attempts to infect the patient or charges of wilful incompetence.

16

9

TRADING INSTITUTIONS

WE have discussed the relationship between *fa'asāmoa* society and production. But, production itself is only part of the economic process, and only one way of earning income in the cash economy. Resources, labour, and capital have not only to be produced and prepared for sale, but actually sold, exchanged for the cash which leads to increases in consumer goods and services. Exchange as this process is usually called, especially the scale and incidence of exchange in a society, directly affects productivity. A corollary of increased exchange is increased specialization. Through specialization concentration on subsistence production declines and exchange is further stimulated. Specialization also increases individual skills, saves time in production and stimulates invention and technological development. Increased exchange also directly affects production by stimulating demand, through the introduction of new goods, and work effort, and through the expansion of wants. Most significantly increased exchange necessitates the introduction of a versatile exchange medium such as money which further facilitates exchange.

In the opinion of many economists and social scientists increased exchange also leads to greater individual freedom and consequently greater production. Trade, by expanding the range of social relationships outside the village, 'shatters' the inhibiting traditional reciprocities, and results in an expansion of production and a heightened 'pecuniary incentive'. Increased exchange and individual freedom also involve the introduction of notions of contract (that is a binding obligation between individuals) which is necessary if an individual is to secure the right to the reward for his efforts.

FA'ASÁMOA TRADE AND EXCHANGE

Trade and specialization were part of *fa'asāmoa* tradition and in many cases these traditions have adapted to or exist with introduced exchange institutions.

There are many reports of a large number of specialists (*tufuga*) in traditional Samoa, i.e. persons who produced part of a good, usually an essential part, and who obtain their livelihood by exchanging their specialized goods and services. People in Malie knew of thirty-six kinds of specialist occupation all of which carried a chief's title.[1] The Samoans themselves explain the frequency of specialization as the best way of using the best man to do the job. 'A coconut crab (*ūū*) has claws to climb the tree, but the fish has not. So the crab climbs and the fish does not try.' Admittedly only a small number of these specialists were occupied full time.[2] This was largely a reflection of prevailing economic conditions. Traditional demand for any product was limited to the village or neighbouring villages (i.e. usually less than 500 people) because the weak development of the traditional transport system (there was no wheeled transport) restricted the movement of specialists themselves or their finished products. Part-time specialization also reflected the low level of technological capital formation and labour requirement needed for most economic activities, especially agriculture. Every man could easily find time and the necessary means to provide food for his family. As transport facilities have improved since the coming of the European, the number of specialists has increased. In all villages Samoans now devote most of their time to cash cropping, wage labour or entrepreneurial activities, using the cash so acquired to use other people's specialist services or goods. The main reason for the decline of certain kinds of *fa'asāmoa* specialist has simply been that their productive functions have been taken over by other Europeans, notably the traders.

Similarly, though it is true to say that *fa'asāmoa* specialists were associated with particular *'āiga*, often as their chiefs, this did not restrict occupational mobility. The *'āiga* was not an endogamous caste or even an hereditary descent group.

---

[1] See Table 22.

[2] The canoe builder (*tava'a*), housebuilder (*tufugālima*), doctor (*taulāsea*) and the fishing expert (*tautai*).

Affiliation to any '*āiga* was possible for all Samoans and succession to title reflected ability first and foremost. In the case of the specialist '*āiga*, affiliation and succession to specialist title usually reflected an aptitude and ability in the particular specialization.

Again although it is true to say that these specialist services were often called on through kinship relationships, it is possible to argue that this was basically an economic relationship, involving definite notions of price and contract expressed in a

TABLE 22

Fa'asāmoa specialists[2] (Tufuga)

Branch of economic activity	Specialist activity	Specific job
1. Agriculture	**Suāu'u**[3]	Making coconut oil
	Māsoā	Making arrowroot
	Matau	Adzemaker
	Tao	Spearmaker
	'*oso*	Making digging sticks
2. Clothing	**Siapo**	Barkcloth maker
	Lega	Preparing turmeric dye
	Lama	Preparing lampblack dye
	'Ie	Making wearing mats, etc.
3. Fishing	**Tāva'a**	{ Canoe builder / Small canoe builder
	mātau	Fishhook maker
	'Upega	Netmaker
	Lā	Sailmaker
	Faga	Fishing pot maker
	Māunu	Fishing bait maker
	Foe	Paddlemaker
4. Housing and household utensils	**Tufugālima**	Housebuilder
	Taumete	Wooden utensils
	Pola	Screen and blind maker
	'*Ato*	Basketwork
	Fala	Sleeping and day mats
5. Medicine	*Foma'i, Taulāsea*	Doctor
	Taula	Priests
	Fofō, Tagata lomilomi	Masseur
	Taulāitu	Spirit medium

TABLE 22 (*cont.*)

6. Political and prestige	Tupe	Maker of the Tupe
	Tatātau	Tattooer
	Tatosiau	Making tattooing instruments
	Selelaula[1]	Barber
	Tanafa ma auta	Drum maker
	Ta uatogi	Club maker
	Tafue	Flywhisk maker
	Tao	Spearmaker
	Savali[1]	Messenger
	Tōga	Making fine mats
	Lagaili	Fanmaker

KEY
(*a*) Words in heavy type indicate that these specialists are still found in many villages.
(*b*) Words in italic type indicate that these specialists are occasionally found.
(*c*) All other categories are no longer found as specialists.
1. Attached only to High Chiefs.
2. See Ch. 7 for full definition of specialist. These are generally people who are regarded as highly skilled in a particular activity and are given the special name indicated.
3. Not traditionally a specialist.

kinship idiom. For example, when a master house-builder[1] was brought in to help in housebuilding he was in a definite sense paid for his services with food and shelter, with gifts before and after the job was done, even if he was a close relative. The house-builders would not start the job unless the initial payments were satisfactory and would not finish the job if the host's funds ran out, or if they were considered inadequate. Conversely, if a satisfactory initial payment had been made the builder was in a definite sense bound to honour his obligation. If he did not, he would face gossip in the village and possibly disciplinary action from the *fono*. Similar comments could be made about other specialists.

There were also examples of regional specialization and trade, in the sense of an exchange of goods based on supply and demand in which economic equivalence or advantage was sought. Throughout Samoa there was traditionally a

[1] This was the villager's (Malie) account, but is confirmed in the literature: Stair 1897: 142, Kramer 1902 v. 2: 221, GCA 1/17b.

regular barter relationship between coast villages and inland villages involving the exchange of marine products for root crops. According to informants in Malie each coastal village had traditionally an inland counterpart; sometimes a section of the coastal village. The inland villages usually managed their own affairs and provided a retreat for the coast villages in times of war, as well as a source of food.

Particular regions or villages also specialized in particular products,[1] Falealupo and Asau in 'ava (kava) bowls, Safotu in 'ava (kava), Manono in cuttlefish hooks, Malua in fine mats, Vaiulu'utai in adzes, North-East Savai'i in dyes, South Upolu in arrowroot and tobacco. There were also larger trading circuits[2] between Samoa, Tonga and Fiji involving the 'export' of bowls and mats and the import of shells and herbal medicines.

It is true that this trade was commonly, though not always, conceptualized in terms of the kinship system. The people say that trading was done through relatives between whom bargaining was thought to be shameful. But again this was often only an idiom by which a basically economic relationship was expressed. In Samoa any person with whom one has continuous and friendly contact is 'āiga, a relative. In traditional Samoa many trading relatives never met as exchange could be a form of 'silent trade' in which piles of goods were left at a certain spot by each party. Many of these and other exchanges were single, discrete transactions in which equivalence could be obtained. There were pressures which made for equivalence in exchange and the honouring of obligations. One of the most important of these was public opinion. If payment was not sufficient, scurrilous epigrams would be circulated which would greatly insult and disgrace the offending village or party.

Such forms of trade, then, were governed very largely by pressures of supply and demand and although perhaps not overtly, equivalence in exchange was considered to be important. On the other hand trading was peripheral to economic activity. Markets or middlemen did not exist and unlike the cash economy, trade was confined to certain goods (not land,

[1] Some of these regions are reported in the literature Kramer 1902 v. 1: 66, 107; v. 2: 157, 288, Wilkes 1847 v.2: 149, NZAJ 1874, 1/34/32, Brown 1910: 305.

[2] These circuits are mentioned also in Stair 1897, Ch. 12, Labouret 1953: 28-9, Ella 1899, though there are no details of how trading was carried out.

labour, etc.) whose transaction did not affect the future use of production factors. More significantly the majority of exchanges were admittedly not primarily governed by such distinctly economic pressures. The majority of goods were exchanged between opposed groups in the social structure ('āiga, villages, village sections,[1] chiefs,[2] chiefs and commoners, certain types of relatives[3]) and were part of a continuous system of prestation and counter prestation in which the regulation of the kinship and political system was more important than economic needs. Goods involved in either side of these exchanges were strictly defined. Goods defined as tōga,[4] goods made by women, were always exchanged for goods called 'oloa,[5] goods made by men. The exchange of these goods did not reflect individual wants but expressed the symbolic separation and identification of these opposed social categories. These categories and their relationships were defined with reference to fundamental symbolic structures in Samoan society. Male categories dispensed 'oloa. These groups included the bridegroom's 'āiga (during marriage and subsequent birth celebrations), chiefs, especially chiefs victorious in war or chiefs who held high mamalu or malo (prestige and power were symbolically associated with the penis), and village sections lying to the front of the village (i.e. the area associated with chiefs' ceremonial sitting positions, cooked food prepared by men). Tōga on the other hand, was always given by the bridal 'āiga, or any person or groups imbued with extensive tapu (which was often associated in song and legend with the female genitalia), the landward section of the village (the source of uncooked food, the sitting positions of unmarried men). Included in these exchange relations were not only goods but courtesies, entertainment, ritual, women, children, feasts, etc. Persons involved were usually particular categories of kin, or kinds of chief (ali'i, tulāfale) and the occasions for exchange were generally occasions of social significance such as rites

[1] Some villages contained up to five sections (pitonu'u), discrete territorial segments containing related or friendly 'āiga. In other villages including Malie there were two or three opposed groups of 'āiga.
[2] That is between ali'i and tulāfale chiefs.
[3] e.g. mother's brother and sister's son.
[4] That is mats, baskets, barkcloth, skirts. Cf. Turner 1884: 179.
[5] Food, tools, canoes, etc., and occasionally land. Ibid.

de passage or important political events. Economic advantage or merely equivalence in exchange was not thought desirable. On the contrary, the man or group who gave most, gained most in terms of *mamalu* (prestige). Liberality was a prime virtue and acquisitiveness a despised trait. Equivalence was in any case in a definite sense very difficult to attain, for unlike 'trading' relations, *tōga-'oloa* transactions were not discrete, but parts of a continuous relationship in which one gift begot another.

Similarly, as we have seen in previous chapters other types of exchanges of goods or services, exchanges within the kinship circle, the obligations to and from chiefs were not trading relations as we have defined the term. For in all cases, the people involved and the occasions for exchange were socially defined, and in most cases liberality was considered to be proper. But these exchanges had secondary functions which were essentially economic. First, as we have pointed out in previous chapters, all types of exchange were reciprocal. Indeed it has been argued, notably by Polanyi[1], that the dispersal of goods in kinship reciprocities, or through chiefs, was an essential means of distribution in a society without markets or traders. Secondly, in large scale ceremonial exchanges particularly, the barter of goods was often an underlying theme. For example, unlike most *rites de passage* certain socially insignificant ceremonials[2] could take place at any time. People say the occasions chosen for these rites were often occasions when goods possessed by people with whom the rites were being celebrated were desired. More significantly, at all important ceremonials goods were bartered and Samoans say that they desire the goods that they will receive on such occasions.

The expansion of trade was not, in fact, limited so much by notions of value and contract as by the areal coincidence of supply and demand in a relatively homogenous environment. Because trading institutions were not highly developed, money in the modern economists' sense was not found. But some traditional goods had some of the characteristics of modern money.

Modern economists consider money to have three important characteristics.[3] First, money should have a wide range of

---

[1] 1957: Ch. 12.
[2] For example, feasts given by the mother's brother for the sister's son.
[3] e.g. Croome 1962. Cf. Dalton 1965.

exchangeability, that is to say, it should be capable of expressing the exchange value of most goods and services in the economy, and should be liquid enough to command purchasing power over them. Secondly, money should express the different exchange values in common terms, that is to say, money should be a standard unit of account. Thirdly, money should provide a store of wealth potential and purchasing power.

It has to be admitted that what is sometimes called money in Samoa (for example, fine mats *i'e tōga*) does not fulfil or fulfil completely certain of these criteria. For example, the exchangeability and liquidity of fine mats was restricted both with regard to the occasions and people involved in exchange, and to the types of goods which could be purchased. Fine mats which formed the most important part of the *tōga* category of goods were only used on the occasions when *tōga* and *'oloa* goods were being exchanged. On such occasions, as we have said, there were definite rules as to who should give and who receive fine mats, and what goods should be received in return for them.

However, because most goods and some services (especially specialist services) could at some time be exchanged for fine mats these mats were an indirect standard of reference for the exchange value of goods and services, and a means of exercising purchasing power, especially as fine mats were used to obtain food which in turn could be used to obtain other goods and services.

If fine mats were an indirect standard of reference for exchange values they could less easily be a standard unit of account. Each mat had an individuality (mats were often named) and could not be consistently expressed in terms of other units. The value of a mat depended traditionally not on any objective criteria such as size or fineness of thread, but on historical association, particularly the rank of previous owners whose *mamalu* had been absorbed and the extent of usage in important ceremonial. Consequently, the relative value of any mat was different at different times.

Fine mats were an important store of wealth in an economy where most wealth was in perishable foodstuffs. Fine mats were durable, easily stored and lost no value in storage. In fact, the older the mat the more valuable it was.

CHANGES IN FA'ASĀMOA INSTITUTIONS

Trade, specialization and in a certain sense, money, were then part of the traditional *fa'asāmoa* economy. These *fa'asāmoa* institutions have persisted, adapting to conditions in a cash economy.

First, some *fa'asāmoa* specialists have reappeared in new forms, turning old skills to new purposes and conducting business essentially in the traditional manner. For example in Malie, house-builders, using labour paid with wages or employed under traditional apprenticeship schemes[1] build most of the village houses, whether Samoan or European style, generally using *fa'asāmoa* technological methods.[2] The initial payment for the house is made as traditionally at a feast. Today cash (usually about 10 per cent of the estimated cash cost of the house) is given to the builder at this feast but fine mats are distributed too. The people say that the exchange of fine mats seals the contract and they claim that this agreement is far less time-wasting than the European methods of signing contracts which involve much time and tedious paperwork. In traditional fashion the employing *'āiga* attends to the felling of trees and the transportation of any materials to the site, after the builder has selected or bought materials. The *'āiga* also provides the unskilled labour throughout the job or the cash to enable the builder to raise extra hands. Payments of goods (*'oloa*) and shelter continue during the housebuilding. There are also payments, generally in cash, amounting to approximately 10 per cent of the total cash cost of the project. These sums are paid at an agreed time-interval, possibly weekly but more often, as traditionally, by piecework at definite stages of the job.[3] Any European or local goods purchased or bartered are paid for at the time by the employing *'āiga*. Finally, when the house is completed the balance of the money is paid and a final feast held. At any stage the builder, even if he is a close relative, can stop work if funds

[1] i.e. where a young man affiliates to an *'āiga*.

[2] People only build cooking houses (*fale umu*) and boatsheds (*fa'asoata*) themselves. Manual methods as described by Buck 1930: 30 ff., were common.

[3] The main stages and their traditional names were (1) *Elega pou*—digging holes for poles or foundations for European houses, (2) *Fu'a tuga*—placing of the poles, (3) *Fuatuatuga*—completion of sides, (4) *Fa'aetaguanau*—completion of ridge poles, (5) *Vaega Pulutuluga*—placing the rafters, (6) *Sunuga-o-so'a*—lashing the rafters, (7) *Usuaga*—completion.

run out or if these funds are considered to be inadequate. If the employer is not satisfied, he can appeal to the village *fono*, or to the Lands and Titles court, though very few appeals come before either body. The employer does not usually want to be called mean, whilst the builder does not want to lose potential business by getting a reputation for extortionist prices or broken contracts.

The kin relationship between the house-builder and the employer does not affect the arrangement. The house-builder's services and profits, as in any other form of cash earning activity, are considered to lie outside *'āiga* demands. *'Āiga* who try to use their relationship to secure a builder's services without specific payments are scorned in the village as mean people, while those builders who give their services without payment are said to be 'soft in the head' or doing an inferior job, unless sickness or great debt prevents the *'āiga* paying.

Builders of small canoes,[1] masseurs, tattooers, traditional doctors, basket, barkcloth, tool and ornament-makers all sell their services in the contemporary village in the *fa'asāmoa* manner, usually collecting payments in cash or kind by specified instalments before, during and after the job, and receiving at least one ceremonial feast and one fine mat.[2]

A number of *fa'asāmoa* specialists also sell their services in the outside world to Europeans. For example, in Malie small canoes (*paopao*) are made for overseas Europeans who want to fish or take home a piece of 'real Samoa'. Introductions are made through relatives in Government departments. The deal is discussed in *fa'asāmoa* fashion in the village at a feast provided by the European buying the canoe. Samoans think that this feast should be *pālagi* (European) style, that is that there should be beer not *'ava* (kava) and food bought in Apia rather than in the village. Another difference from *fa'asāmoa* practice is that there is only one payment (though seldom completely in cash) when the job is finished and the European comes to collect the canoe.

There are also *fa'asāmoa* handicraft specialists. Mats and baskets are manufactured in the villages for tourists and the

---

[1] See Table 22.
[2] Payments were usually in goods and cash. For example in Malie 1964, for a small canoe 2 5-lb tins of pisupo (beef) plus £10 cash.

curio market, usually by the women. Woodwork experts continue to make items of traditional culture for the same market using new tools and techniques. Traditional craft experts have also taken up new crafts, such as shell and toothbrush[1] ornaments, and even silverwork. In general, however, these handicrafts are sold in *pālagi* (European) rather than *fa'asāmoa* fashion, that is by payment at one direct sale rather than by cash instalment, feasting and fine mats. Most handicrafts are sold in the village to itinerant merchants and often the villagers are so glad to have the cash from the merchant's fat wallet that they provide the feast. Some handicrafts, especially ornaments, are sold by vendors on the verandah of a large store in Apia.[2] These goods are sold mainly to local Europeans and particularly to tourists who come on the fortnightly banana boat or the occasional cruise ship, or who stay at Aggie's Hotel.[3] These vendors, corpulent ladies, who sit on the verandah from Monday morning to Friday night also sell *fa'asāmoa* products particularly *suāu'u* (coconut oil in Coca-Cola bottles) and plaits of *tapa'a* (Samoan tobacco smoked in long cigars). For the tourists and Europeans, terms are strictly cash, but for the local Samoans, for *fa'asāmoa* products only, terms are more elastic and food is accepted for bartering and credit given for at least one purchase. Since these ladies are virtually the only and certainly the cheapest source of such indispensable luxuries as coconut oil and tobacco, debts are usually repaid.

The inter-island canoe trade routes had certainly disappeared by 1964. One important reason for this situation was the declining demand for Tongan or Fijian products (for example, medicines, ornament shells) which had been replaced by European goods which had become as easily obtainable in Samoa as anywhere else. There is still much inter-island exchange of goods which are not easily procured locally. Much of this traffic is carried on by migrants or travelling parties who crowd as deck passengers on every available form of transport in and out of Samoa.[4] But the Samoan crews of

---

[1] i.e. ornaments made from toothbrush handles.   [2] See Table 23.

[3] Aggie Grey the manageress is, according to local legend, the Bloody Mary of Michener's *South Pacific*.

[4] These deck passengers provided their own food and beds (mats) for a cost of £5 to Tonga or Fiji on Union Company ships.

TABLE 23

Sales of Samoan handicraft and accessory[8] vendors[1]
September, October 1964

Type of goods	Quantity sold	Amount of sale
		£. s. d.
Necklaces—shell	252	25 5 0
Bracelets—shell	105	20 3 0
Basketwork	151	15 4 0
Plaited goods[5]	104	10 3 6
Polished seashells	107	10 0 0
Necklaces—bead	47	8 5 6
Plastic ornaments[2]	27	3 2 6
Carved wooden goods	17	2 2 3
Other coconut goods[3]	6	0 18 6
Other shell goods[4]	5	0 17 3
Coconut oil (*Suau'u*)	742 bottles[6]	74 8 0
Local tobacco (*Tapa'a*)	283 coils[7]	14 3 0
Total		184 12 6
Average sale per vendor		26 7 6

1. There were seven vendors who regularly sold on the Apia Streets. All were old women (average age 60) from Apia (4) Aleisa (1) or nearby villages in North-West Upolu. These seven vendors congregated outside the Burns Philp store under the awnings. A small number of handicrafts were sold singly by children walking up and down the street or occasionally by fruit and vegetable sellers. The period during which sales were checked was claimed to be representative of all 1964 sales, according to vendor's estimates. This estimate is probably accurate since there were in the two-month period exactly one-sixth of all tourist ship arrivals for the preceding twelve months. An estimated 80 per cent of total sales occurred during the period when the tourist ships were in the harbour.
2. Mainly broaches and pins made from toothbrush handles and sunglass rims.
3. Balls, gourds, nets, brushes, etc.
4. Ornaments, purses, etc.
5. Mainly place mats, etc.
6. Standard price of 2s. for Coca Cola bottle.
7. Standard price of 1s. for a coil.
8. By Samoan accessories we mean those *fa'asāmoa* goods which Samoans no longer manufacture for themselves but still greatly desire.

these ships also carry considerable stocks of goods, mainly clothes, tools, and luxury goods including liquor, purchased from the Suva Indian traders. These goods are easily smuggled ashore, or sent by canoe to a neighbouring village where they are quickly disposed of amidst great feasting and excitement, or sold more quietly to the local trader.

In some areas the coast-interior exchange pattern between villages has remained[1] while in many villages there are frequent exchanges of fish and root crops between the coast and sections of the *'āiga* or village now living inland in order to exploit virgin land for cash crops or to be near a European road along the crest of a mountain ridge.

In these exchanges trading parties refer to each other as relatives (*'āiga*) whether in fact they are related or not. But these 'traders' have a very good idea of the exchange value of goods they are exchanging and without appearing to mind are always anxious to drive home a bargain. 'Relatives' might be relatives for only one transaction.

More significantly *fa'asāmoa* kinship exchanges and other ceremonial journeys (*malaga*) have become a very significant means by which goods,[2] especially cash economy goods, are distributed, as well as being the most important mechanism whereby the individual can transform goods into highly desired status. In recent years there has been an expansion in the number of ceremonials and particularly in the volume of goods in them. Traditionally, the volume of exchange goods was limited by transport difficulties. There was no wheeled transport and only narrow tracks through the rain forest or along the jagged coast, whilst navigation was treacherous in the coral seas. Inter-village exchange was restricted to light-weight goods, usually *tōga* goods.[3] But the building of roads,[4] the introduction of a ubiquitous and frequent bus service, a wide range of durable goods, and an even more light-weight exchange medium than fine mats, that is money, made greater and more frequent ceremonial possible.

First, the exchange category *'oloa* has expanded. *'Oloa* now

---

[1] e.g. Fagaloa.   [2] See Table 3.

[3] *Tōga* goods went out of the village on the most important *rites de passage* initiated by marriage since women especially married outside the village.

[4] Now (1964) reaching all but two villages, Uafato and Tafua.

not only includes local foods but also European tinned foods and usually any European consumer goods. The consumption of these European goods through ceremonials forms a major part of consumption patterns and expectations.[1] One man in Malie said, 'We do not buy tinned food these days, someone will soon be born or die.' The acquisition of European goods through ceremonials is favoured for other reasons. The people say that these European goods are made 'more Samoan' by their participation in ceremonial, whereas goods obtained at the trader remain European goods (*mea pālagi*). More significantly, the goods symbolize and connote the festive surroundings in which they are received. Many people also feel that goods received at a ceremonial are rewards for laudable effort and endeavour. Most people will not buy tinned and luxury goods considering that these should only be acquired at ceremonials. The exchange functions of the *tōga* category of goods has also increased. First, as the goods category *'oloa* has expanded, fine mats, which are exchanged for *'oloa*, come much nearer to resembling cash economy money. As fine mats are exchanged for cash economy goods or money which has a precise value they also come to have a more precise value, as well as a greater exchangeability. Since the end of the nineteenth century at least, the use of fine mats as a quasi-currency has expanded.[2] Fine mats came to be accepted for goods purchased in the trading stores at a fixed rate. In the early twentieth century this process was encouraged by the New Zealand administration.[3] In 1916, it was decided that all fine mats should be valued and a trial scheme was adopted to mark all mats with their value. Later it was stipulated that mats should be generally used as payments for goods and services. The Mau disturbances (1925–36) and the administration's prohibition of *fa'asāmoa* ceremonials prevented the full implementation of the scheme but fine mats continued to be used as cash economy money in many villages. For example in Malie today there still remain certain old mats with great historical associations and without a precise

---

[1] Much tinned food is left unopened at ceremonials.

[2] This has been the experience with some other so-called primitive currencies. Fine mats are now much more like the African iron bars and cowrie shells.

[3] The history of these efforts is in NZAJ A4B 1927: 267 ff.

exchange value. But these mats are only used occasionally in high-ranking exchanges. In many other exchanges in the village[1] there are lesser fine mats without names which have a fixed price attributed to them often depending on size and fineness of thread.

Not only have fine mats become more like cash economy money, but also cash economy money has come to be regarded as a form of *tōga* in *fa'asāmoa* exchanges. Many ceremonial exchanges[2] simply involve the movement of European goods *'oloa* against a cash equivalent which is called *tōga*. Most *tōga* money is current local legal tender or New Zealand or United States currencies which are constantly moving in and out of ceremonial relations and being used in cash transactions with the European world. But there are also in some ceremonial exchanges an assortment of obsolete, legally inconvertible European currencies (Tahitian francs, South American currencies dating back to the nineteenth century) which remain solely within the sphere of ceremonial exchange.

SPECIALISTS

The cash economy also introduced a new kind of exchange institution, the market, where, mainly through European traders and merchants, local products and labour are sold and European goods are bought. Samoans generally participate successfully in these market institutions. Most Samoans have become specialists in the sense that they are engaged in the production of part of the good rather than the whole of it. All cash crops are processed after leaving the gardens and there has been a growing tendency to leave the producer with fewer and fewer functions. Even if we accept a narrower definition of specialists as those who sell only their skills[3] there have still been significant increases in the number of specialists. For instance, the 1951 census mentions 615 'skilled native operators' in secondary or tertiary industries, but in 1956, there were 1042 in this category.[4] Admittedly, the proportion of skilled specialists to the total Samoan working population (less than 10 per cent) is low in comparison with Europeans or part-Europeans (about 60 per cent) as is the proportion of skilled

[1] See Table 14.　　　　　　　　　[2] See Table 14.
[3] See Table 17.　　　　　　　　　[4] WSDF Statistics, latest available.

specialists in proprietary and managerial positions. But these figures do not necessarily mean, as they are often taken to mean, that Samoans have little desire or ability to learn specialist skills because of a preference for short-term economic goals, or that they feel repugnance towards profit or wages, or a dislike of working away from the group in an individualist occupation. One significant reason for the relative absence of skilled labour is the tendency in the post-war period for skilled workmen to leave the territory in search of the higher wages and greater opportunities which exist in New Zealand or the United States.[1] Another important reason is the weak demand for skilled tradesmen outside the main town of Apia. This demand situation not only affects people's job preferences in the villages but also their job preferences when they come to the towns. Because many men prefer to return to their villages eventually they see little point in spending long years in learning skills which they might not be able to use at home. Consequently they prefer the quick returns of labouring or more often the prestige or possible power of jobs in a government associated with the European overlord or the local aristocracy through whom the Europeans work. The proportion of white collar government workers, as in many other underdeveloped areas, is high, approximately 4 per cent of the Samoan work force, and absorbs the ablest people into varying degrees of non productive activity. Finally, as we have seen the most important reason of all for the shortage of skilled labour is the weak development of training facilities, especially technical schools or apprenticeship schemes.

MARKETING

Similarly, *fa'asāmoa* society has little to do with the economic problems of marketing. Traditionally there was much contact between villages. Villages were generally exogamous units and often the focii of exchange were widely separated. For example, villages in North West Upolu had traditionally marriage and exchange relationships with villages in South Upolu or Savai'i rather than with their immediate neighbours. Patterns of exchange were also often part of the political systems which

---

[1] WSDF Statistics Department.

17

involved villages of different districts. The coming of the cash economy led to much greater contact between all villages as roads and bus routes opened and especially between the villages and Apia. As we have seen in previous chapters, this world outside the village was socially and economically an integral part of the village and the *fa'asāmoa* social structure.

The main problem in marketing was not, in fact, lack of contact with, or knowledge of the world outside the village, but a technical problem of transport, the solution of which was largely beyond the villagers' control. Traditionally transportation of goods was simple because both the *tōga* goods which moved out of the village, and the most important inter-village trade goods (fish-hooks, *'ava* (kava), dyes, etc.) were light-weight and durable enough to be carried by foot or by canoe, whilst the heavier, more perishable goods, especially foods, were consumed locally. Cash crops on the other hand are bulky, and either perishable (bananas) or require specific delivery dates at specific destinations. The Samoans are fully aware of these marketing requirements for efficient cash cropping. But they often find it difficult to meet requirements because they cannot raise enough capital to buy their own transport or improve roads round the village, or install communications with the town which allow a detailed and accurate knowledge of market conditions and movements. Consequently they are forced to rely on European marketing institutions which are usually very inefficient. For example, in Salani, the messages concerning the arrival and departure of banana boats and growers' allocations on the boats often do not reach the village until the boat has sailed. Even when the message does arrive on time or even a few hours before the boat sails there is no difficulty in preparing suitable bananas for dispatch. The chiefs of each *'āiga* individually, or collectively in *fono*, organize the young men to gather bananas and pack them. This is done, if time is short, throughout the night. If young men are not available for any reason (e.g. working in town) the chiefs themselves will go to the gardens. There are even cases of ceremonial being quietly interrupted to get the bananas off. The troubles begin after the bananas have arrived back from the gardens. Often there are insufficient crates, or nails to pack the fruit because the Banana Board has not sent the materials out in time. There are usually, too, great problems with the part-European contractors who are supposed to pick up the bananas. Most contractors will not work at nights, some never keep their appointments and many run faulty trucks which break down just outside the village. Finally, even when arrangements have run smoothly bananas may arrive bruised and battered in Apia because the roads are in such poor condition.[1] Similar comments can be made about the marketing of other cash crops.

ENTREPRENEURIAL ACTIVITY

The most significant aspect of Samoan participation in marketing (and a very significant index of the compatability of *fa'asāmoa* institutions and cash economy exchange institutions) has been the development of successful Samoan trading, that is activities involving the purchase of cash crops and the sale of European consumer goods and other entrepreneurial (i.e. profit-making) activities. The history of entrepreneurial activity in Samoa has two distinct and interrelated phases. First, until after the Second World War the majority of entrepreneurs were Europeans or part Europeans and the Samoans were generally customers and clients.

In this stage the Samoans were able to do business successfully with the Europeans.[2] Most of the European entrepreneurs were traders, i.e. persons who bought local cash crops and sold European consumer goods. From the arrival of the first traders there were many attempts at the exploitation of villagers, mainly because most European traders were agents of large firms who paid them little or no salary and only a commission on sales.[3] The most common methods of exploitation were fake weights and measures, overcharging and underpaying, circulating[4] coins of debased currency or of high denomination (e.g. shillings—so that no change could be given and so all goods

---

[1] The Banana Board files show (WSDF Banana Board) that the number of rejected cases increases as the distance from Apia increases.   [2] See Table 24.

[3] The early traders were mainly castaways, but increasingly young men, including missionaries' sons, or ex-missionaries, tried to make their fortune by trading. Most of the agents were employed by the German firm of Godeffroy established in 1857 (cf. Schmack 1938).

[4] But this rebounded when Samoans used this money to pay for goods. Churchill 1902: 721.

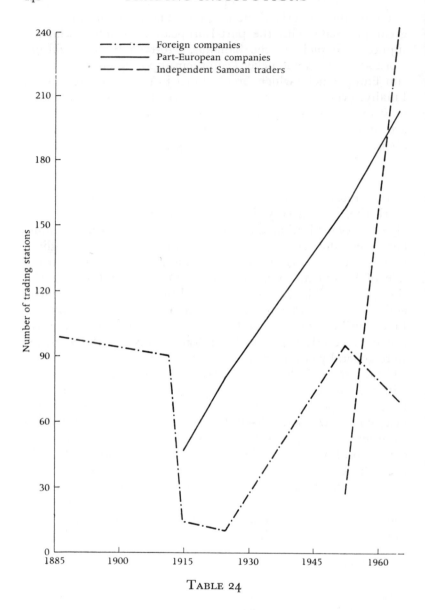

TABLE 24

Growth of village trading in Samoa 1885–1964. Sources: GCA 1/2/3, LMS—Annual Calendar 1915, NZIT 69/78, NZIT—Annual (1952) Report—App. 25, WSDF—Statistics Dept.

had a high minimum price), charging very high rates of interest on any deferred payment or cash loan. Credit was also often used as a means of securing permanent rights over village production. Many villages mortgaged land, or when this was prohibited in 1893, cash crops, sometimes for years in advance to secure goods or cash used mainly for ceremonial.

These attempts at exploitation provoked strong reactions in the village. The villagers generally did all they could to control exploitation and to exploit the trader themselves. There were attempts to secure lower prices for goods, higher prices for copra and easier credit terms. If the trader had already married locally or participated in village society this was done by informal pressures within the *'āiga*, or by direct edict from the village council, the *fono*. The *fono* also attempted to control traders outside village society by prohibiting villagers from buying, selling, bartering or repaying debts until the trader agreed to the villagers' terms.[1] The *fono* also refused to extend its protection to the trader's store and the trader would then be exposed to a constant threat of physical violence from the unruly young men of the village (*taulele'a*) and continual theft. Little redress could be obtained from the European courts who were reluctant to interfere with village affairs. The picture of a bloated village trader exploiting oppressed and abjected villagers was true of very few villages in Samoa. More often dejected and impoverished European village traders[2] were frightened to step outside their huts. They watched stock disappear whenever they turned their backs, slept under the counter at night, and waited day after day looking out to sea ignored by the disapproving villagers.

After the establishment of a centralized native government in 1873 there were also attempts by Samoan leaders to secure wider controls on village trading,[3] and from 1900 the European administrations generally assisted these attempts. Both the German and New Zealand administrations prohibited unfair practices and credit[4] whilst the New Zealanders controlled both retail and cash crop prices and organized the marketing of bananas, and for a time, copra as well.

---

[1] e.g. GCA 2/XVII/B4/V4/51.   [2] e.g. Churchill 1901.
[3] Malietoa Laws, Ch. 11, FO 58/137/81.
[4] The relevant legislation is NZO 5/1924; 4/1924; 1929 and GCA 2/XVII/AI V2/3.

More important than the village control over traders was the active participation of Samoans in trading itself. From 1900 villagers became traders in their own rights. Under the German administration there were a handful of Samoan agent traders and the number increased[1] greatly when part-European companies based on Apia took over the German trading stations during the First World War.[2] There were also a number of attempts[3] by Samoan chiefs to form large-scale co-operatives to market copra and sell consumer goods. These schemes collapsed, partly because of ignorance of business procedures, but mainly because of pressure from the administrations which suspected that the chiefs had rebellious motives as well as entrepreneurial ambitions. The most significant increase in independent Samoan traders, as well as Samoan agent traders, has been since 1945 and especially in the last few years. In 1964[4] there were 400 Samoan village traders (three quarters of all village traders) of whom 240 operated independently. There was also in the post-war period a great increase in Samoan participation in other forms of business, particularly taxi and bus driving, or urban stores.

There were two important reasons for the great increase of Samoan participation in trading. First, there was a general withdrawal of European and part-European traders from the inhospitable villages, or from Samoa itself, to enjoy the urban creature comforts and conveniences of Apia or overseas, or to make profits, greater profits than from village trading, by selling retail goods wholesale to village traders and buying export cash crops from them. Secondly, there was a widespread desire amongst Samoans to become traders. For although the alien trader may have been heartily despised in the village, there has always been a deep respect and desire for European goods. From the first explorers, Europeans have always been amazed at the rapid rate at which moveable objects disappear in Samoa. The desire for goods increased significantly when the affluent United States Marines arrived during the Second

[1] See Table 24. Many of the part-Europeans (e.g. Nelson) were originally village traders.

[2] Notably Nelson's which had been founded by a Swede in 1867. Many of the Samoan traders of this period were connected by marriage with the part-Europeans.

[3] e.g. The Oloa Trading Co. (1905). The Tu'u fa'atasi ma Toeina Co. (1918).

[4] WSDF Statistics. There were six in Malie and two in Salani.

World War, and when a wide range of attractive consumer goods appeared in the Apia stores after the war. Prestige and an aura of sophistication attaches to the man who handles European goods even if he does not make a profit. And if he does make a profit there is not only the opportunity to enjoy a better standard of living, but also the chance to secure or enhance rank which is closely related to the ability of a man to disburse European goods in ceremonial distribution. Trading is also a means of earning money and staying in the village and is preferred to the sweat of cash cropping, if the 'āiga has cash crop land available,[1] or the separation from village society which wage labour usually entails. Taxi and bus driving also usually allow village residence and most drivers live in villages near Apia. Driving is a prestige occupation, as a bus or taxi is constantly travelling to or from Apia or to such sophisticated places as the nissen hut and kerosene lamp flare path of Faleolo airfield where an ancient DC 3 arrives once a week. Ownership of urban stores or companies also carries great prestige, since most people think that such businesses lead to great wealth. Store owners, like other Apia residents, often retain their links with village society, participating particularly in ceremonial activity.

Though the desire to trade is widespread, Samoan entrepreneurs as a group have some particular and non-traditional characteristics. Entrepreneurs are usually relatively young, ambitious men with strong personalities, who have been more exposed than their fellow-villagers to European influences, especially secondary schooling or a job in Apia or abroad. A sample of independent taxi drivers in Apia, for example, indicates considerable physical separation from village society.[2] But most retain their links with village society and some have chiefly titles, sometimes high titles.

In general, Samoan entrepreneurs manage to keep their businesses going within fa'asāmoa society,[3] though approximately one in ten fail[4] and profits are low absolutely and in

---

[1] In Malie and elsewhere, traders were often from 'āiga where there were land shortages.　　　　　　　　　　　　　　　　　　　　[2] See Table 25.

[3] Most accounts of entrepreneurial activity tend to emphasize the importance of 'difference' and non-traditional influences in the development of entrepreneurs—e.g. Cole 1959: 6, Aitken 1965, Barth 1963.

[4] Estimate from Statistics Department, Apia.

TABLE 25

History of independent[1] Samoan taxi drivers, 1964

	Proportion of total sample
	%
1. Job history[4]	
Carpenter	12
Civil servant	12
Labourer	24
Mechanic	6
Shop assistant	12
Plumber	6
Village cash cropping	24
2. Residence history	
(a) Village of birth	
Apia	54
Elsewhere Upolu	36
Savai'i	6
(b) Employment abroad	
New Zealand	30
American Samoa	48
Average duration	18 months
3. Occupation of other nuclear[3] family members	
Abroad	24[2]
Apia wage labour	60
Village cash cropping	12
Other (prison)	6
4. Average age	23.6 years

1. That is self employed and owning a cab or cabs which were officially licensed as taxis. There were eighteen cab owners in the sample, all owning a single cab. These comprised approximately 75 per cent of independent Samoan cab owners. Most taxi drivers (there are 179 taxi drivers in Samoa) were employed by the large firms, only one of which was Samoan. The sample was conducted in September 1964.
2. Proportion of nuclear family members totalling thirty-two in the sample.
3. Parents, siblings, children.
4. Employment prior to present employment.

relation to turnover, capital, etc. The following table summarizes the nature of Samoan entrepreneurial activity in 1963.[1] This modest success is made possible by an adaption to, and compromise with, *fa'asāmoa* society, whilst the major reason for

[1] See Table 26.

TABLE 26

Turnover, profits, and investment in
Samoan businesses[1] 1963

Type of business	Number	Average turnover[3]	Average profit[3]	Profit[10] turnover ratio	Profit[11] capital ratio
		£	£	%	%
1. Village traders	243[2]	521	173	30	28
2. Apia traders	9	8,010[5]	2,005	24	32
3. Bus owners	8	1,410	530	39	25
4. Taxi owners	7	1,405	601	38	33
5. Truck owners	7	928	496	45	26
6. Multiple transport[4]	7	—[6]	—[6]	—	—
7. Traders and transport[7]	6	4,002[8]	1,723	38	26
8. Dressmakers	3	423	105	25	120
9. Plumbers	3	982	331	35	150
10. Carpenters	3	621	143	22	175
11. Bakers	2	723	204	28	25
12. Barbers	2	662	175	24	100
13. Traders and planters	2	1,005	382	35	33
14. Repairs[9]	2	1,111	395	35	30
15. Petrol pump	1	—[6]	—[6]	—	—
16. Tailor	1	—[6]	—[6]	—	—
17. Restaurateur	1	436	89	20	22
Total	307				
Average turnover	£723				
Average profit	£289				

1. Source—Department of Inland Revenue, Apia.
2. In three cases profits, etc., unknown.
3. Average for all in type of business in 1964.
4. Any two or more of categories 3–5.
5. Includes one business with £30,000 turnover.
6. Profits and turnover unknown.
7. That is transport services sold separately from trading business.
8. Includes one firm with £2,980 turnover.
9. Mechanical repairs.
10. Profit as a proportion of turnover.
11. Profit as a proportion of capital expenditure on the business, not including usable stock (e.g. traders goods), labour skills, etc., but including plant, land, rentals, etc.

failure where it occurs, and for the low level of profits, lies outside the village and beyond the villager's control.

Village trading is not *per se* regarded as a *fa'asāmoa* activity, but when the Samoan entrepreneur does business with his *'āiga*[1] as often happens today, the relationship is felt to be part of the *'āiga* relationship. In many ways this relationship is an asset rather than a liability.

First, relatives provide a secure market for buying and selling. Patronage is considered to be part of kinship obligations. Relatives often assist in running the store, help to expand business,[2] or help when the entrepreneur is sick or involved in ceremonial activities, in particular relatives help to take over the store if the entrepreneur has another job in town where he obtains extra cash and possibly valuable experience. Relatives often provide capital to buy the bus or taxi, to build the store, or to increase stock and purchase capital equipment which leads to increased profits. For example, a trader who can afford a kerosene fridge sells a wider range of goods, especially frozen meat, and attracts more custom. A trader who can afford a superior hot-air copra drier fetches premium prices for his copra in Apia. Some *'āiga* recognizing the advantages of *'āiga* co-operation formally register themselves as co-operatives[3] with the Government bureau in Apia, and share any profits which are made.

The entrepreneur is expected to recognize and reward his relation's co-operation and patronage. For example, traders are expected to sell below competitors' retail prices and buy above competitor's cash crop prices,[4] though it is also recognized that the trader should make a profit. Secondly, the entrepreneur is expected to give limited credit for day to day

---

[1] All the Samoan traders in Malie and Salani did business with their *'āiga* in Malie and Salani or with relatives in the neighbouring villages.

[2] One trader was able to use relatives to establish an ancillary bakery, another to run a petrol pump and a bus.

[3] By 1964 forty-eight co-operative societies with retail functions had been registered, of which three had officially closed (Co-operative Register, Apia). Many others, however (including the Malie Society), had run down because of debt, stock shortages, and quarrels. These, however, were largely village societies. The smaller informally run 'co-operatives' described here were much more successful. There were also a number of successful Samoan companies, especially the Kolone Brothers, who included village trading in their activities. See Table 15.

[4] The cut to relatives was expected to be about 10 per cent. This left the trader with approximately a 20 per cent profit.

purchases, and unlimited credit for *'āiga* ceremonial needs, though all debts are contractual and usually repaid. The following table indicates the pattern of trading and debt in Malie and Salani in 1964.[1] Rewards for specific labour services or capital contributions vary with the kin relationship. No reward is expected for capital and services provided by parents or children which are seen as part of normal filial and parental duties. Specific rewards are occasionally expected by real brothers and sisters and usually expected by relatives outside the nuclear family. In the case of traders, labour services are rewarded, as traditionally, by food, from stock. A day's work is rewarded with a meal for the worker's nuclear family. The cash value of the food is always considerably less than the wage that would be expected when working for non-relatives, and the current wage-rate in Apia. Capital contributions are considered to involve greater rights in stock or profits, though limits are recognized, and the price of the capital is still usually much cheaper than loans offered by the 'big firms' in Apia at high interest rates and on difficult repayment terms.[2] If the entrepreneur feels that demands are likely to be excessive, he conceals his stock, or puts his profits in the bank, though these subterfuges often lead to quarrels. A preferred method of acquiring capital is to borrow it from a relative in New Zealand or the United States. Generally this relative is too well off to care about a tin of fish and too far away to doubt the letters telling him that business is very bad, though loans may take time to come through.

Demands for personal contributions from the entrepreneur as part of his *'āiga* obligations are not usually serious. Demands only occur occasionally, when there is a ceremonial (*fa'alavelave*). On these occasions an entrepreneur contributes as much or as little as he wishes, and excessive personal ceremonial contributions are not usually a cause of failure. Where excessive contributions occur they are often deliberate choices, preferences for the social returns, for the status increment of disbursement, rather than the profits, the physical increment of business success. This is particularly true of chiefly traders who feel most keenly that it is their duty to make great contributions on ceremonial occasions and not be outdone by

[1] See Table 27.   [2] e.g. involving purchase rights over cash crops.

TABLE 27

Samoan trading in Malie (May-July) and Salani (September-November) 1964
(all figures percentages of totals)

Type of transaction	Number of 'Aiga[4] involved		Value of transactions		Number of 'Aiga[4] with outstanding debt[3]		Value of outstanding debt		Value of transactions involving relatives[5] of trader		Value of outstanding debts incurred by relatives[5] of trader	
	Malie %	Salani %	Malie %	Salanie %	Malie %	Salani %	Malie %	Salani %	Malie %	Salani %	Malie %	Salani %
1. NON CREDIT												
Barter sale	80	30[1]	8	9	—	—	—	—	6	8	—	—
Cash sale	100	100	48	19	—	—	—	—	30	18	—	—
2. CREDIT												
Normal sale	78	90	24	27	5	0	2	10	18	22	1	0
Fa'alavelave sale	50	60	10	36	15	20	59	29	14	35	8	3
Traders personal credit	100[2]	100[2]	10	9	100[2]	100[2]	39	61	22	17	91	97
Totals	45 'aiga	25 'aiga	£3,942	£655	45 'aiga	25 'aiga	£532	£97	£948	£352	£272	£58

1. During part of the period there was a Sa (Tapu) on coconuts.
2. Proportion of number of traders involved. There were seven in Malie, two in Salani who co-operated.
3. Debts recognized by creditor or debtor to be outstanding.
4. i.e. the local segment of the 'Aiga poto poto.
5. i.e. any relatives but mainly in the local segment of the 'Aiga poto poto.

untitled people or chiefs of lesser rank. When '*āiga* pressures exceed the trader's willingness to disburse, the subterfuges of concealing money in the bank or stock are again used.

Apart from a personal contribution the entrepreneur also usually supplies goods or services for the '*āiga* ceremonial contribution. This contribution[1] varies from a few shillings for small ceremonies of insignificant and distant relatives, to thousands of pounds for a high chiefly wedding or funeral in the '*āiga*, or the use of a taxi or bus for as long as a month. For the more important and expensive ceremonials, and especially for funerals, where there is little time to harvest a cash crop or raise cash, debts, sometimes large debts, are incurred.

These debts,[2] or any other kin debts incurred through normal purchases are, however, not usually difficult to reclaim. It is recognized that any goods supplied for '*āiga* purposes, as opposed to goods which the trader contributes personally, are an '*āiga* responsibility and have to be paid for by the '*āiga*. It is generally thought to be bad to default on debts to relatives, and strong pressures can be exerted by senior members of the '*āiga* or even by the *fono* on the recalcitrant, though sometimes the productive ability of the '*āiga* cannot cover the debt.

The entrepreneur is usually successful trading with '*āiga*, but despite the fecundity of Samoans few have only '*āiga* for customers or clients and many do business entirely with non-relatives or distant relatives. Sometimes untitled traders leave the village because the chief does not like a rival power in the '*āiga* with some control over cash crop production. Rarely do traders leave their village because they fear '*āiga* demands, though agent traders may be prohibited by their employers from trading with relatives.[3] The trader is generally worse off doing business with non-relatives than with relatives, indeed worse off than the European or part-European trader. The Samoan cannot command the same grudging admiration as the European can simply for being European and to some extent he is still exposed to village attempts at exploitation by trading in bad copra, thieving stock and not paying debts. The trader

---

[1] See Tables 3, 14.

[2] By debts we mean here outstanding debts which trader and debtor know would not normally be repaid. Most Samoans had running debts which did not remain permanently outstanding.

[3] They are moved to villages where they do not have relatives.

without relatives does not have any of the advantages of
patronage, or the use of *'āiga* land, labour or capital. Nor,
since no village is more than a day's trip from any other, is he
usually immune from the demands of his own *'āiga* personal
ceremonial contributions, whilst there are strong pressures
on him to affiliate to a local *'āiga* whether he has any local
relatives or not.

Credit is also a problem. Prohibiting or restricting credit
means losing some custom, but debts can be difficult to recover.
The trader cannot usually use formal or informal pressures
in the village, nor is European court action effective. The
courts are usually lenient on debtors, since there is seldom
any documentary evidence (receipts, books)[1] and since the
court (consisting of European judges) mistrusts Samoan
witnesses. The courts will not enforce large debts or debts
contracted by women, and seldom send anyone to prison,
which in any case is regarded as a cheap way of living in town.
There are very few ways of securing debts and making some
recovery in this way. The mortgaging of village land or cash
crops is prohibited in law, and in any case, this security could
seldom be recovered.[2] Most traders try to compensate for the
risk of debt by charging high prices on credit sales.

When Samoans are selling goods to Europeans there are
fewer difficulties. Europeans do not prefer to patronize Samoan
stores in Apia as they are regarded as 'dirty hovels', or use
Samoan taxis or buses which are thought to be inferior or
dangerous. But as part-European businesses have curtailed
their activities, there is an increasing demand for services
which Samoans provide. In general the Samoan vendor does
very well in these transactions. The Samoans do not usually
haggle over price. Most do not care when they sell their produce or services since they have few other demands on their
time (indeed they enjoy sitting on the pavement or in the
store chatting), and since their goods are not perishable[3]

---

[1] Receipts were seldom given or asked for. Books consisted usually of a dog-
eared page where debts and credits were recorded by crossings out in a single
column.

[2] The *fono* would usually not help and there were always other traders who
would secretly take a man's produce. At one time fine mats were seized, but this
was prohibited in the German administration (GCA 17b/16/9/01).

[3] e.g. the curio vendors.

or can be consumed by the '*āiga*. Most know they are operating in a sellers' market, where demand far exceeds the supply of goods or services. The price of goods in fact[1] varies little between vendors, and most entrepreneurs know of, and charge, what they consider to be a proper price for any particular goods or service. Usually this is considered to be a just price, i.e. a fair return to sellers and also a good bargain for buyers since most prices are 20–25 per cent lower than European competitors' prices, if indeed there are competitors.

The pressures of credit and the difficulties of recovery in the village are sometimes important reasons for debt, failure, or low profits, but much more important reasons originate directly or indirectly outside the village. For example, certain serious types of mismanagement,[2] such as insufficient notice of depreciation or insurance, miscalculation of unit costs, poor book-keeping can be attributed to the almost complete absence of commercial education facilities. Business competence is important but even the most competent, and those who have established good trading relations with the villagers, are usually unable to make more than slender profits because the margin within which they operate is so very small. In a definite sense the most important reasons for failure or low profits result from the monopolistic position of the big firms in Apia who ultimately control the buying and selling of most goods and many services. The big firms pay their agents a very small salary and a very low commission on profits, while they sell wholesale only limited amounts of goods to independent traders on the most stringent credit terms, possibly at Apia retail prices or even higher. These high wholesale prices are charged, according to the big firms, to cover the risk of debt. On the other hand, relatively low prices are paid for traders' cash crops. Official price controls, on copra for example, are not universally effective, whilst there is no price control on retail goods or cacao. Fluctuations in import or export prices, or increased tariffs or duties are usually handed on to the village trader by the big firms. Competition between the big firms does not significantly affect the

---

[1] e.g. the fruit and vegetable sellers.
[2] Less important reasons for failure were falsification of the books, bribing of supervisors who came to check the books, etc.

independent village trader's bargaining position, for there are informal agreements amongst some firms, whilst most have purchase rights over the independent trader's cash crops in return for loans made to him. The big firms are also often in direct competition for the custom of villagers who live near Apia (over a half of the total population of Samoa) by giving higher cash crop prices, or discounts on cash croppers' purchases leaving village traders to handle less lucrative retail sales. The big firms are able to perpetuate this monopoly by excluding Samoans from the European social group. This social group is an important reason, in fact, for part-European and European economic success. Capital, advice and expertise are readily available to group members, often flowing along social connections created by marriage. Contracts and debts are honoured as there is social as well as economic pressure forcing a man to do so. If, for example, a man does not honour a debt he might sever social as well as economic links with his creditor and face public criticism and possibly ostracism. Because part-European and European business is on a secure footing, because contracts and debts are honoured, overseas European big business which monopolizes external trade prefers to deal with these firms. The existence of long-term contractual and credit relationships is an important reason for the success of many of the European firms.

In general, the village trader cannot hand on, or charge, higher prices in the village. Many try to combat big firms' competition by emphasizing the convenience and accessibility of their services, staying open or operating at all hours or buying or bartering unprocessed nuts, though this transaction benefits traders as well as producers, since the traders can properly process the nuts in hot air driers and sell at higher prices in Apia.

The Samoan entrepreneur can also offer a more personal service than the large European companies. The village store is a good place to gossip. The atmosphere is more informal than in town. The village trader will probably let the customer examine the goods at length and experiment with them. The villagers feel more relaxed in the village store or on the Samoan bus or taxi, which they feel is part of the Samoan rather than the European world. Although the trader like the village pastor or Government representative might be introduced into or appointed in the village to represent and to further outside causes, he is often regarded as representing the village in the outside world, protecting village interests against outside interference, and introducing new goods and new ideas into the village. There are even cases where the trader has been appointed by the *fono* and where any trading losses are regarded, as are contributions to the pastor or costs incurred by the Government, as part of proper and necessary relations with the outside world.

CONCLUSION

THE major conclusion of this study is that local economic development can be internally generated, achieved mainly through traditional (*fa'asāmoa*) values and institutions.

The external European contribution to local development is weak. This weakness stems partly from a scarcity of altruistic motives amongst Europeans, but mainly from the separation of European society from Samoan society which prevents both effective contribution or exploitation. Those most closely associated with Samoan society, e.g. the village traders, have contributed most, despite their limited altruism, whilst the efforts of missionaries and administrators, who live in their own little worlds, are largely dissipated.

Conversely, the internal generation of economic development is strong, despite, perhaps because of, European indifference. Just as the weakness of the external contribution can be explained in terms of the separation of European society from Samoan society, the strength of the internal generation is the result of the successful Samoan participation in the European world, and particularly in the cash economy.

The most important dynamic in this internal generation is the strong desire for European goods. As in the ideal capitalist system, acquisitiveness, hard work, productive use of resources are most important values in Samoan society. The allocation of time, resources, and expenditure is carefully calculated. European goods and services are preferred because they are more efficient and have a higher symbolic value in the Samoan status system. For although Samoans want European goods they also want to live, at least ultimately, in *fa'asāmoa* society, in the *'āiga* and the village according to traditional norms.

In general traditional institutions are a suitable vehicle for the realization of the basic ambition of acquiring European goods. An important means of acquiring goods traditionally was through direct subsistence activities (producing and consuming goods within a single small social unit). Subsistence activities remain important especially when or where it is difficult to obtain cash. But European goods are difficult to produce in the village mainly because the means of production are not available and because locally produced goods are of lesser status than imported goods.

Consequently when there are opportunities for earning cash to purchase desired European goods, Samoans relinquish subsistence activities. Traditional institutions (*fa'asāmoa*) allow successful participation in the cash economy providing a relatively efficient framework for production and exchange and adequate production incentives. First, the individual has, in the context of *fa'asāmoa* society, adequate access to the factors of production and adequate rights in the rewards for economic activity. The first kind of reward for successful economic activity is in status. Economic ability in cash earning activity is the most important criterion for obtaining a title, or rank and prestige generally. The second kind of reward is in property. Private property is an important *fa'asāmoa* institution. Individuals either own goods (including land) absolutely or have extensive rights of use and consumption. Property rights are protected by a wide range of sacred and secular sanctions. The economic rights of chiefs and communal groups are limited by convention, strong secular sanctions and by the fear of losing prestige. Any goods or services an individual contributes to the chiefs or communal groups are given willingly and are rewarded adequately, either in status or goods. Both the chiefs and communal groups play, in fact, important functions in cash earning activities, the chiefs as leaders and managers, the communal groups as producer, consumer and marketing co-operatives or in a wide range of welfare activities.

Traditional institutions have then adapted to cash economy conditions and also these traditional institutions co-exist with new introduced institutions. Successful individual cash croppers work away from the village earning cash which they spend on leisure and prestige activities in the village. Conversely, the greatest failures are those farmers who sever all ties with *fa'asāmoa*.

A similar pattern emerges in the wage labour structure. *Fa'asāmoa* demographic institutions, producing a large number of children, provide a large labour force with considerable potential in a relatively unskilled labour market. *Fa'asāmoa* society also provides significant production incentives for wage labourers. Migrants, although often separated from their *āiga* and village for weeks, months, or years, still retain a deep and vested interest in *fa'asāmoa* leisure and prestige. The cash earned by wage labourers and sent back to the village as prestige payments offsets the economic disadvantages caused by the depletion of rural manpower.

Traditional institutions are also compatible with capital formation. There is a tradition of conservation, and savings and investment are widely accepted as worthwhile aids to cash earning activity, whilst human capital formation, the acquisition of knowledge, and good health are thought by many to be as important as the acquisition of goods. This capital formation has been achieved despite administrative indifference and neglect.

There is also a tradition of trade and specialization. Traditional institutions, embodying mechanisms of reciprocity and redistribution, account for a significant part of the distribution and exchange of goods and services. Traditional specialists still operate in the traditional manner, though possibly selling European goods and services. Money has been incorporated into *fa'asāmoa* society, and traditional exchange media have taken on the functions of money. Successful traders and other entrepreneurs operate successfully within the context of *fa'asāmoa* society utilizing *'āiga* resources, whilst the failures are usually the lone wolves. In all exchange activities the Samoan is able to compete successfully in the European market.

But if traditional institutions have been apparently successful in promoting economic growth why is Samoa still described as an underdeveloped country in the conventional economists understanding of the term?[1] One possible reason is that levels of development in advanced industrial areas and in rural underdeveloped regions are not strictly comparable. Clearly Samoa, and undoubtedly many other Afro-Asian societies, are only underdeveloped in a relativist sense. First, the low levels of *per capita* output and consumption may simply be a statistical distortion due to the undercollecting of data. Nor need these low *per capita* levels necessarily indicate economic deprivation. There is often a misplaced emphasis on the

[1] A clear definition is Liebenstein 1966.

importance of population increase. As in most economic equations the relationship between population and production or consumption does not vary exactly. Population increases do not mean proportionate decreases in output or increases in consumption, as there is a diminishing effect in all spheres. In Samoa, as elsewhere in Afro-Asia, there is often a considerable potential in the existing usage of labour and capital, as well as in unused factors, so that increased numbers may have little effect. For example in Samoa, land use may be extended, or extra crops planted without significant additions to labour input, or some capital items (e.g. copra driers, tools) may be shared as easily amongst 200 as 20. Finally, of course, output may be increased by population increase, especially in rural situations where relatively unskilled labour can be absorbed.

In the calculations of output or consumption, inadequate notice may be taken of the importance of the subsistence sector. Certainly in Samoa and other rural areas of the Pacific the subsistence sector is flexible and provides goods to bring consumption up to what is locally considered to be an acceptable level. Especially when there are downturns or disappointments in the market this subsistence production may be considerable. Economists and statisticians drawing their data largely from urban institutions may be largely unaware of the scale of these endeavours, or unwilling or unable to calculate them into the national equations.

The 'overpopulation in the agricultural sector' often held up to be a criterion of underdevelopment need not have adverse effects in a rural tropical environment. Rural living, at least where there is available land, can support a greater population than the squalid city slums. The traditional milieu also gives a stability and security to the country people. Conversely hunger, sickness and insecurity are often the background to the lawlessness and unhappiness of many tropical towns and cities.

Capital, too, is liable to misrepresentation and miscalculation. Production potential is not always in the form of money, modern machines or medicines, and their absence does not necessarily denote capital deficiencies. What in Western eyes is crude capital may be suitable in rural Afro-Asia and there are considerable and unrecognized sources of purchasing power and production potential within the traditional capital complex. Perhaps there is not 'take-off' in the Rostowian phrase but this is only possible within a very large capital unit and is an unsuitable analogy for the dynamics of small-scale capital units.

Finally the levels of consumption may be an inadequate index of wealth or economic satisfaction. The Samoan, for example, has his own idea of proper consumption and in most cases he is reasonably satisfied with his standard of living and very satisfied with his way of life. In general economists have ignored the considerable symbolic, as well as monetary, value of the social context of economic activity. 'We may not be wealthy', said one Samoan chief, 'but we are happy with *fa'āsamoa*. We do not envy the rich European in his caddy (Cadillac). His money leads him only to trouble.' Many Samoans believe that they would be wealthier if they move outside the orbit of *fa'asāmoa* but few think they would be happier.

Underdevelopment, at least in Samoa, is from different points of view a chimera, an economist's convention, or merely a measure of that exchange with European markets which can be exactly monitored. In this exchange the form of the local society, as Geertz[1] has noted elsewhere, is in a definite sense irrelevant. Development, in the sense of increased exchange with European or urban markets, can take place whatever the form of local society, for what is significant is the relationship between the local and urban sectors. In the Samoan and many Afro-Asian cases the reason for the relatively low level of European goods or local cash production is the restrained demand by Europeans for tropical products. Coconuts or cacao are not usually the sinews of war or industry and Afro-Asian labour is thought to be unskilled, as well as conducive to racial troubles. Ultimately the Europeans do not feel the kind of social or political affinity with the underdeveloped world which enables the maximum flow of capital, advice, and assistance.

Much recent international aid has attempted to redress the imbalance. But as long as development is seen largely as an effort to form the Afro-Asian economies into Western moulds

[1] Geertz 1963(b): 154.

success will be limited. More recognition should be given to local or traditional resources, capital, and incentives. If nothing else this recognition would help establish a much closer rapport between incoming experts and local leaders, creating new channels along which available European wealth and expertise could flow. Samoa may be an extreme though not unique example of a modern state pervaded by traditional influences, but the traditional way of life is still a vital force in much of rural Afro-Asia, and a force which can be turned to productive purposes.

APPENDIX 1

Inventory of household goods—Salani, Malie and Apia[1]

Type of goods	SAMOAN GOODS			
	Description of goods	Number All figures *per capita*		

Type of goods	Description of goods	Number — All figures *per capita*
A. SAMOAN GOODS 1. Food	*Crops* (a) *Coconuts (niu)*—varieties—*'afa, 'ena, vai, mea, ui, la'ita, nuikini.* (b) *Bananas (fa'i)*—varieties—*papalagi, fua'naulalo, samoa, misiluti. pata, soa'a, aumamae, pupuputa, niue, manifi, pipi'o, talua, mili, suka, vaivai, lefa.* (c) *Yams (ufi)*—varieties—*paloi, laupalai, ufitau, ufivao, ufisina, ufilei, ufipoa, ufilega, ufimasoa.* (d) *Talo*—varieties—*vale, magasive, sugalu, sasauli, pula, mutale, putemu, manu'a, pa'epa'e.* (e) *Ta'amū*—*niukini, toga, sega, lauo'o.* (f) *Breadfruit (ulu)*—*puou, maopo, momolega, Aveloloa.* (g) *Tolo (sugar cane)*—varieties—*vaevaeuli, folouli, tolotea.* (h) *Other*—*Papaia, mango.* *Fish and Meat*—mullett (*anae*), herring (*atule*), bonito (*atu*), octopus (*fe'e*), prawns (*ula*), crabs (*pa'a*), seaweed (*limu*), turtle (*laumei*), sea-cucumber (*tuitu*), chicken (*moa*), pig (*pua'a*), etc.	Food is acquired from the gardens or sea as required. See Table 9 for land use. In Apia many of these foods are bought.

Type of goods	Description of goods	Salani	Malie	Apia
2. Clothing	*Pulou* (plaited hat) *Siapo* (tapa—barkcloth)	1 0·5[2]	0·5 0·2[2]	0·2 0·1[2]

3. Household implements	*Mats and Platters*
	    Papa (Coarse floor mat)
	    Fala (Sleeping mat)
	    Ma'ilo (Food platters)
		
		2·0
		2·2
		4·1
			
			1·8
			1·7
			3·9
				
				1·5
				1·5
				3·7

APPENDIX 1 *(contd.)*

	SAMOAN GOODS			
		Number (*per capita*)		
Type of goods	Description of goods	Salani	Malie	Apia
3. Household implements —*contd.*	*Containers*			
	pū niu (coconut cup)	0·5	0·5	0·1
	afo (basket)	1·2	1·1	0·8
	soni (coconut water bottle)	0·2	0·1	—
	'umete (wooden bowl)	0·7	0·5	0·1
	tanoa'ava (Kava bowl)	0·1	0·1	—
	Other			
	pulumu (brush)	0·1	0·1	—
	iofi (coconut fire tongs)	0·1	—	—
	tuai (coconut grater)	0·1	0·1	—
	tauaga (coconut wringer)	0·1	0·1	—
	pele (bamboo knife)	0·1	0·1	—
4. Furniture and fittings[4]	*Ali* (bamboo pillow)	0·1	0·1	—
	Pupuni (barkcloth curtains)[3]	0·1	0·1	—
	Pola (blinds on outside of house)[3]	0·3	0·2	0·1
5. Capital goods	*Paopao* (small canoes)[5]	12	27	16
	Oso (digging sticks)	0·1	0·1	—
	Tao (spears—fishing)	0·1	0·1	—
	Faiva (nets)	0·2	0·1	—
	I'e tōga (fine mats)[5]	20[6]	53[6]	54[6]
6. Houses	*Fale*[5] (dwelling house built in Samoan style)	80	170	38
	Fale umu[5] (cooking house built in Samoan style)	30	65	22
	Fale tele[5] (guest house built in Samoan style)	2	2	1
B. EUROPEAN GOODS 1. Food	(a) *Meats* Tinned bully beef (*pisupo*) or corned beef Tinned fish—mainly herrings and pilchards (*eleni*) Mutton (frozen)—*manoe* Sausage—*sosisi*	Food is brought from the trader as required. See Table 1 for expenditure.		

APPENDIX 1 (contd.)

	EUROPEAN GOODS			
Type of goods	Description of goods	Number (*per capita*) Salani	Malie	Apia

1. Food —contd.	(b) *Bread (Falaoa) Dripping* (c) *Tea (ti) Cacao (koko)* (d) *Condiments*—salt (*masima*), pepper (*popa*), sugar (*suka*), mustard (*sinapi*) (e) *Vegetables*—Onions (*aniani*) (f) *Sweets*—Cake (*keke*), biscuits (*masi*) (g) *Cereals*—flour (*falaoa*), rice (*alaisa*), cornflakes (*koni*) (h) *Ice*—*aisa*			
2. Clothing	Cotton kilt (*lava*) and dresses	1·5	2·0	2·2
	Sandals or shoes (*se'evae*)	0·8	1·1	1·2
	Shirts, blouses (*'ofutino*)	2·1	3·2	3·0
	Ties (*tae*)	0·3	0·5	0·4
	Umbrella (*fa'amalu*)	0·1	0·2	0·1
3. Household implements	*Mats and platters* Linoleum (*Lino*)	—	—	5[7]
	Plates (*ipu māfolafola*)	0·8	1·0	1·3
	Containers ipu (cups—tin, pottery or plastic)	1·0	1·1	1·3
	'umete (bowls)	0·1	0·5	0·7
	taga (bag)	—	—	0·3
	fagu (bottles)	0·5	0·5	0·8
	pani(pans)	0·2	0·3	0·6
	Other pusa (safe)	0·1	0·2	0·3
	naifi (knife)	1·0	1·1	1·3
	sipuni (spoon)	0·8	0·9	1·0
	'āuli (charcoal irons)	—	0·1	0·2
	uālesi (radios)[8]	14	43	134
	pulumunifo (toothbrushes)[8]	10	21	56
	laulau (serving implements)	0·1	0·2	0·4

APPENDIX 1 *(contd.)*

	EUROPEAN GOODS			
		Number *(per capita)*		
Type of goods	Description of goods	Salani	Malie	Apia
4. Furniture and fittings[4]	*Pusatoso* (drawers)	0·1	0·4	0·5
	'Aluga (pillow)	0·1	0·2	0·3
	Laulau (table)	0·2	0·2	0·4
	Lamepa (Coleman Lamp)	0·1	0·2	0·3
	Ta'inamu (Mosquito nets)[3]	0·1	0·1	0·2
	Pupuni palasi (cloth curtains)[3]	0·1	0·3	0·4
	Moega (bed)	0·1	0·2	0·3
	Lamepa uila (electric light)[9]	—	—	0·2
	Nofoa palagi (chairs)	—	0·1	0·6
	Kapoti (cupboards)	0·1	0·2	0·2
	Pusa (trunks)	0·3	0·2	0·2
	Pusa (cases)	0·2	0·2	0·3
	Pusa aisa (icebox)[8]	—	1	35
	Aisa pālagi (refrigerator, electric)[8]	—	—	6
	Kītala (guitar)[8]	5	9	23
5. Capital goods	*Metei apa* (Dehusking (Copra) Spike)	0·1	0·1	—
	La'au su'isu'i (sewing machine)[5]	20	42	110
	Uila (bicycles)[5]	—	25	75
	Ta'avale (motor vehicles)[5]	3	16	20
	Fale niu (Copra drier)[5]	3	10	1
	Vati (Cacao fermentation vats)	6	10	—
	Fao (nails)	15	25	20
	Faoseku (screws)	10	10	8
	Suo asu (spades, shovels)[5]	29	49	175
	Naifi (bush knives)	0·2	0·3	0·2
	Suo (hoes)[5]	5	7	5
	To'i (axes)[5]	49	82	165
	Fagota pālagi (fishing lines—cord)	0·2	0·3	—
	Matau apa (steel fish hooks)	10	12	7
	Faiva pālagi (nets—cord)	0·2	0·3	—
	Mata tiota (fishing goggles)	0·8	0·4	—
	Lagai (shanghais)	0·1	0·1	—
6. Houses	*Fale apa a luga*[5] (tin roofed fale)	2	2	24
	Fale pālagi[5] (house with wooden walls, concrete floor and tin roof)	7	24	45
	'Ekālisa[5] (Church)	3	4	5
	Laititi[5] (Earth toilets)	7	10	11

1. Survey conducted in Malie—5–19 May, 1964, Salani—9–16 September, Apia—22 November–4 December, 1964. Only the more frequently found items (over 0·1 *per capita*) or more valuable (over 1*s.* cash value) were included.
2. Pieces.
3. Piece.
4. There were also in Apia one each of the following: organ, toaster, washing machine, electric massager.
5. Total number.
6. Estimate from informants.
7. Number of houses with lino.
8. Total number.
9. In Apia 30 per cent of the houses have electricity.

APPENDIX 2

Village income and its distribution in Malie, Salani and Apia, 1964

(All figures per capita)

INCOME

Source	Salani			Malie			Apia		
	£.	s.	d.	%	£.	s.	d.	%	£.	s.	d.	%
Cash cropping	12 16 4[3]		65	8 12 0[2]		29	0 2 3		
Wage labour	2 6 8		10	12 8 0		41	39 12 0		79
Migrant remittances	3 12 6		11	3 10 6		12	7 19 0		16
Local business	1 0 6		7	3 10 6		12	1 2 6		2
Other[4]	1 0 3		7	1 2 6		4	2 4 0		4
Totals[1]	20 16 3			29 3 6			50 19 9		

EXPENDITURE

Object	Salani			Malie			Apia		
	£.	s.	d.	%	£.	s.	d.	%	£.	s.	d.	%
Subsistence	9 1 0		45	14 2 0		44	19 1 0		38
Ceremonial	5 14 0		29	7 9 0		23	11 7 0		24
Luxury—Personal items	1 2 3		6	3 5 6		10	9 1 0		18
Capital goods	3 0 9		15	5 6 0		17	7 12 0		15
Other[4]	1 0 0		6	0 19 6		4	1 18 6		4
Totals[1]	19 18 0			31 2 0			48 19 6		

1. Errors in balancing arise mainly through distortion caused by small size of subsistence sample, and also by erroneous figures given for savings and hoardings.
2. Includes handicrafts, £1 10s.
3. Includes Handicrafts, 10s.
4. Gifts, gambling winnings or debts, soliciting and gifts from relatives, theft, etc.

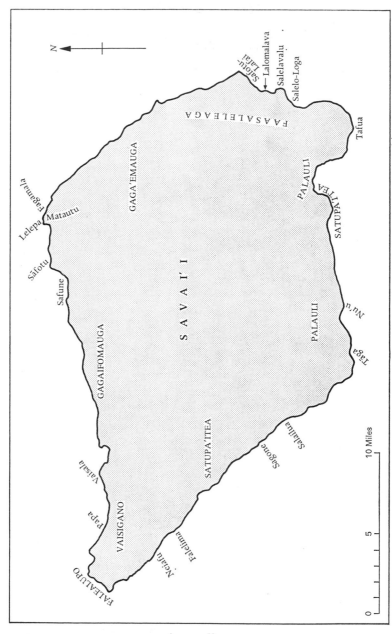

Appendix 3

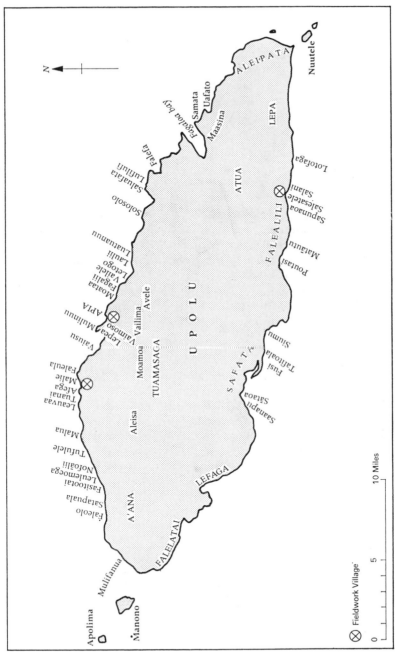

N

Nuutele

ALEIPATA

Samata
Uafato
Maasina

Faggaloa bay

LEPA

Faleta

Lotofaga

Salani
Salesatele
Saleaoaoa
Sapunaoa

Salualala
Lufilufi

Solosolo

ATUA

FALEALILI

Maiautu
Poutasi

Luatuanuu
Lauli
Letogo
Vailele
Fagalii
Moataa

UPOLU

Avele

APIA

Vailima

Lepea Mulinuu
Vaimoso
osomoe

Moamoa

Siumu

Vaiusu

Tafitoala

SAFATA

Fusi

Falelua

Malie
Alega
Tuanai
Leauvaa

TUAMASAGA

Aleisa

Saaoa

Sanapu

Malua

Tufulele

Nofoalii
Leulumoega
Fasitootai

LEFAGA

A'ANA

Falelolo
Satapuala

FALELATAI

Mulifanua

Apolima

Manono

10 Miles

⊗ Fieldwork Village

5

0

Appendix 3 (*contd.*)

BIBLIOGRAPHY

Abbreviations used in Bibliography

JPS JOURNAL OF THE POLYNESIAN SOCIETY
N NELSON LIBRARY, APIA
NZ NEW ZEALAND, DOMINION ARCHIVES
SPC SOUTH PACIFIC COMMISSION
T TURNBULL LIBRARY, WELLINGTON, NEW ZEALAND

AITKEN, H. J. 1965 *Explorations in Enterprise*. Harvard University Press, Cambridge.
APIA MUNICIPALITY 1879–94. 'Municipal Regulations.' T.
APPLEYARD, R. T. 1965. *British Emigration to Australia*. Weidenfeld and Nicholson, London.
BALANDIER, G. 1951. 'La Situation Coloniale', *Cahiers Internationaux de Sociologie*, vol. 9, pp. 44–79.
BANTON M. (Ed.) 1965–6. *Association of Social Anthropologists Monographs*. Tavistock, London.
BARFF, C. and WILLIAMS, J. 1830. Journal of a Voyage, MS. Mitchell Library, Sydney.
BARNES, J. 1954. 'Classes and Committees in a Norwegian Island Parish', *Human Relations*, vol. 7, pp. 39–58.
BARTH, F. (Ed.) 1963. *The Role of the Entrepreneur in Social Change in Northern Norway*. Norwegian Universities Press, Bergen/Oslo.
BASCOM, W. R. 1948. 'Ponapean Prestige Economy', *Southwestern Journal of Anthropology*, vol. 4, pp. 211–21.
BAUMAN, Z. 1964. 'Economic Growth, Social Structure, Elite Formation', *International Social Science Journal*, vol. 16, pp. 203–17.
BELSHAW, C. S. 1955(a). 'In Search of Wealth: A study of the Emergence of Commercial Operations in the Melanesian Society of South-Eastern Papua', *American Anthropologist*, Memoir 80.
1955(b). 'The Cultural Milieu of the Entrepreneur: A Critical Essay', *Explorations in Entrepreneurial History*, vol. 7, pp. 146–63.
BENEDICT, B. 1966. 'Sociological Characteristics of Small Territories' in M. Banton, 1966, vol. 4, pp. 23–36.
BLACKSTONE, J. 1773. *Commentaries on the Laws of England* (5th edition). Clarendon Press, Oxford.

BOEKE, J. H. 1942. *The Structure of the Netherlands Indian Economy*. Institute of Pacific Relations, New York.

1953. *Economics and the Economic Policy of Dual Societies*. Institute of Pacific Relations, New York.

BROWN, G. C. 1910. *Melanesians and Polynesians*. Macmillan & Co. Ltd., London.

BROWN, G. C. 1937. The Congregational Church of Samoa, MS. Sinclair Library Honolulu.

BUCHER, K. 1893. *Die Entstehung der Volkswirtschaft*, Tubingen.

BUCK, P. H. 1930. *Samoan Material Culture*, BP. Bishop Museum. Bulletin, 75. Honolulu.

CATT, A. J. L. 1955(a). The National Income of Western Samoa. SPCTP.

1955(b). 'Western Samoa Agricultural Census', *SPCQB*, vol. 5, n. 4, pp. 32–3.

CHURCHILL, L. P. n.d. At the Traders Station in Samoa, n.p. T. (1902?)

1925? Sports of the Samoans, MS. T.

CHURCHWARD, W. B. 1887. *My Consulate in Samoa*. Bentley, London.

CLARE, B. L. and TAMATI, P. 1962. Social and Labour Conditions in Western Samoa, Report to South Pacific Conference, Tahiti, TS. Mulinu'u.

COLE, A. H. 1959. *Business Enterprise in its Social Setting*. Harvard University Press, Cambridge.

COOK, P. H. 1942(a). 'The Application of the Rorschach Test to a Samoan Group', *Rorschach Research Exchange* no. 2.

1942(b). 'Mental Structure and the Psychological Field: Some Samoan Observations', *Character and Personality*, vol. 10, pp. 296–308.

COOK, S. 1966. 'The Obsolete "Anti-Market" Mentality', *American Anthropologist*, vol. 68, pp. 323–45.

COPP, J. D. 1950. *The Samoan Dance of Life—An Anthropological Narrative*. The Beacon Press, Boston.

CROOME, H. 1962. *Introduction to Money*. Methuen & Co. Ltd., London.

DALTON, G. 1965. 'Primitive Money', *American Anthropologist*, vol. 67, pp. 44–66.

1966. *Tribal and Peasant Economies*. American Museum of Natural History, New York.

DANA, J. 1935. *Gods Who Die—The Story of Samoa's Greatest Adventurer*. The Macmillan Co., New York. T.

DANHOF, C. H. 1959. *Change and the Entrepreneur*. Harvard University Press, Cambridge.

DAVENPORT, W. 1959. Non-unilineal Descent and Descent Groups', *American Anthropologist*, vol. 61, pp. 557–72.

DAVIDSON, J. W. 1947. The Government of Western Samoa, Unpublished Survey, Prepared for the Department of External Affairs (Confidential), MS. NZ.

n.d. Induced Cultural Change in the Pacific: Political Organization—The Transition to Independence in Western Samoa: The Final Stage, TS. Apia, New Zealand High Commission.

DAWS, A. G. 1961. 'The Great Samoan Awakening of 1839', *JPS*, vol. 70, pp. 326–37.

DEBEAUVAIS, M. 1962. 'The Concept of Human Capital', *International Social Science Journal*, vol. 14, pp. 660–76.

DEEKEN, R. 1901. *Manuia Samoa—Samonische Reiseskizzen und Beobachtungen.* Gerhard Stalling, Oldenburg.

DEMANDT, E. 1913. *Die Fischerei der Samoaner.* Museum für Völkerkunde, Hamburg, Mitt. 3, Heft 1. T.

DUBE, S. C. 1964. 'Bureaucracy and Nation Building in Transitional Societies', *International Social Science Journal*, vol. 16, pp. 229–37.

DUBOIS, C. 1936. *The Wealth Concept as an Integrative Factor in Tolowa—Tututni.* University of California Press, Berkeley.

DUNCAN, H. G. 1954. Labour Conditions in Western Samoa, TS. Apia, Statistics Department.

ELLA, S. 1899. 'The War of Tonga and Samoa and the Origin of the Name Malietoa', *JPS*, vol. 8, pp. 231–4.

ELLISON, J. W. 1938. *Opening and Penetration of Foreign Influence in Samoa to 1880.* Oregon State Monographs, Studies in History No. 1.

EMBER, M. 1962(a). 'Political Authority and the Structure of Kinship in Aboriginal Samoa', *American Anthropologist*, vol. 64, pp. 964–71.

1962(b). 'The Nature of Samoan Kinship Structure', *Man*, Art. 203.

EVANS, P. C. C. 1962. 'Western Education and Rural Productivity in Tropical Africa', *Africa*, vol. 32, pp. 313–23.

FA'ALUPEGA 1958. *O le Tusi Fa'alupega o Samoa.* Samoan Church Press, Malua.

FAATONU-O LE, Newspaper—American, Samoa 1920–60. Sinclair Library, University of Hawaii, Honolulu.

FAIRBAIRN, I. 1961. 'Samoan Migration to New Zealand', *JPS*, vol. 70, pp. 18–30.

1963. The National Income of Western Samoa, Ph.D. Thesis, Australian National University.

O LE FETU AO, Methodist Newspaper, Mulinuu (Legislative Assembly).

FIRTH, R. 1941. 'The Analysis of Mana: An Empirical Approach in Polynesian Anthropological Studies', *Memoirs of the Polynesian Society*, vol. 17, pp. 189–216.

FIRTH, R. and YAMEY, B. S. (Eds) 1964. *Capital Savings and Credit in Peasant Societies*. George Allen and Unwin Ltd., London.

FIRTH, R. 1964(a). 'Introduction—Leadership and Economic Growth', *International Social Science Journal*, vol. 16, pp. 186–92.

FRANKEL, S. H. 1954. *The Economic Impact on Underdeveloped Societies*. Basil Blackwell, Oxford.

FREEMAN, J. D. 1959. 'The Joe Gimlet or Siovili Cult: An Episode in the Religious History of Early Samoa', in J. D. Freeman, and W. R. Geddes, 1959, *Anthropology in the South Seas*. Avery, New Plymouth.

GEERTZ, C. 1963(a). *Agricultural Involution—The Processes of Ecological Change in Indonesia*. University of California Press, Berkeley. 1963(b). *Peddlers and Princes*. University of Chicago, Press.

GENTHE, S. 1908. *Samoa Reiseschilderungen*. Allegmeiner Verein für Deutsche Literatur, Berlin.

GERMANY. Colonial Administration Archives (1900–14). Secretariat. NZ.

Colonial Administration, Tulafono. NZ.

Consular Archives, 1879–99. NZ.

Samoanische Gouvernement Gazetz-Blatt. NZ.

Reichstag No. 110, 7 Legislatur, Periode IV Session 1888/9. NZ.

Deutschen Seewarte, 1890–1906, Deutsche Ueberseeische Meteorologische Beobachtungen, Hamburg. NZ.

GLUCKMAN, M. 1947. 'Malinowski's Functional Analysis of Social Change', *Africa*, vol. 17, pp. 106–9, 118–21.

GOO, F. C. and BANNER, A. H. 1963. A Preliminary Compilation of Samoan Animal and Plant Names, Hawaii Marine Laboratory, University of Hawaii, mimeo. Department of Agriculture, Apia, W. Samoa.

GREAT BRITAIN. Colonial Office, Records in the Public Record Office, Correspondence. CO 209/New Zealand.

Foreign Office, Pacific Islands, Consul for the Navigator Islands 1846–78, FO 58, Correspondence, Reports etc., Public Record Office.

Foreign Office, Foreign Various 1845–1913, FO 58. Public Record Office.

Miscellaneous MS. Reports in Public Record Office:
1. Maxwell W? 1848, Information regarding the Islands of the Samoan Group, FO 58/63/232–54.
2. Trade Reports FO 58, 1858.

280 BIBLIOGRAPHY

Miscellaneous Printed Reports. Public Record Office.
1. Municipality of Apia, Municipal Regulations, 1879–80, Griffiths & Co., Apia. FO 58/169/249H.
2. Memorandum by Sir George Grey, Upon Despatch No. 50, 1878 respecting Alleged Cruelties to Polynesian Labourers in the Navigator Islands. FO 58/107/6.
3. Cruise of H.M.S. *Miranda* Fiji and Samoa 1883, Commander Acland RN. FO 58/189/86.
4. Correspondence respecting the Affairs of the Navigator Islands 1865–76.
5. 1877–8, Confidential Paper 5305, 3846. FO 534/9/10.
6, 7, 8. Further correspondence respecting the Affairs of the Navigator Islands.
9. Secret Correspondence respecting Samoa and Tonga, 1886–7, FO 534/35.
10. Further correspondence respecting the Navigator Islands, January-March 1889. FO 534/44.
Parliamentary Papers. Public Record Office
1. Correspondence respecting the Question of Diplomatic and Consular Assistance to British Trade Abroad. Parl. Papers 1886, LX 89.
2. Opinions of H. M. Diplomatic and Consular Officers on British Trade Methods Parl. Papers 1899, XCVI.
3. Report from Select Committee on Consular Service and Appointments. Parl. Papers 1857–8, VIII.
4. Treaty of Friendship between Her Majesty and the King and Government (Malo) of Samoa 1879. Samoa No. 1, 1881.
5. Convention between Her Majesty and the King and Government of Samoa for the Government of the Town & District of Apia 1879. Samoa No. 2, 1881.
GREEN, R. C. 1964. Preliminary Report on Archeological Fieldwork in Western Samoa, December 1963 to June 1964, mimeo, Department of Anthropology. University of Auckland.
GREY, J. O. n.d. Manuscript Notes on Samoa, General Assembly Library, Wellington. New Zealand.
GUDGEON, T. W. 1905. Mana Tangata, *JPS*, vol. 14, pp. 44–66.
GURR, E. W. Manuscript Papers. T.
HAGEN, E. E. 1962. *On the Theory of Social Change*. Dorsey, Homewood Illinois.
HALL, D. M. and WINSTEN, C. 1959. 'The Ambiguous Notion of Efficiency', *Economic Journal*, vol. 69, pp. 71–86.
HARALDSEN, S. S. R. 1963. Public Health Conditions in Western Samoa, TS. Apia.

1964(a). Recommendations on Public Health in Western Samoa, TS. Apia.

n.d. (1964?)(b). Special Recommendations concerning Rural Health in Western Samoa, TS. Apia.

HARRÉ, R. 1963. Maori, Pakeha Mixed Marriages, Ph.D. Thesis. London School of Economics.

HAYEK, F. A. 1940. *The Pure Theory of Capital*. Routledge and Kegan Paul, London.

HIRSH, S. 1956. A Study of Socio-economic Values of Samoan Intermediate School Students in Hawaii, M.A. Thesis. University of Hawaii.

HOCART, A. M. Manuscript Papers relating to Samoa, T. 73 MS. Notes on Samoa, n.d. (1913?)

HOLMES, L. D. 1957. 'Ta'u—Stability and Change in a Samoan Village', *JPS*, vol. 66, pp. 301–38, 398–435.

HOSELITZ, B. (Ed.) 1960. *Sociological Aspects of Economic Growth*, The Free Press of Glencoe, Illinois.

HOYT, E. E. 1956 'The Impact of a Money Economy on Consumption Patterns', *The Annals of the American Academy of Political and Social Science*, May.

JANNE, H. 1964. 'Relations Dynamiques des Elites Traditionnelles et des Elites Nouvelles dans les Pays en Voie de Developpement', *International Sociological Association, Transactions 5th WorldCongress*, vol. 3, pp. 285–95.

KEESING, F. M. 1934. *Modern Samoa*. George Allen and Unwin Ltd., London.

1937. 'The Taupo System of Samoa—A Study of Institutional Change', *Oceania*, vol. 8, pp. 1–14.

KEESING, F. and M. 1956. *Elite Communication in Samoa*. Stanford University Press, Stanford.

KIRCHOFF, A. 1880. Die Sudsee Inseln und der Deutsche Sudsee handel, in Frommel und Pfaff, Sammlung von Vortragen, vol. 3, Heidelberg.

KNAEFFLER, TOMI 1965. 'Samoan Migration to Hawaii', *Samoa Bulletin*, June-August. Apia.

KRAMER, A. 1902. *Die Samoa Inseln*. Nagele, Stuttgart.

LABOURET, H. 1953. L'Exchange et le Commerce dans les Archipels du Pacifique et en Afrique Tropicale, in *Historire du Commerce*, ed. J. Lacour-Gayet, tome III, livre I., pp. 5–129. Edition Spid. Paris.

LACHMANN, L. M. 1956. *Capital and its Structure*. Bell, London.

LAUFASI, OLA 1956–64. Department of Agriculture, Information Circular (to Planters). Apia, Western Samoa.

LEACH, E. R. 1954. *Political Systems of Highland Burma*. Bell, London.

LEWIS, W. A. 1955. *The Theory of Economic Growth*. George Allen and Unwin, London.

—— 1961. The Strategy of Educational Development in Relation to the Economic Growth of Underdeveloped Countries. OECD Policy Conference on Economic Growth and Investment in Education.

LIEBENSTEIN, H. 1966. 'Economic Development', *Encyclopedia Britannica*, vol. 7, pp. 926–8.

LONDON MISSIONARY SOCIETY. Candidates Papers. Livingstone House, London.

Missionaries Journals. Livingstone House, London.

    1. Barff, C.   1836
    2. Buzacott, A.   1836
    3. Hardie, C.   1837
    4. Murray, A.   1840
    5. Platt, G.   1835
    6. Powell, T.   1870
    7. Vivian, J.   1871

O le Kalena Samoa. LMS Press, Malua.

Manuscripts (South Seas), Letters.

Miscellaneous Manuscripts. Livingstone House, London.

    1. Biographical Notes of Mrs. Alexander Chisholm, typescript, n.d., 56 pp.

    2. T. Heath, On certain Defects in the Polynesian Missions of the London Society, February 1842, B15/FS/JA

    3. Extracts from the Rev. Charles Wilson of Tahiti (1770–1857) with notes about his ancestors in Scotland and descendents in Tahiti, Sydney, Samoa etc., compiled by W. F. Wilson, Honolulu 1925, South Seas, Personal Box 1.

Newell Papers, Livingstone House, London.

Pamphlets. Livingstone House, London.

    1. A Defence prepared at the request of H. E. Governor Solf by the Staff of LMS in German Samoa in reply to certain charges made by a correspondent of the Schleissche Zeitung, Malua 1901 (in N. P.).

    2. Castle Captain, Round About Apia, Samoa. United Service Institution N.S.W., 1890.

    3. Rev. John Angell James, An address to the Children of the Congregation and the Sunday Schools, 1885. Hamilton Adams & Co., London.

    4. G. Turner, 55 years Work in Samoa. London, 1886.

    5. W. Harbutt, Extracts from the Correspondence of Rev. W. Harbutt, Missionary in the South Seas to a Friend in England. B. H. Byles, Bradford, n.d.

6. Private and Confidential, to the Board of Directors and especially the members of the Southern Committee, May 1905, n.p. (Malua?)

Quarterly News of Woman's Work, 1887–95. Livingstone House.

Register of Missionaries, Deputations, etc., 1796–1923. LMS London, 1923.

Reports (Annual) of the London Missionary Society, 1840–1962. Various publishers, London.

Reports, Medical Mission. LMS Press Leulumoega, Samoa.

Samoan Reporter, Apia, Samoa, Nos. 1–22, 1845–61.

Station Reports (South Seas) 1886. Unpublished MS.

McArthur, N. n.d. (1956). The Populations of the Pacific Islands, Part 4, Western Samoa and the Tokelau Islands. Unpublished mimeograph. Australian National University.

McClelland, D. C. 1961. *The Achieving Society*. Van Nostrand, Princeton.

Ma'ia'i, F. 1957(a). 'Education in N.Z.'s Pacific Dependencies', *Overseas Education*, vol. 29, pp. 54–9.

—— 1957(b). A Study of the Developing Pattern of Education and the Factors Influencing that Development in New Zealand's Pacific Dependencies, mimeograph, Islands Division, Department of Education. Wellington.

—— 1957(c). '*O le tulipe uliuli*, Department of Education. Wellington.

—— 1958(a). '*O le Motu o 'oloa*, Department of Education. Wellington.

—— 1958(b). '*O 'oloa a Solomona*, Department of Education. Wellington.

—— 1960. Bilingualism in Western Samoa: Its Problems and Implications for Education, Unpublished Ph.D. Thesis. University of London.

Malinowski, B. 1922. *Argonauts of the Western Pacific*. Routledge and Kegan Paul, London.

Maps 1924 Plan of Malie District—MS—Lands and Survey Department—Apia (1:2500)

—— 1956. Aerial Photograph Survey of Western Samoa, Mosaics, Lands and Survey Department. Apia.

Marsack, C. C. 1961(a). Notes on the Practice of the Court and the Principles Adopted in the Hearing of Cases affecting (1) Samoan Matai Titles, (2) Land held according to Customs and Usages of Western Samoa, TS. Lands and Titles Court, Apia.

—— 1961(b). *Samoan Medley*. Robert Hale, London.

Masterman, S. 1934. *The Origins of International Rivalry in Samoa*. Allen and Unwin, London.

Mauss, M. 1954. *The Gift* (translated by I. Cunnison). Cohen and West Ltd., London.

MEAD, M. 1928. 'The Role of the Individual in Samoan Culture', *Journal of the Royal Anthropological Institute*, vol. 58, pp. 481–96.
—— 1930. *Social Organization of Manua*, B.P. Bishop Museum Bulletin 76. Honolulu.
—— 1943. *Coming of Age in Samoa*. Penguin Books, London.
—— 1949. *The Mountain Arapesh*. American Museum of Natural History, Anthropological Papers, 41, pt. 3.
MILNER, G. B. 1961. 'The Samoan Vocabulary of Respect', *Journal of the Royal Anthropological Institute*, vol. 91, pp. 296–317.
—— 1966. *Samoan Dictionary*. Oxford University Press, London.
MITCHELL LIBRARY. Manuscript Collection—SYDNEY.
MONFAT, P. A. 1890. *Les Samoa ou Archipel des Navigateurs, Etude Historique et Religeuse*. E. Vitte, Lyon.
MURRAY, A. W. 1876. *Forty Years Mission Work in Polynesia and New Guinea from 1835 to 1875*. James Nisbet & Co., London.
MUSGRAVE, F. 1963. *The Migratory Elite*. Heinneman, London.
NADEL, S. F. 1951. *The Foundations of Social Anthropology*. Cohen and West, London.
NAYACAKALOU, R. R. 1963. Fijian Leadership in a Situation of Change, Ph.D. Thesis. London School of Economics.
—— 1964. 'Traditional and Modern Types of Leadership and Economic Development among the Fijians', *International Social Science Journal* vol. 16, pp. 261–75.
NEW ZEALAND. British Military Occupation of Samoa, Despatches from the Administrator. Files at Army Department, New Zealand and in Governor Series. NZ.
British Military Occupation, Miscellaneous Files. NZ.
    1. Bankruptcy File.
British Military Occupation of Samoa, Native Affairs, Unsorted Material Relating to. NZ.
Village Files
    1. Solosolo.
    2. Sataoa.
    3. Faleasiu.
    4. Fasitootai.
    5. Siumu.
    6. Leulumoega.
    7. Fusi.
    8. Samoan Officials in the Government Service. Record Book.
    9. File relating to Trader Boycotts.
  10. Lands and Titles Commission Proceedings 1914–18.
  11. Files of the Native Clerk, Mulinuu 1914–18. (Laupue).
  12. Population Figures of Apolima, Upolu and Manono.

British Military Occupation of Samoa, Proclamations. T.
British Military Occupation, Tulafono and Ordinances, TS.
Legislative Assembly, Mulinu'u.
External Affairs Department, n.d. Samoa (1925?). L. T. Watkins, Wellington. T.
Instructions to Officials (Village), Malua, 1922. T.
Islands Territories, Department Archives. NZ.
Island Territories, Miscellaneous Office Papers, Series 4, NZ.

    1. Documentary Record and History of the Lauati Rebellion (O Le Lauati) in Western Samoa 1909, 3 vols., 1932–3, TS.
    3. Reports on the Mau 1935–6.
    5. Documents Relating to Ex-Enemy Property, 1929.
    9. Miscellaneous Papers on Samoan Life.
    13. Vailima Education Conference 1946.
    15. Commission of Enquiry into the Public Works Department, 1955.
    16. Constitutional Convention 1955.

Journals of the House of Representatives, 1918–64 (Appendices). NZ.
Labour, Department of, Western Samoans Personal Files, Sample Survey 1958–63.
Ordinances of Western Samoa, 1920–62.
Statutes, 1958. Reprinted Act with Amendments Incorporated, Samoa, vol. 2. Government Printer, Wellington.
NURKSE, R. 1953. *Problems of Capital Formation in Underdeveloped Countries*. Oxford.
PACIFIC ISLANDS MONTHLY 1930–65. Pacific Publications. Sydney.
PACIFIC ISLANDS YEARBOOK 1963. Pacific Publications Pty. Ltd., Sydney, 8th Edition.
PEARCE, D. 1956. Establishment of a Literature Committee and Bookselling and Library Facilities in Western Samoa, South Pacific Commission, Unpublished MS., Island Territories Department. NZ.
PIRIE, P. 1964. The Geography of Population in Western Samoa, Ph.D. Thesis. Australian National University Canberra.
POLANYI, K. 1947. 'Our Obsolete Market Mentality', *Commentary*, vol. 3, pp. 109–17.
POLANYI, K., ARENSBERG, C. M. and PEARSON, H. W. (Eds.) 1957.
Trade and Market in the Early Empires. Economics in History and Theory. The Free Press, Glencoe, Illinois.
POLYNESIAN SOCIETY. Archives, Wellington. Alexander Turnbull Library.

PRATT, G. 1911. *Grammar and Dictionary of the Samoan Language*, 4th Edition (1960 reprint). Malua Printing Press, Western Samoa.

PRITCHARD. W. T. 1866. *Polynesian Reminiscences of Life in the South Pacific Islands*. Chapman and Hall, London.

REES, W. J. 1956. 'The Theory of Sovereignty Restated', in P. Laslett, (Ed.), *Philosophy, Politics and Society*. Blackwells, Oxford.

RIEDEL, O. 1942. *Der Kampf um Deutsch Samoa*. Deutscher Berlin.

ROSS, A. 1964. *New Zealand Aspirations in the Pacific in the 19th Century*. Oxford University Press, London.

ROSTOW, W. W. 1960. *The Process of Economic Growth*. Oxford University Press, London.

RUOPP, P. 1953. *Approaches to Community Development*. W. van Hoeve, The Hague.

RYDEN, G. H. 1933. *The Foreign Policy of the United States in Relation to Samoa*. Yale, New Haven.

SAHLINS, M. D. 1956. 'Production, Distribution and Power in a Primitive Society', in *Men and Cultures* A. F. C. Wallace (Ed.). University of Pennsylvania Press, Philadelphia.

1965. 'On the Sociology of Primitive Exchange', in M. Banton, (Ed.), vol. 1, pp. 139–236.

SALISBURY, R. F. 1962. *From Stone to Steel*. Melbourne, Cambridge University Press.

SAMOA Government, 1873–1900. Archives of. NZ.

Malo, Malietoa Government, Laws of. 1892 MS. NZ.

Government, Official Papers. NZ.
1. Samoan Constitution and Laws, 1873.
2. Declaration of Rights, 1873.

Malo, Malietoa Government, Ordinances 20/2/1892. NZ.

Malo, Malietoa Government, *O Sina Tala i le Fa'aaogina o Tupe i le Malo o Samoa*, 1893. NZ.

Samoa Bulletin. 1950–64. Newspaper, Apia. N.

Samoan Leader. 1923–64. Newspaper, Apia. NZ.

Samoa mo Samoa. 1938–39. Newspaper, (Mau), Apia. NZ.

Samoa Times. 1920–40. Newspaper, Apia. N.

1920. Western Samoa, Samoa's Problems. A Series of Reports compiled by the Citizens Committee, in view of the forthcoming visit of the New Zealand Parliamentary Party. The *Samoa Times*, Apia, T.

Samoana. 1961. Newspaper, Apia. N.

Samoanische Zeitung. 1900. Newspaper, Apia. T.

Savali, O le 1920–64. Legislative Assembly. Apia.

SCHAPERA, I. 1947. *Migrant Labour and Tribal Life*. Oxford University Press, London.

SCHEURMANN, E. 1927. *Samoa, Ein Bilderwerk Herausgageben und Eingeleitet.* Verlag Konstanz.

SCHMACK, K. 1938. *J. C. Godeffroy und Sohn.* Verlag Broschek & Co., Hansestadt Hamburg.

SCHNEE, H. n.d. about (1922). *Die Deutschen Kolonien unter fremder Mandatherrschaft.* Verlag von Quelle & Meher, Leipzig.

1926. *German Colonization Past and Future.* George Allen & Unwin, London.

SCHULTZ, E. 1910. 'Das Falealii', *Globus*, vol. 98, n. 19, pp. 300–2.

1911. 'The Most Important Principles of Samoan Family Law and the Laws of Inheritance', *JPS*, vol. 20, pp. 43–53.

1926. *Erinnerungen an Samoa.* Scherl, Berlin.

SINGER, H. W. 1961. 'Trends in Economic Thought on Underdevelopment', *Social Research*, vol. 28, pp. 387–415.

SOLF, W. 1907. Samoa, The People, the Missions and the Europeans. Report prepared for Imperial Colonial Office 21 November 1907. Photostat Turnbull.

1919. *Kolonialpolitik.* Hobbing, Berlin.

SOLOSOLO. 1962. *Iuni Faa'une Tupe—Faamatalaga toe Faafo'i faaletau-saga*, mimeograph. Economic Development Secretariat, Apia.

SPOEHR, F. M. 1963. *White Falcon, the House of Godeffroy and its Commercial and Scientific Role in the Pacific.* Pacific Books, Palo Alto.

SRINIVAS, M. and BÉTAILLE, A. 1964. 'Networks in Indian Social Structure' *Man*, vol. 64, pp. 165–8.

STACE, V. D. 1954. The Pacific Islander and Modern Commerce. SPCTP.

1956. Western Samoa, An Economic Survey. SPCTP.

1962. Capital Formation in the South Pacific, Unpublished TS.

STAIR, J. B. 1897. *Old Samoa, or Flotsam and Jetsam from the Pacific Ocean.* Religious Tract Society, London.

STEINER, F. B. 1954. 'Notes on Comparative Economics', *British Journal of Sociology*, vol. 5, pp. 118–29.

1956. *Taboo.* Cohen and West, London.

Sudsee Handbuch die Samoainseln. 1911. Mittler, Berlin.

THOMPSON, R. 1963. *Race Relations in New Zealand.* New Zealand Church Council.

THURNWALD, R. 1932. *Economics In Primitive Communities.* Oxford University Press, London.

TROOD, T. Private and Business Papers of Thomas Trood. NZ.

1912. *Island Reminiscences.* McCarron Stewart & Co., Sydney. T.

TURNER, C. H. 1958. Broadcasting in the Life of Pacific Peoples, Western Samoa. Unpublished MS. Apia.

TURNER, G. A. 1861. *Nineteen Years in Polynesia, Missionary Life, Travels and Researches in the Islands of the Pacific.* John Snow, London.

1884. *Samoa—A Hundred Years Ago and Long Before.* MacMillan and Co., London.

TURNBULL LIBRARY. MS. Samoan Collection.

TUVALE, T. 1918. History of Modern Samoa, MS. WS Legislative Assembly, Apia.

UNITED NATIONS 1948. *The Population of Western Samoa.* Department of Social Affairs, New York.

1951. *Measures for the Economic Development of Underdeveloped Countries.* Department of Economic Affairs, New York.

UNITED STATES. Consuls in Apia, Despatches 1843–1906. The National Archives, General Services Administration. Washington.

Department of Labour, 1957, Economic Report on American Samoa, Division of Territorial Wage Determinations, Stat. Dept. Apia.

VANSINA, J. 1965. *Oral Tradition.* Routledge and Kegan Paul, London.

VEBLEN, T. 1953. *The Theory of the Leisure Class.* New American Library, New York.

WALLERSTEIN, I. 1966. *Social Change: The Colonial Situation.* Wiley, New York.

WALPOLE, F. 1849. *Four Years in the Pacific in H.M.S. Collingwood, 1844–1848,* 2 vols. Bentley, London. T.

WATTERS, R. F. 1958. 'Cultivation in Old Samoa', *Economic Geography,* vol. 34, pp. 338–51.

WESTERN SAMOA. Bank of. Annual Reports 1960. Statistics Department. Apia.

Chamber of Commerce, Annual Reports, 1932–, Apia. British Museum.

Constitutional Conventions 1955, 1960, Resolutions. Legislative Assembly. Apia.

Constitutional Conventions 1955, 1960, Debates. Legislative Assembly. Apia.

Customs Department, 1923, Return of the Trade, Commerce and Shipping of Western Samoa. Wellington and Apia.

District and Village Affairs, Commission of Inquiry into District and Village Government. Records of Evidence from Village Meetings, 1950.

Department Files, Apia.

Agriculture 1956–64.

Banana Marketing Board 1960–4.

Co-operatives 1953–64.
Copra Board 1948–64.
District and Village Government 1900–64.
Economic Development Secretariat 1963–4.
Inland Revenue Department 1955–64.
Justice 1956–64.
Lands and Survey Department 1960–4.
Land and Titles Court 1900–64.
Labour 1956–64.
Legislative Assembly 1920–64.
Public Trustee 1920–64.
Statistics, Bureau of 1963–4.
Economic Development Committee, Report 1961.
Education Department, Miscellaneous Papers 1. Syllabus for Grade II and III Schools 1943. T.
Financial and Banking Survey. Government Printer, Wellington, 1957.
Fono of Faipule and Fono of all Samoa Proceedings, 1936–62. NZ.
Acts Passed by the Legislative Assembly after Independence, 1963. Apia.
Legislative Assembly, Departmental Reports, Presented to the Apia, 1962.
Legislative Assembly, Memoranda presented to, 1964
   1. Alienation of Customary Land.
   2. Bunchytop.
   3. Civil List.
   4. Judgement Summonses.
   5. Samoa Customs.
   6. Workers Compensation.
1965—1. Economic Development.
   2. Handicrafts Industry.
   3. Samoan Companies (PP. 60/1965).
   4. Water.
   5. Enterprise Incentives (PP. 56/1965).
Legislative Council, Legislative Assembly Minutes and Debates, 1936–64.
Census, Population, 1951, 1956, 1961. Government Printer, Wellington.
Statistical Bulletin. Bureau of Statistics, 1964.
Statistics Department. Income and Tax Survey, 1964, mimeograph.
(Samoa i sisifo), Tulafono mo Samoa i Sisifo. LMS Press, Malua, 1926. NZ.

WILKES, C. 1847. *Narrative of the United States Exploring Expedition During the Years 1838, 1839, 1840, 1841, 1842*, n.p. Philadelphia.

WILLIAMS, J. 1837. *A Narrative of Missionary Enterprises in the South Sea Islands with remarks upon languages, traditions and usages*. J. Snow, London.

WILLIAMSON, R. W. 1924. *The Social and Political Systems of Central Polynesia*. Cambridge University Press, London.

WILSON, G. and M. 1954. *An Analysis of Social Change*. Cambridge University Press.

WORSLEY, P. 1964. *The Third World*. Weidenfeld and Nicholson, London.

WOHLTMANN, F. 1904. 'Pflanzung und Siedlung auf Samoa', *Tropen Beihefte*, vol. 5, pp. 1–164.

YAUKEY, D. 1955. 'A Metric Measurement of Occupational Status', *Sociology and Social Research*, vol. 39, pp. 317–23.

ZIESCHANK, F. 1918. *Ein Jahrezehnt in Samoa 1906–16*. Haberland Leipzig.

INDEX

Administration, 21ff, 121, 124, 141ff, and economic development 22ff, in the villages 172ff, and education 220, Germany 22ff, New Zealand 23ff, United Nations 24

Adult education, 223, see also Education

Adultery, 111n

Affiliation, 117n

Agriculture, see Cash Crops

'Āiga, 7, 41, 58, 70ff, 84ff, 87, 99ff, 115ff, 136, 138ff, 159, 195, 210, 231, 234, 238, 242, 254, and chiefs 68ff, and land 99ff, demands on goods 137ff, mother's brother 139, and community development 141, and marriage 160, and agriculture 195, and credit 210, and specialists 231, 238, and trade 242, 'āiga potopoto, 70, terminology 139n, see also Land

Aitu, 92, 225ff

Alcohol, 41n, 158

Ali'i, see Matai

Ali'i Sili, 85n

Ao, 84ff, see also Matai

Apia, 9ff, 17, 45, 113, 114, 124, 135, 147, 177ff, 251, 254

Asau, 234

Asiata, 69

Aogā, 30, 45

Aualuma, 87n, 146n, 163, see also Women

'Aumāga, 87n

Authority, see Matai, Pule

'Ava, 197n, 239

Bananas, 36, 47, 59, 64, 206

Banks, 201ff, 207, 213ff

Barkcloth, 27, 41

Birth, 127ff

Birth control, 158, 163

Bunchytop Virus, 61, 195

Bureaucracy, see Administration, Pulenu'u

Buses, 94, see also Transport

Bush, 60n, see also Land

Buzacott, Rev. A., 5

Cacao, 36, 47, 59, 196

Cannibalism, 158n

Canoes, 94, 239, see also Capital

Capital, 4ff, 43ff, 148ff, 190ff, 265, attitudes 43, definitions 190, domestic 191, wealth 192, technological 192, conservation 192, increasing production 194ff, savings 201ff, investment 205, 'social overhead' 206, see also Money, Savings, Credit, Human capital

Capitalist spirit, 1ff, 262ff

Cash crops, 10, 36, 47ff, 59ff, see also Copra, Cacao, Bananas

Castaways, 15ff

Ceremonial, 39ff, 127ff, 255

Chiefs, 68ff, see Matai

Children, 94, 159, 199

Chinese, 16, 18, 148, 211

Cleanliness, 30n

Coconut oil, 240

Coconuts, 195

Co-existence, institutional, 8

Communal groups, 7, 41, 58, 70ff, 84ff, 87, 99ff, 115ff, 136, 138ff, 159, 195, 210, 231, 234, 238, 242, 254, see also 'Āiga, Community development

Community development, 141ff, administration and 142, reasons for failure 142, co-operatives 143, successful examples 145, women in 146ff, see also Communal groups, 'Āiga

Consuls, 15ff

Consumption, 26ff, 28n, see also Goods Consumption, conspicuous, 42n

Contract, 238

Co-operatives, 143ff, 254

Conversion, 56

Copra, 36, 47, 59, 61, 64ff, 197, see also Coconuts

Copra driers, 94, see also Capital

Credit, 207ff, history of 207, and advice 208, in villages 208, credit unions 209, approved loans 209, private lending 210, interest 211, low interest investment 213, forced

Credit (*contd.*)
 savings 214, high interest investment
 214, gambling 215, in trading 258,
 see also Capital, Savings
Credit unions, 209
Crime, 111n, 121n

Death, 73, 127ff
Debts, 257ff, see also Credit
Decision making, see *Fono*, *Matai*
Demographic changes, 156ff
Demand, 35, see Goods, Cash crops
Depression, 58, 66
Development, defined, 1, prerequisites
 for 2ff, Europeans and 15ff,
Descent, 99, see also *'Āiga*
DH and PG, 65
Dido H.M.S., 15
District works, 139ff
Divorce, 160
Doctors, 167ff, in the village 227ff
Documentary record, 11
Drought, 61n

Education, 21, 46, 217ff, desire for
 217, history of 217, obstacles in
 village 218ff, mission schools 219,
 administration and 220, use of
 vernacular 220, teaching 220, agricultural education 221, technical
 and commercial training 221, adult
 223, reading material 224
Efficiency, 29, 198
Electricity, 30n, 173
Entrepreneurs, 2, 247, history of 247ff,
 agent traders 250, Samoan participation in trading 250ff, taxi
 drivers 251–2, turnover profits and
 investment 253, village trading 254,
 debts 251, see also Trade
Environment, 9ff
Epidemics, 156ff
Europeans, 7, 15ff, 161n
Expenditure, 32, 38, 39, 45 App. 1,
 see also Goods

Fa'alavelave, see Ceremonial
Fa'alupega, 78ff, see also *Matai*
Fa'apalagi, 7
Fa'asamoa, 7
Faipule, 179
Fale, see House
Falealupo, 234

Faleolo, 251
Faletua ma Tausi, 87n, 146n, see also
 communal groups.
Family, see *'Āiga*
Fertility, 159, 161, in agriculture 195
Filaria, 73
Fiji, 234
Films, 39
Fine mats, 237ff
Fishing, 30n, 94, 193, see also Sub-
 sistence
Fono, 75, 87n, 88, 93, 108, 119ff, 146,
 249, 258n, 261, see also *Matai*
Food, 41n, see also Goods, *'Oloa*

Gafa, 12, 77
Gambling, 215
Germany, 22ff, 62, 249
Geertz, C., 266
Gifts, 235ff, see also Prestige
Godeffroy, J. C., 16, 64, 154
Goods, 26ff, 268, as necessities 26ff,
 satisfaction 29, utility 29, and status
 33, 'free' 36, luxury and ceremonial
 27, 127ff, capital 43, property 90ff,
 soliciting 137ff, inventory 268, see
 also Property
Government, 54, 165, see also Ad-
 ministration, *Pulenu'u*, *Matai*

Handicrafts, 147, 239ff
Health, 156, 225ff, traditional beliefs
 225, and germ theory 225, de-
 ficiencies in programme 226, see
 also Capital, Doctors
Hoarding, 204, see also Savings
Housebuilding, 233, 238
Housing, 30n
Human capital, 215ff, see also Health,
 Education
Hurricanes, 61, 200n

I'e Toga, see Fine mats
Ifoga, 121
Incentives, and status 69, and goods
 90, and chiefs 113, and communal
 groups 126, and wage labour 154,
 and capital 190
Income, 35n, 54n, 273, see also
 Labour, Capital, Cash crops
Indentured labour, 16
Individual farmers, 148ff, see also Land
Infanticide, 158

Intelligence, 217
Interest, 211, see also Capital, Credit
Intermarriage, 17
International Commission, 1893, 177, see Land
Investment, 205ff, low interest 213, high interest 214, gambling 215, in business 253, see also Capital

Kava, 239
Keesing, F., 11, 113
Kinship, see 'Āiga

Labour, 16, 47ff, 54ff, 154ff, wage labour history 154, occupations 155, traditional influences and labour force 157ff, war 157, fertility 159, 161, marriage 159, European influences 163ff, labour productivity 164, working conditions 164, legislation 164, labour relations 165, types of wage labour, migrants 166ff, see also Work, Trade unions, Migrants
Land, 94ff, rights in 94, housesites 94, use and tenure 95, rent 97, security 97, housesite land in court 98, gardenland 98ff, land use Malie, 100, 'āiga and 99, rights in Malie 102, rights and affiliation, individual rights 103ff, duties and tautua (services) 104, succession 104, New Zealanders and 105, rents 106, changes 107, as gift 108, fono grant 108, purchase 109, squatting 109, exchange 109, and Europeans 109, International Commission 1893, 110, bushland 110, open sea 111, sale of in Apia 179
Land and Titles court, 12, 70, 76, 78, 98, 105ff, 122, 239, see also Land, Matai
Lagoon, 111
Lauati Mau, 29n, see also Mau
Lava Lava, 94
Leadership, see Matai
Leisure, see Relaxation, Ceremonial, Gambling
Lewis, W. A., 2
Libraries, 223
Literacy, 21, see also Education
London Missionary Society, 4, 14, 33n, 45, 57

Magic, 225
Malae, 111
Malaga, 41, 224, see also Ceremonial
Malie, 9ff, 30, 32, 38, 39, 45, 49ff, 60, 61, 69ff, 79, 81, 95, 96ff, 107, 127, 128ff, 142, 168ff, 181, 185, 192, 194, 202, 208, 218, 231, 233–4, 238, 239, 243, 255, 256
Malietoa, 33n, 85n, 158n, Law 122n, see alo Matai
Mālō, 158, 235
Malua, 234
Mamalu, 74, 76, 117, 235, see also Prestige, Status
Mānaia, 88
Market (Street, Apia), 148ff
Marketing, 245ff
Markets, overseas, see Cash crops
Marriage, 76, 159, 161n, 184
Mass Media, 223ff
Matai, 7, 27, 68ff, 113ff, splitting titles 69, selection 70, ability 71, age 72, succession 73, wills 73, acquisition of title 74, cash needed 75, mobility 77, tulāfale 77, 80ff, fa'alupega 78, ali'i 80, multiple titles 82, precedence 81, untitled people 87, economic disabilities 88, restrictions on power 113ff, tribute 116, pule 116, decision making 119, and 'āiga 120, and courts 121ff, leadership functions 123, and administration 124, pulenu'u 125, communal demands 126, and wage labour 168ff, and specialization 231, and gift giving 235, Europeans holding titles 72n, 86n, women holding titles 88n
Mau, 8, 29n, 62, 85, 125, 179n, 243
Mavaega, 73
Mē, 19
Mead, M., 7, 113
Melanesians, 16, 148
Methodology, 9ff
Migrants, 167ff, population movement 168, types of migrant 168, adaption to village life 170, commuting 172, chiefs 176, longer term migrants 176ff, return to the village, obtaining titles 180, status and 181, overseas 182, relations with Europeans 184, socio-economic effects of 185ff, Samoan attitudes to 188, social

Migrants (contd.)
conditions in receiving areas 188–9, see also Labour
Missionaries, 18ff, and introduction of goods 30, education 20, health 20, and work 53, and conversion 56, titles 61, and trading 62, and agricultural beliefs 215, and education 219, see also London Missionary Society, Wesleyans, Roman Catholics, Mormons
Money, 46ff, 204, 236ff, fine mats as 237, see also Trade
Monotaga, 121, see Matai, Gifts, Tōga, 'Oloa
Mormons, 57, 58n, 62
Mosquito, 126n
Mūmū, 73
Murder, 111n

Networks, 8
Newspapers, 223
New Zealand, 23ff, 62, 105, 108, 147, 181ff, 218ff, 243, 249, 255

Old Age, 88, 198
'Oloa, 235ff, 242ff
Occupations, 155, 181, 187, see also Labour, Migrants

Papālagi, 7, 33n
Papali'i, 69
Part-Samoans, 17, 259ff
Pastors, 115, 167, 170
Pega, 27
Pests, 61ff, see also Rhinoceros Beetle, Bunchytop, Rats
Planters and Plantations, 16, 58, 198
Polanyi, K., 236
Polygamy, 160
Population growth, 59n, 156
Prestige, 27, 33, 74ff, 78, 117ff, 135, 181, 235, 251, see also Matai, Mamalu, Status
Price, 35, 59, Land 110n, see also Goods, Cash crops, Capital, Trade
Price control, 59n, see also Trade
Productivity, 164, 194, 198, see also Labour, Capital
Property, 90ff, private 90ff, communal 93, land 94, see also Goods, Land
Psychological tests, 217
Pule, 115ff, see also Matai

Pule (titles), 84n, see also Matai
Pulenu'u, 1, 14n, 125ff, 166, see also Matai
Parsons, T., 2

Radio, 223, see also Mass Media
Rank, see Matai
Rebellions, see Mau
Rats, 61
Reading Material, 224
Reciprocity, 9n, 235ff, see also Soliciting, Prestige, Gifts
Relaxation, 47n, 52ff, see work
Religion, Traditional, and agricultural activity, 215
Rent, 106n, see also Land
Rhinoceros beetle, 10, 61ff, 195
Rites-de-passage, 68, 73n, 75, 127, 159, 235, see also Birth, Death, Marriage
Roman Catholics, 58n, 62, 163

Sā, see Tapu
Sahlins, M., 9
Salani, 9ff, 32, 38, 39, 45, 49ff, 69ff, 79, 81, 95ff, 128ff, 152, 168ff, 185, 192, 198, 202, 208, 246, 255, 256
Saniatu, 57
Savings, 201ff, history of 201, deficiencies in 201, facilities 203, hoarding 204, education and 204, investment 205ff, forced savings 214, see also Capital, Credit
Sea, 111
Sexual contact, 23, 184
Siapo, 27, 41
Snakes, 72n
Soliciting, 137ff
South Pacific Commission, 142ff
Specialists, 137, 231ff, 239
Spirits (aitu), 92, 225ff
Stace, V. D., 3
Status, 33, 64, 69ff, 135, see also Matai, Prestige
Structural flexibility, 8
Suāu'u, 240
Subsistence, 2n, 58n, 60, 147, 194, see also Goods
Substantivists, 1
Syphillis, 15

Tafa'ifa, 33n, see also Matai, multiple titles
Talo, 194

Tamafafine, 70n, 75
Time, 36n, see also Labour
Tamasese, 85m, 179n
Tapa'a, 240
Tapu, 92, 192, 195ff, 235
Taulupega, 75
Tāupou, 88, 163
Tautua, 74, 76, 104, see also *Matai*,
   Land
Taxes, 62, 63n
Taxi Drivers, 251
Theft, 56, 92, 166
Tithes, 61
Titles, see *Matai*
Tobacco, 40n, 240
Tōga, 235ff, 242ff
Tonga, 18, 105n, 234
Tools, 193, see also Capital
Tourists, 239
Trade, 230ff, specialization 231, region-
   al specialization 233 *tōga* and *'oloa*
   goods 235, money 236, modern
   specialization 238, inter-island trade
   233, 240, marketing 245, entrepren-
   eurs, 247ff
Trade unions, 54, 165, see also Labour
Traders, 15ff, 247ff, see also Trade,
   Entrepreneurs
Transport and communications, 173,
   206
Tufuga, see specialists
Tuimalaeifono, 85n

Tulāfale, see *Matai*
Tumua (titles), 84n
Turner, Rev. G., 4, 21, 157

United Nations, 24, 87n, 127
United States, 25, 57, 185, 255,
   Marines, 25, 154, 250, American
   Samoa 188n
Usufruct, 93ff, see also Land, Property
Utility, 30, 45

Vaiulu'utai, 234
Vegetable growing, 147ff
Village employees and officials, 114n,
   166ff, see also *Pulenu'u*, Labour,
   Migrants
Village works, 139ff, see also *Fono*,
   Matai

Wages, 54, 137, 165, 171, 180n, see
   also Labour, Migrants
Warfare, 74, 157
Wealth, see Capital
Wesleyans, 19, 57, 58n
Women, 146ff, 199, holding titles 88n,
   see also Marriage
Women's goods, see *Tōga*
Work, 47ff, attitudes to 47ff, seasonal
   cycle 52, relaxation 52ff, incentives
   to 53, missionaries and 53, pro-
   ductivity 55, wages 54